P9-DCR-732

Applied Sociology

Applied Sociology

Research and Critical Thinking

Thomas J. Sullivan
Northern Michigan University

Macmillan Publishing Company
NEW YORK

Maxwell Macmillan Canada
TORONTO

Maxwell Macmillan International
NEW YORK   OXFORD   SINGAPORE   SYDNEY

Editor: Bruce Nichols
Production Supervisor: Katherine Evancie
Production Manager: Paul Smolenski
Cover Designer: Robert Freese

This book was set in Century Schoolbook and Helvetica by Monotype
and was printed and bound by Book Press.
The cover was printed by New England Book Components.

Copyright © 1992 by Macmillan Publishing Company,
a division of Macmillan, Inc.

PRINTED IN THE UNITED STATES OF AMERICA

All rights reserved. No part of this book may be reproduced or
transmitted in any form or by any means, electronic or mechanical,
including photocopying, recording, or any information storage and
retrieval system, without permission in writing from the Publisher.

Macmillan Publishing Company
866 Third Avenue, New York, New York 10022

Macmillan Publishing Company is part of
the Maxwell Communication Group of Companies.

Maxwell Macmillan Canada, Inc.
1200 Eglinton Avenue East
Suite 200
Don Mills, Ontario M3C 3N1

LIBRARY OF CONGRESS CATALOGING-IN-PUBLICATION DATA

Sullivan, Thomas J.
    Applied sociology: research and critical thinking /
Thomas J. Sullivan.
      p.   cm.
    Includes index.
    ISBN 0-02-418355-5
    1. Sociology—Research—Methodology.   2. Sociology—
Methodology.   I. Title.
HM48.S85   1991
301′.01′1—dc20   91-24884
                      CIP

Printing: 1 2 3 4 5 6 7   Year: 2 3 4 5 6 7 8

**To Nancy,
a delightful spirit who has been with me
on all of our journeys**

Preface

This book was born out of my frustration with the materials available to introduce the promise of sociology to students. Over the years, I have introduced thousands of college students to the field of sociology. Most have found it an exciting journey. Some were sufficiently compelled to pursue it as a major or a career. Many left my courses with the recognition that sociological insight offered them a new and enlightened viewpoint from which to understand what goes on around them and with broadened horizons regarding human beings. However, when reading the text materials available to them in sociology, a not insignificant number were a little puzzled, asking, What exactly do sociologists *do*? Other than conducting research on human social behavior and teaching others about what they have learned, what do sociologists *do*? Do they do anything that actually has a tangible impact on the world? Psychologists counsel clients, bus drivers transport passengers from one location to another, and business executives make decisions about what products to manufacture and sell. What do sociologists do? Most texts in sociology present the content of the field, which is very interesting to most students, but don't address the issue of the impact sociology has on the world. This book provides college students with a clear answer—actually a number of answers—to that question. It explores applied sociology—what sociologists do that has an effect on the world, and how they do it.

Applied sociology can take a number of forms, and each is discussed in this book, but common to all is a reliance—either directly or indirectly—on the systematic observations of the scientific method. So, I have organized this book around a basic introduction to the logic and use of scientific research methods in the social sciences. Applied interventions, such as program evaluations or social impact assessments, can be fully appreciated only by recognizing the logic and value of such elements as theory and hypothesis development, sampling, multivariate analysis, and so on. To this end, I have provided an overview of how sociologists make systematic observations of the social world.

However, the scientific method is not totally alien to the thinking of nonscientists. In fact, science is, in part, a more organized, systematic, and disciplined version of the way laypeople sometimes think. So, a second organizational feature of this book is meant to encourage the student to develop critical thinking skills by adopting some of the discipline and logic of scientific analysis. In fact, this incorporation of critical thinking skills is another application of sociology to our everyday lives.

Applied research often results in some change in social policy or practices. So, a third organizational feature of this book involves documenting some of the interesting ways in which this has happened or could happen and showing how applied research can be a part of the policy-making process—and that what sociologists *do* in the world does make a difference.

Features

To achieve these goals, I have incorporated the following features into this book:

1. Each chapter opens with a *case study* describing a problem affecting a particular individual. Later in the chapter, I show how applied research was used, or could be used, to ease this person's problem.
2. Each chapter contains at least one *Research in Action* section that describes some applied sociological research and shows how it changed programs or policies and thus impacted on people's lives.
3. Each chapter closes with a *Critical Thinking* section that shows how the logic of the scientific techniques discussed in that chapter can enhance the student's ability to think carefully and critically in everyday life.
4. The last element in each chapter is a set of *Exercises* that encourages the reader to review the content of the chapter and to practice the critical thinking skills that have been developed in that chapter.

In addition to these features, each chapter contains a list of the key terms in the chapter and a list of suggested readings for those who want to pursue a particular topic in greater depth. The Appendix at the end of the book lists journals and organizations in the field of applied sociology. Some students, especially those who are considering a career in applied sociology, may find it helpful to review these journals or contact the organizations to learn more about applied sociology.

Acknowledgments ―――――――――――――――――――――

All teachers assume (hope?) that they have an impact on their students. A good teacher recognizes that the students also can and should shape the teacher. I am acutely aware of how my students have delighted, challenged, charmed, intrigued, and at times frustrated me. But they have always spurred me on to greater efforts as a teacher. So, I feel compelled to acknowledge their contributions to this book. Much of the material was originally prepared for them and revised and updated because of feedback from them. This book is an effort to make the same material available to a wider audience of students.

Many faculty and administrators at Northern Michigan University also deserve acknowledgment for providing me with the time and intellectual environment that made writing this book possible. I have had the opportunity to work with two talented editors at Macmillan Publishing Company: Chris Cardone, who recognized the worth of the project from its inception, and Bruce Nichols, who expertly guided it to its completion. I also want to thank the following reviewers who read and commented on the complete manuscript: Raymond Adamek, Kent State University; Richard Wallace, Berry College; Herbert Danzger, Herbert H. Lehman College; Wilbert Leonard, II, Illinois State University; and Joseph DeMartini, Washington State University.

It is my hope that many students gain from this book a better grasp of what sociology does in and for the world—of how it can be used to shape and reshape the world. Possibly a few of these students will be sufficiently excited by the prospect of such possible reforms that they will be motivated to learn about applied sociology in greater depth. I would be delighted to hear from any such students and to offer them whatever help I can.

T.J.S.

Contents

Applied Sociology

Sociology: Its Uses and Applications

OUTLINE

This book is about applied sociology: the use of sociological and social science research to help us understand problems that people face and to help ease those problems through changes in social policy or other practices. Throughout this book, I discuss the application of social research to the alleviation of some of society's most important and disturbing problems. The field of applied sociology has been one of the most exciting and fastest growing developments in the social sciences in the past 20 years, and I use some of the more interesting and useful parts of it to illustrate the logic of social research. In mastering the fundamentals of this process, the student will also develop a more disciplined and critical way of thinking about and analyzing the world and its problems.

Problems can take many forms. Society as a whole must deal with crime and violence; corporations must find and assess markets for their products; professional organizations like the American Medical Association must evaluate the need for services of different medical specialties. All of these problems enter the lives of people in the form of everyday events and experiences and become very real and very personal. Consider the following events that occurred during two days in the lives of two very real women.

March 9, 1977 was proving to be distressingly like many of the other recent days in Francine's life. Her husband Mickey was loud, drunk, and abusive. They argued about the groceries she had bought, the disruptiveness of the children, and her attendance at business college. He punched her in the face a couple of times and dragged her into the living room. He called her a whore and worse, and he threatened to blacken both her eyes and disable her car with a sledgehammer if she continued going to college. He ripped up her textbooks and notebooks— a semester's worth of work destroyed as she watched. He slapped her and grabbed her by the neck and choked her.

The argument continued through the day. At one point, Mickey splashed beer on Francine and punched her numerous times. He chased her through the house, cornering her in the dining room where he threatened to kill her. At this point, Francine shouted to one of her children to run to a neighbor and call the police. The police arrived 20 minutes later. Although Francine was visibly injured and Mickey admitted hurting her (he threatened to kill her in front of the police), their only offer was to take Francine to a relative's house if she wished to go.

Francine had been assaulted repeatedly by her husband over many years. She despaired of things ever getting better. She didn't feel the police could do anything. The police believed that under the Michigan statutes where Francine lived, they had no authority or responsibility to act unless they observed the assault in progress. The result was as tragic as the years of beatings Francine had been forced to endure. The police left without doing anything. Later that day, Francine poured gasoline around the bedroom in which her husband slept in mindless drunkenness and lit a fire in which he died. (A full account of this episode can be found in McNulty, 1980.)

A decade later, also in Michigan, Wayne got into an argument with his wife Cindy (Betzold, 1989). Wayne had a history of wife beating, and he now had his wife on the floor and was beating her again. When she threatened to call the police, he handed her the phone, saying "Go ahead. They won't do anything anyway." She called and, to the surprise of both of them, the officers took the incident very seriously and immediately arrested Wayne. If she had not filed a complaint, the police would have had a magistrate authorize immediate arrest. Cindy reported no assaults following the arrest. The arrest seemed to put an end to her husband's tendency to use violence against her.

What had happened in the decade between Francine's and Cindy's episodes? There has, of course, been an upsurge in concern about spouse abuse and a growing recognition that women should never have to suffer such attacks. In addition, however, some crucial applied research conducted by social scientists has helped us understand the dynamics of spouse abuse and what can be done to intervene effectively. This applied research has been translated into new social policies that provide the police with some direct tools to intervene in such troubling episodes. It is directly because of this research that Cindy's call to the police led to a very different and much more aggressive response on the part of the police.

We will look at this research a little later in this chapter. First, however, I want to focus on the *social* aspect of applied social research. I begin by looking at the sociological enterprise in order to provide a clear understanding of what we mean by *social* behavior. Then I analyze the nature and importance of the scientific method in understanding human social behavior. Next I discuss applied research and applied sociology. Finally, I describe how understanding the scientific approach can increase one's ability to think critically in everyday life.

Understanding Social Behavior: A Challenging Task _____

Sociology is *the study of human societies and of human behavior as it is influenced by groups and other social factors.* Sociologists study subjects that people often think they know a great deal about: families, crime, divorce, education, relationships, and generally why human beings do what they do. Most of us have opinions about these and many other issues that relate to human behavior. We read about these things in the newspaper, watch programs about them on television, and see them unfolding all around us. We may even become highly impassioned about some of these topics, feeling that we know exactly how to stop assaults or reduce poverty. In recent years, for example, a great deal of controversy has arisen over the death penalty. Those in favor of it proclaim that it deters people from committing major crimes because of the severity of the punishment. Those opposed to it rebut that crimes such as murder are often committed in the heat of passion when people are not likely to consider the future consequences of their behavior. Many other arguments for and against capital punishment have been propounded.

Although these issues generate much heat, it is often notoriously difficult to achieve any consensus about many of them. Opinions at wide variance with one another persist. How do we decide who is right and who is wrong? Is one person's opinion as good as another's? Unfortunately, the decibel level at which such debates rage often goes up while people's critical faculties decline. However, this failure of critical thinking is not inevitable. This book offers a set of procedures that can be applied in such situations—a systematic way to sift through the opinions and information that surround us and to determine which parts have some validity. These procedures rest on the scientific approach used by the modern social sciences. They can't answer all questions, as we will see, but in those realms in which they are appropriate, they provide one of the most valuable ways of separating fact from fancy. They don't eliminate all debate and controversy by any means, but they do provide guidelines to help us find our way through the thickets of distortion, misinformation, and half truths in which we so often find ourselves. Learning about this approach can lead us to a more systematic and disciplined way of thinking about the world and its problems.

Why Are People So Difficult to Understand?

One of the reasons that understanding people can be so difficult is the rather beguiling nature of human social behavior. Now *beguile* is a word that has two quite different meanings. One meaning is to "fascinate" or "captivate," and human beings can certainly do that. I was reading an account of a day in the trial of Bernhard Goetz, the New York subway passenger who gunned down four young men who he claimed were about to rob him. It is difficult to imagine the social pressures that led him to pack a gun and to be willing to use lethal force while doing such a mundane thing as riding a subway. And Goetz was not a man who routinely used force or weapons to gain his way. His behavior is horrifying but also captivating by its rarity, its bizarreness, its seeming assault on the social fabric. Such individual reliance on violence seems to threaten the very basis of the social order; yet, Goetz found many sympathizers because his actions touched a nerve of fear or revenge or self-confident bravado that can be found in many of his fellow Americans. That fear, revenge, or bravado is a product, in part, of the social conditions and circumstances in which people live.

So, human actions can frighten, confuse, charm, repulse—but they are always captivating and absorbing. The second meaning of the word *beguile* is to "deceive," and human behavior can certainly do this, although in a way different from what the reader might at first think. I don't mean deceive in the sense of deliberately tricking or cheating someone (although people certainly do enough of that), but rather deceive in the sense that we can easily allow ourselves to believe something to be true about human behavior that is either inaccurate or overly simplified. In other words, we can delude ourselves into thinking that we know more about people than we actually do. In fact, this is a normal part of our nature. We simplify the world in order to be able to comprehend it. We look around at the information immediately available to us, and we use that to generalize and establish "truths" about human behavior and group life. I was reading a magazine article about the International Society of Krishna Consciousness, a rather unconventional religious group by the standards of many Americans. The article described people who left their families and turned their backs on worldly pleasures to become Krishna devotees, living in Krishna temples and wearing long flowing robes. The article suggested that these groups trick, coerce, and possibly brainwash troubled young people in order to gain new adherents. Why else, the article assumed, would these Americans join such a seemingly foreign group? This belief fits in with many people's preconceived notions about such unconventional religious groups. Yet, rare is the person who has direct experience with such groups, and even more unusual is the individual with direct experience of 5, 10, or more of them. Most people have only read about them in the newspaper or heard about them indirectly from others. Social scientists, on the other hand, have visited many of these religious groups to see what really goes on (Levine, 1984). For the most part, they find healthy, young people who, although troubled by some issues, are no more troubled than those youngsters who never join such groups. They also find a lot less coercion than most people believe occurs. The vast majority of devotees join willingly because the group has considerable appeal for them and is seen as a way of overcoming some personal difficulties. The vast majority also leave the group within a few years and resume a relatively conventional life.

So, a lot of the knowledge gained from magazines and newspapers and by word of mouth about these groups is deceptive because it is overly simplified or incomplete. When we accept such knowledge as truth, we are deceiving ourselves; human behavior is beguiling because we *want* so desperately to understand it that we are often willing to accept incomplete or inaccurate information, especially if it fits in with our preconceived ideas. Sociology and the other social sciences attempt to overcome this tendency by utilizing a special perspective and the scientific method to help comprehend the world.

The Sociological Perspective

Although this book is about the sociological method more than the sociological perspective, the two are so intertwined that we need to have a basic grasp of the latter in order to fully comprehend what sociologists do and why they do it. In addition, some of the insights provided by the sociological perspective are important in understanding the use of science by social scientists, especially its limitations.

The sociological perspective involves a way of thinking that is very different from the everyday way that people think about their lives. People tend to view their lives in terms of events, such as having a baby or graduating from college. It is these personal events that give our individual lives shape and meaning in our own minds. Furthermore, people assess themselves and others in terms of these personal events and in terms of individual qualities and capabilities. We say of someone that he wanted to have a child or she chose to go to college or that she is a strong, intelligent, or forceful person. This way of approaching things is called an *individualistic* perspective because it sees human beings as creatures who make choices in their lives and whose opportunities and accomplishments are shaped by their own individual qualities, characteristics, and decisions.

Sociologists and other social scientists recognize the importance of human volition and human qualities and characteristics. They are well aware that variations in personal dispositions or choices and behaviors can be influenced by many things, including biologically shaped temperament and character. But sociologists also recognize that there is another important level of reality: Human beings live in *societies* that transcend individuals and the personal events of their everyday lives. Societies are organized into *social systems—groups, organizations, and institutions—that shape, and sometimes control, people's lives*. All these elements are collectively called the **social structure,** a very important term in sociology. The sociological perspective involves the fundamental insight that human beings are social creatures whose behavior is profoundly influenced by other people and by the social structure in which they live. The social structure includes groups, organizations, social institutions, and cultural values that make up the social world. Social scientists disagree among themselves about many of the specifics, but they do agree that most problems can be completely understood only when these social factors are taken into account and that solutions and policies flow from, are influenced by, or are hindered by these same social forces. Furthermore, it is through these social forces that problems, solutions, and policies enter people's lives.

The social structure is passed on from one generation to the next and, along with all the beliefs, practices, and material things that are also inherited, comes to constitute human cultures. Thus, social scientists recognize the immense importance of the *sociocultural* context in human life: the social structure and cultural content that make up human societies. Each person is shaped by his or her sociocultural environment, whether that environment is the family, peer group, or society. Through the socialization process, people come to have qualities and characteristics viewed as appropriate or desirable in their group or society. The point here is that groups and societies attempt to shape and mold people, and we can understand human behavior only by recognizing the fact that individual behavior results from this process.

People occupy different positions in the social structure, and their experiences are strongly influenced by their position. One way to conceive of the various positions in the social structure is in terms of social characteristics: age, gender, occupation, race, ethnicity, and religion, to name but a few. Each characteristic refers to a group or social category to which a person can belong and indicates a position in the social structure. Being a member of the social category *female* means, in most societies, that one is treated differently and has different opportunities in life than those in the category *male*. For example, very different social forces impinge on a 19-year-old Hispanic male who is unemployed than on a 45-year-old Anglo female lawyer. The neighborhoods they live in, the people they associate with, the opportunities they have, the resources available to them—all are likely to be vastly different for each of them. In addition, their reactions to events are likely to be quite different. Being turned down for a job may well precipitate feelings of hopelessness, cynicism, or anger in the young man, whereas the same rejection might well be a minor event for the already employed lawyer with many alternate opportunities. The important point is that their behaviors and reactions are shaped largely by their positions in the social structure.

So, the sociological perspective recognizes that people often can't act as completely isolated or "free" individuals but rather are constrained by the social structural position they occupy. This *structural* approach contrasts sharply as an explanation of human behavior with the individualistic approach that people often use in their everyday lives. From this structural perspective, people have children or go to college not simply because they choose to do so; rather, people's opportunities, outlooks, and choices are constrained and limited by their position in the social structure. In fact, in this structural view, the very notion of *free choice* is much more complex than people routinely imagine. For example, the structural environment of one person may discourage any aspirations to choose college and provide few opportunities to do so. It might be easy for a 19-year-old unmarried woman from an affluent family to "choose" to go to college; a 38-year-old single parent with four children and a minimum wage job may feel she has no other "choice" but to continue working and forego college. For sociologists, it is people's position in the social structure (in this example, age, parenthood, and socioeconomic status) that strongly influences their behavior. In many cases, choices are really selections from a very limited range of alternatives that do not include options available to those in different or more advantageous positions in the social structure. One of the major assets that social scientists bring to the debate over social problems is their knowledge of the complexity of the social structure and its influence. This knowledge is crucial because virtually all efforts to solve society's problems either change the social structure or impact on people differently depending on their position in the social structure.

In addition to emphasizing the importance of structure, the sociological perspective recognizes that there is an *interpretive* dimension to human social life: People help to create the social world by the way they interact with one another. Out of interaction, we establish social meanings and interpretations that serve as the foundation for how we relate to other people and ourselves. We respond to the world as we perceive and understand it rather than to the objective reality of it. A person like Francine who believes that women have no alternatives other than to accept a certain amount of physical abuse from men will act on the basis of that perception. For her, that interpretation or meaning is reality, and she may not pursue avenues that other women see as feasible. Her acceptance of the abuse communicates to others— and to herself—the "reality" that men can and will dominate women. The point is that we, to an extent, construct our own social worlds out of the social meanings, values, and interpretations with which we are surrounded. The prostitute, for example, who internalizes the social meanings implied by the label "cheap whore" will accept a world in which she can aspire to no other way of life. Her world is shaped by the fact that she accepts the stigmatized label, even though another woman might have quite different perceptions of the situation. So it is misleading to talk of an objective social reality that exists independently of people's perceptions and interpretations because people act on the basis of their perceptions, not on the basis of objective conditions.

So, there is a subjective quality to human life, in the sense of a personal element in each of our lives that others cannot fully comprehend and experience. The meanings and values that I hold are my personal property, and, although I can tell you about them, you can never directly experience them yourself. Even though this subjective world is personal, we are not totally free to shape it as we wish. Our sociocultural environment provides us with cultural values and norms that serve as the foundation for our perceptions and interpretations. In fact, much of what make up that personal world are the group values and norms that we have internalized. In addition, because of our social nature, we constantly look to others for validation of our perceptions. Especially in realms that are complex or ambiguous, we are influenced by those around us as to how to assess or interpret what is happening. And our position in the social structure affects who is around us and likely to influence our judgments. So, our subjective perceptions are strongly influenced by our position in the social structure and by others' reactions to us. Francine's subjective understanding of the world was shaped by the dominance of men that she saw around her, on television, and in the lives of other women. It was reinforced by the response of the police who, although disturbed that she had been beaten, did nothing to stop it and by their inaction added to the impression that the abuser had some legitimate right, or at least the power, to do what he had done. It is by these routine actions in the everyday lives of people that the social world of meanings and interpretations is constructed. (A little later in this chapter, we will return to this aspect of the sociological perspective in terms of what it tells us about our ability to study people scientifically.)

So, social scientists approach problems and policies with expertise in understanding the nature and operation of the social structure and social interaction. They bring to bear an understanding of the complexity and variability that can be found in social life. In fact, sociologist C. Wright Mills (1959) used the term *sociological imagination* to refer to the ability to see the link between what is happening in people's personal lives and the social forces that surround them. Most people have some degree of sociological imagination. Recognizing that our adult personality is shaped in part by the way our parents treated us as children is a part of the sociological imagination. But the social forces in our lives are far more extensive and complex, and often far more subtle, than this bit of common sense suggests. The sociological perspective recognizes that human biology and psychology play their part, but our behavior is also strongly influenced by social forces in very complex combinations. Human beings are not, however, robots. We can make choices and change directions. In fact, one of my reasons for studying sociology is to better understand our social nature so that we are better equipped to make considered choices and change directions when desirable.

The Social Sciences

The term **social science** is used to refer to *the disciplines that focus on the study of human behavior, groups, and society.* Sociology is only one of the major social science disciplines. Political science, for example, studies political behavior, the operation of government, and the exercise of power in general. Economics focuses on the production, distribution, and consumption of goods and services and on people's behavior as consumers in the marketplace. Anthropology is most directly concerned with human cultures, customs, and beliefs, as well as the origin and evolution of human beings.

Each of the social sciences has an important contribution to make to our understanding of human behavior, and the line between the different social sciences is difficult to draw in any absolute way. However, there are some differences among them, especially with regard to sociology. One difference is that sociology is the most general and encompassing of the social sciences in that it studies all forms of human social behavior, whether in economic, political, or other contexts. Second, the social sciences differ among themselves in terms of the emphasis each gives to training in scientific research methods. Sociologists receive extensive training in a broad range of research methods that can be applied to the scientific study of human behavior. The other social sciences are somewhat more limited in the range of research methods they routinely use. Political science, for example, tends to emphasize survey methods, and some political scientists even discount the value of scientific research and focus more on political philosophy as a way of understanding political institutions. Anthropologists focus on the in-depth study of particular groups. However, when political scientists and anthropologists do receive training in scientific research methods, their competencies can equal those that sociologists have. But such training is not as integral to the education in the other social sciences as it is to virtually all training in sociology.

So, this book is really about applied social science research, but it is written by a sociologist. In fact, many social scientists work in the area of applied research, and such research often has an interdisciplinary character, with sociologists, political scientists, economists, and others making significant contributions (Berk, 1981). They each bring a special substantive knowledge from their particular social science discipline that is valuable given the complexity and variability that exist in social life.

Studying People Systematically: The Scientific Approach

Given the beguiling nature of human beings, then, how is it possible to acquire accurate knowledge of them as social creatures? Sociologists have found that the tools and techniques of science provide one of the most valid ways of doing so. **Science** is *a method of obtaining knowledge about the world through systematic observations*. Some people are skeptical about studying human beings scientifically. One reason for such skepticism is the belief that people are too spontaneous or too unpredictable to ever be understood by science. Yet it doesn't take a great deal of probing to see that some human behavior is highly predictable: If we just look around ourselves each day, we see people driving on the right side of the street, wearing clothing in public, and shaking hands on meeting. Furthermore, social scientists have established many strong generalizations about human social behavior, including the following: People with strong social ties to family or other groups are less likely to commit suicide than people with weaker ties; groups that are isolated from one another and in competition will develop stereotyped images of one another and prejudice and discrimination will likely emerge; and increasing levels of education in a society lead to smaller family size (Collins, 1989). Over and over again, looking at many different groups of people, we find these things to be true. So, commonsense experience, along with established scientific findings, give evidence that some social behavior is highly predictable. This does not mean that all human behavior is predictable. There may well be some degree of spontaneity that is beyond the scientific reach, but much of our behavior is predictable and we can locate the causes of it.

Another reason why some people are skeptical about studying human behavior scientifically is that many people misunderstand the nature of the scientific process. They think that *science* means the natural sciences, such as physics, chemistry, and biology. These sciences deal with matter, energy, and their interrelationships and transformations; they study the natural and physical world. Gravity and thermodynamics, gases and molecules, lungs and frogs—these things seem especially amenable to scientific investigation. You can measure them, dissect them, and watch them change. Yet this confuses the *subject matter* of a science with the *process* or *method* of science. What makes any discipline scientific—whether physics or chemistry, psychology or sociology—are the methods used for acquiring knowledge. All sciences strive to follow the same basic methods in acquiring knowledge.

So, this book is about scientific research on human social behavior, especially research that is used to attack problems that people face. The purpose of the book is to impart an understanding of what it means to make *systematic* observations of human behavior and why it is so important to do so. Along the way, I describe the basic ways in which social scientists collect, arrange, and present data to make some sense out of it. (The term *data* simply refers to the observations that are made, and these are the foundation of the scientific enterprise.) The sociological perspective involves a rigor and a discipline in analysis that is not often present in everyday efforts to understand the world.

However, once people are aware of what systematic observation involves, they are better able to incorporate some of it into their everyday lives and to think and analyze critically and with a trained eye.

The Characteristics of Science

The scientific approach can be summarized, at least in the ideal, by five characteristics (Popper, 1965; Merton, 1973). First, all scientific knowledge is based on *observation*. This is why sciences are called empirical: Knowledge is based on experience or experiment in the world. Science is not, as some people mistakenly believe, the equivalent of theorizing, philosophizing, or speculating (although each of these may play a part in the scientific process). Scientists must at some point make observations in the world to see if their theories or their speculations accord with the facts. For example, people have speculated over the years that providing teenagers with education about the consequences of using alcohol, tobacco, or other drugs would reduce the likelihood that they would use these substances. In fact, it has gone beyond speculation with policies establishing such programs and considerable money being spent on them. The scientific approach to such issues would be to observe in the world whether such interventions work: Let's look and see if teenagers who go through such educational programs use less alcohol, tobacco, and other drugs than do teenagers not in such programs. The policies on which these programs are based would have a scientific foundation if they were based on the outcomes of such observations.

Second, scientific knowledge is based on *systematic observation*. I can't overemphasize the importance of this characteristic of science. In fact, much of this book is an elaboration of this point. Systematic observation is based on organized, methodical, and public procedures that other scientists recognize as the most likely to achieve an accurate picture of whatever is being studied. Notice that I said that scientists recognize that these methods are "most likely" to achieve accuracy. They do not guarantee error-free results, but they do reduce the likelihood of errors when compared to other methods of acquiring and analyzing information. To make a *systematic* analysis of the educational programs described in the previous paragraph, we would need to compare two groups: one that goes through the program and a control group that does not. Why not just look at the record of the group that receives the education? Suppose we did that and the group used less drugs and alcohol after going through the program than before. Does this mean that the educational program reduced drug use? Maybe. But logically it could also be that the group would have reduced its drug use without the program, possibly because the drug supply had dwindled and drugs became more expensive during the time of the program. Without a control group to compare it to, we can't say whether it is the educational program or some other factor that produces a certain pattern of behavior, and we have very weak grounds from which to assess the impact of the educational program. So, the use of control groups is one illustration of what is meant by *systematic* observation, and their use is discussed in Chapter 4. Other procedures used to make observations systematic are introduced in later chapters. (Incidentally, assessments of the effectiveness of drug education programs using control groups have been equivocal. A Rand Corporation analysis of numerous studies concluded that the results have been contradictory and ambiguous [Polich et al., 1984].)

A third characteristic of scientific knowledge is that it focuses on *causation*. Causality refers to the reasons *why* something happened. Scientists assume that there is order in the universe, that there are reasons why everything happens, and that scientists, using the procedures of science, can discover what those reasons are. Much of this book, but especially Chapters 3 and 4, are devoted to the logic and techniques that social scientists use to discover the many causal factors that play a part in any social event. This element of science goes to the heart of an erroneous belief about sociology's status as a science: that people are unpredictable. Certainly there may be aspects of behavior that we will never be able to predict, but sociology is based on the assumption that we can observe the associations between different elements in social life. We have already observed the link between social class background and educational achievement (people from the lower classes are much less likely to attend college) and between social integration and suicide (people involved in family, church, or other important groups are less likely to commit suicide). As scientists we assume that many other associations can be found. This assumption fuels our search. To assume that human behavior does not have a cause is to say that there is no order or pattern to social life, and that contradicts what we seem to see around us and what we can see throughout human history. This is not to say that the search is easy or that some things may not always be beyond our powers to explain through the methods of science.

Fourth, scientific knowledge is *provisional*, which means that the results of science are always considered tentative; they are always open to question and refutation. There are no final, unquestioned, irrevocable truths in science. There are no scientists who are held in such esteem that their work cannot be criticized and rejected. Rather, scientists view science as a process of constant closer approximations to a more accurate vision of reality. Scientists stand on the shoulders of the previous generation of scientists, hoping to see even further into the murkiness of reality. As scientists disclose more, they also typically learn of the shortcomings or inadequacies of previous knowledge and earlier scientists. This provisional nature of science keeps all of us constantly aware that the quest never ends; we may never achieve a picture of reality that is ultimate and final. We need to constantly expand and develop our knowledge.

A fifth and final characteristic of scientific knowledge is that of *objectivity,* which means that scientists incorporate procedures that will minimize the impact of their own personal biases and values on the outcomes of their research. This does not mean that scientists have no values or biases or passions that inflame them. Scientists are as intensely involved in the issues of the day as are other citizens. Sociologists may be even more impassioned about them than other scientists because it is often an interest in "people issues" that first drove sociologists to the study of human behavior. However, scientists recognize that values and passions can, and probably will, distort their view of the world. After all, both common sense and science tell us that people tend to see what they want to see, and scientists (being people) will have a tendency to find what their values lead them to want to find. We cannot depend on scientists to set aside their values or biases. In many cases, they may not be aware of what their biases are or how they might influence their research. Instead, science incorporates *procedures* that help reduce the impact of bias and thus bring research closer to the goal of objectivity.

One such procedure is the publication of all research techniques and findings so that they can be assessed by other scientists. Nonscientists often find scientific journals deadly boring because the articles in them go into great detail about seeming minutiae. People understandably want the exciting conclusions: Which people beat their spouses? How can we get juvenile gangs off the streets and back into the classroom? Will a workfare program help reduce the welfare rolls? But the minutiae help us assess whether the conclusions are biased. To this end, papers on scientific research always include a section titled something like "Methods" or "Research Procedures" where we can see exactly how observations were made and whether the conclusions that were ultimately drawn were justified by the observations made. This is also where we learn about control groups, sampling procedures, and the other techniques that make research systematic. Reviewing these procedures can help us assess whether the conclusions are justified or whether there may be some bias in the research.

A second procedure that can enhance objectivity is *replication,* or repeating studies a number of times to see if the same results are found. Scientists are very cautious about accepting one observation by one scientist. There is too great a chance that there is bias or error in the research, even if no one can detect it. (Some of the reasons why bias might go undetected are discussed in Chapter 2.) If the research is to be used as a basis for expending social policy funds, repeated observations would be especially necessary.

So, scientists strive after objectivity but probably never totally achieve it. It may well be the most controversial characteristic of science because some would argue that given human nature and social reality, objectivity is an impossible ideal to achieve (Kuhn, 1970; Richardson, 1988; Signorile, 1989). We mentioned earlier the interpretive approach in sociology—the idea that human beings live in a socially constructed world in which they attach subjective meaning or significance to information. If this is true, as all sociologists believe it is, then science, which is a human activity, must also have this interpretive dimension. Scientists, being human, perceive the world—including their own research—through a filter of values that is shaped by their position in the social structure. The data or information that scientists collect is interpreted in one fashion by one scientist, but differently by another scientist; laypeople may invest the same information with quite different meanings. Rather than searching for objective social reality, scientists may be simply revealing layer upon layer of subjective meanings. The very choice of a research problem is often a reflection of fundamental cultural values. For example, there is much research on spouse abuse today, but there was little 40 years ago. Does this reflect the fact that the problem is more widespread today? Or is it the outgrowth of new scientific discoveries? Actually, it reflects shifting cultural values in the United States regarding men, women, and the family as an institution. In a more male dominated society, the abuse of women might be seen as normal or possibly even unimportant and thus not worthy of scientific attention. The increasing interest in spouse abuse also reflects changes in the social sciences, particularly the involvement of more female researchers in the field. When social scientists were mostly male, abuse of women was more likely to be ignored or not seen as a problem because most male social scientists were not adversely affected by it. So the choice to investigate a particular problem is not just an objective scientific judgment but rather a reflection of cultural values and biases.

So, cultural values can never be completely removed from scientific work, and thus the ideal of objectivity is one that can be approximated but probably never completely achieved. I address this problem of objectivity throughout this book and am especially sensitive to the many ways in which poor or unsystematic research methods can lead to serious violations of the principle of objectivity. Possibly the best that can be hoped for is constant vigilance regarding threats to objectivity.

These five characteristics of science, then, are what scientists strive to achieve. They stand as ideals against which we can measure particular scientific activity. Although social scientists would agree that we can apply the methods of science to the study of people, most would also argue that we need to be careful in doing so, especially in applied sciences where the point of the research is to accomplish something practical in the world.

Basic and Applied Sociology

All sciences, including sociology, draw a distinction between basic (or pure) and applied science. The primary focus of basic sciences is to advance the theoretical understanding of some phenomenon; applied sciences focus on solving some real-world problem. Figure 1.1 describes three distinct realms in which basic or applied sciences operate: the theoretical realm, where the focus is on developing theories of some phenomenon; the observational realm, where data are collected; and the policy or action realm, where actions are taken to solve a problem in the world. Both basic and applied sociology are based on observation, and thus are in the observational realm. However, what they do with these observations is quite different. The primary focus of basic sociology is in the theoretical realm: developing theories of human social behavior and testing hypotheses derived from those theories. **Basic sociology,** therefore, refers to *sociological research whose purpose is to advance our knowledge about human social behavior with little concern for any immediate practical benefits that might result.* **Applied sociology** consists of *research and other activities designed to focus sociological knowledge or research tools on a particular problem identified by some client with some practical outcome in mind.* The primary focus of applied sociology is on the policy or action realm: making recommendations about social programs or policies that might be implemented or changed (DeMartini, 1982). Notice in Figure 1.1 that both basic and applied research take from the theoretical knowledge base as well as contribute to it; this is a primary focus of basic research but a secondary focus of applied research. This distinction is discussed in more detail in Chapter 2.

Table 1.1 provides an outline of the major differences between basic and applied sociology. Basic sociology is an attempt to develop theories that explain how societies work and why people behave the way they do. Hypotheses are derived from these theories and subjected to empirical tests. Confirmation of the hypotheses provides some verifica-

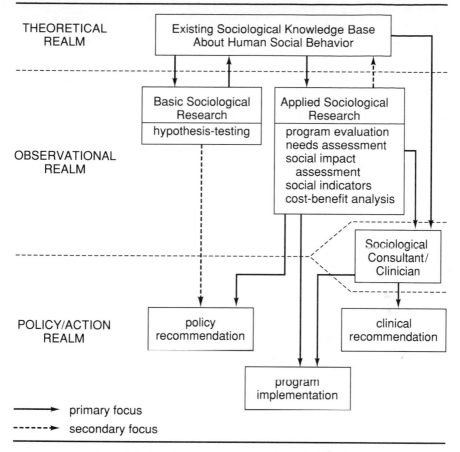

THEORETICAL REALM

Existing Sociological Knowledge Base About Human Social Behavior

Basic Sociological Research

hypothesis-testing

Applied Sociological Research

program evaluation
needs assessment
social impact
  assessment
social indicators
cost-benefit analysis

OBSERVATIONAL REALM

Sociological Consultant/ Clinician

POLICY/ACTION REALM

policy recommendation

clinical recommendation

program implementation

→ primary focus

------► secondary focus

Figure 1.1 The Focus of Basic and Applied Sociology

tion for the theory. The overall goal is to advance our knowledge of human behavior. Applied sociology, on the other hand, uses sociological theories and research tools to tackle some particular problem that somebody wants solved: How well does some program or practice work? Does it achieve its goals? What consequences does it have? The overall focus is to use existing knowledge and research tools for some practical end. We may learn something new about human behavior along the way, but that is not the main goal.

Basic and applied sociology also differ in how a problem is chosen for study. In basic sociology, sociologists themselves decide what research questions are most important based on their assessment of the state of our knowledge and their judgment about which research directions would produce the greatest advances. In doing this, they rely on the evaluations of their work by other social scientists. In

TABLE 1.1   Basic Versus Applied Sociology

	Basic Sociology	Applied Sociology
Orientation	theory building/ hypothesis testing	program effects/ consequences of practices
Goal	knowledge production	knowledge utilization/ problem solving
Source of Research Problem	self- or discipline generated	client-generated

Source: Adapted with permission from NTL Institute. "Basic and Applied Sociological Work: Divergence, Convergence, or Peaceful Coexistence?" by Joseph R. DeMartini, pp. 205–206, *The Journal of Applied Behavioral Science,* Vol. 18 (no. 2) Copyright 1982.

applied sociology, on the other hand, the problem to be addressed is suggested by a client who needs the problem solved. The sociologist's task is to develop a systematic assessment of the problem, given the needs and goals of the client. A final point to be made at this stage is that even though the distinction between basic and applied science can be made in the abstract, it is often difficult in reality to draw a hard and fast line between the two. Many research endeavors and problem-solving efforts contain elements of both.

Applied sociologists can work in a number of different spheres (DeMartini, 1979; Iutcovich and Iutcovich, 1987; Rebach and Bruhn, 1991). One is that of the *applied researcher,* in which a client's problem calls for the collection and analysis of data in order to recommend solutions to the problem. Applied researchers may work in a variety of settings, such as government agencies, private corporations, private research organizations, or under individual contract with some agency or organization. They also conduct many different kinds of research, which will be discussed shortly. An applied sociologist can also be a *sociological consultant,* whose role is to make recommendations to clients for changes in programs or practices based on the existing body of sociological knowledge about human groups and human social behavior. Unlike applied researchers, consultants don't collect and analyze data themselves but rather rely on the conceptual and theoretical knowledge distilled from the basic and applied research of others. Using this knowledge, the consultant offers a solution to a problem or offers a general understanding of the sociocultural environment relevant to a client. For example, a sociological consultant might use past research on the link between socioeconomic status and attitudes toward crime to help a lawyer pick a jury that would be most favorably disposed toward the lawyer's client. A third sphere in which applied sociologists work is that of the *clinical sociologist* who attempts a sociological diagnosis of group problems and behavior and develops a planned program of change. Some clinical sociologists, for example, conduct family counseling directed toward helping families overcome problems; others help people change undesired behaviors such as overeating or alcohol abuse (Roberts, 1991; Vissing and Kallen, 1991; Fritz, 1991). As do sociological consultants, sociological clinicians utilize existing sociological knowledge without conducting research themselves (Glassner and Freedman, 1979). These three spheres taken together (applied researcher, sociological consultant, and sociological clinician) constitute what is called *sociological practice*.)

Figure 1.1 shows that sociological consultants and clinical sociologists operate in a slightly different realm from basic and applied researchers. They are sort of in between the observational and policy realms: They do not collect and analyze data themselves, although their work does rest on the observations of other social scientists. In addition, all three types of applied sociologists—researchers, consultants, and clinicians—make direct contributions to the policy or action level where something is actually done with the knowledge: Policy recommendations are made, programs are implemented or changed, or clinical recommendations are made. Basic research, on the other hand, impinges on policy only indirectly. An illustration of applied social research and of the link between the theoretical, observational, and policy realms is presented in Research in Action 1.1.

RESEARCH IN ACTION 1.1 ══════════════════════════════════

Stopping Spouse Abuse

Consider again the abuse victims Francine and Cindy. How did social research make a difference in Cindy's life as compared to Francine's? Agonizing problems such as domestic violence have been one of the major targets of applied social research. There are many points at which to attack this problem. One is to figure out the best way for police to intervene in such cases: Should they mediate between the couple, counseling and advising but then walking away, as they did so frequently with Francine? Or should they aggressively pursue the arrest option, as they did in Cindy's case? Or is there some other effective option, such as sending the abuser away in the hope that a

period of separation will calm the passions that led to the violence?

For many years, this decision was left to the judgment of the individual officers at the scene. Those judgments were shaped in part by the experiences of the officers but also by each one's personal feelings about spouse abuse, about the relationship between men and women, and by many other social and cultural factors. Some officers had a favorite approach that they believed worked, but no one had any systematic knowledge about which strategy was actually most likely to stop future outbreaks of domestic violence. In the early 1980s, criminologist Lawrence Sherman and sociologist Richard Berk

(1984) developed an innovative program to collect systematic observations to begin resolving this issue. They based their approach on two competing theories of the effect of punishment in controlling crime. One theory, the specific deterrence doctrine, posits that punishment, such as an arrest, tends to stop people from committing future crimes because they fear further punishment. The opposite approach, labeling theory, argues that punishment by an official law enforcement agency increases the likelihood of future crimes because it starts the person down the path of becoming a career criminal.

The police in Minneapolis cooperated with Sherman and Berk in their data-gathering venture. The researchers gave each officer a pad of police report forms that were in three different colors, with each intervention—separation, mediation, and arrest—represented by one of the colors. The different colored forms were ordered randomly in each officer's pad, and the officer took whatever action was called for by the color of the form on the top of the pad when called out on a domestic dispute. Thus each type of intervention was used an equal number of times and was chosen without the judgment of the officers coming into play. Sherman and Berk then looked to see which perpetrators of spouse abuse were most likely to be involved in repeat offenses over the next six months. (For ethical reasons, these procedures were followed only in cases of simple, or misdemeanor, assault where there was no severe injury or life-threatening situation.)

This was a complex piece of applied research to conduct, but basically Sherman and Berk discovered that arrest was the most effective form of intervention: Those who were arrested were less likely to be involved in another domestic assault over the next six months than were those who experienced mediation or separation. This was true even though those arrested were released very quickly and thus were free to commit further episodes of abuse.

These research findings have made a difference in the lives of many women and men because they have been used as the justification for changing social policies. As a result of these findings, the Minneapolis police were ordered by their superiors to "aggressively utilize arrest powers" in dealing with domestic assault cases, which resulted in a three-fold increase in such arrests ("Arrests of Wife-Beaters. . .", 1984). Many other police departments, including those in New York City, Houston, and Dallas, have given their officers similar orders (Barth, 1984). It was because of findings such as these that a program of aggressive intervention was established in the police jurisdiction that responded to Cindy's call, and this explains why Cindy's experience was so different from Francine's of a decade earlier. In Cindy's jurisdiction, as in many others today, police are given authorization to arrest in such cases even if the victim does not make a complaint—a vast improvement over the past neglect. By 1988, a number of other police jurisdictions, including Milwaukee, Atlanta, and Charlotte, North Carolina, were repeating versions of the Minneapolis experiment to see if the same results would be found in cities with different traditions and with people who have different sociocultural characteristics (Garner and Visher, 1988).

The Sherman and Berk study and the ones that followed it illustrate some of the central features of applied social research:

1. Applied research rests on an existing body of knowledge about human

behavior (in this case, theories about the effect of punishment on people's future involvement in crime);

2. Applied research is founded on systematic observations (e.g., randomly assigning interventions on each domestic dispute call and carefully following up to see who becomes a repeat offender);

3. Applied research uses replication (e.g., repeating the study in a number of different communities);

4. Applied research culminates in policy recommendations (e.g., establishing standing orders for the police to utilize the arrest intervention); and

5. Applied research is typically interdisciplinary in nature (in this case, involving a sociologist and a criminologist).

Types of Applied Sociological Research

This book focuses mostly on the applied research activities of applied sociologists because research is the foundation for what all applied sociologists do. The major types of applied research are listed in Figure 1.1 and are discussed at length and with illustrations in Chapter 6. A brief definition of each at this point, however, provides an orientation to the kind of work done by applied sociologists. To briefly illustrate each, I will state the type of research question each might address if an evaluation of a program to reduce repeat pregnancies among teenage mothers were being done.

Program evaluations assess whether programs are achieving their goals and whether they are creating new problems while alleviating preexisting ones. (Do the teen mothers in the program have a lower rate of repeat pregnancy than teen mothers not in the program?) *Needs assessments* involve an evaluation of how extensive some problem is, what resources exist for meeting the problem, or whether some goods or services are needed by a particular group. (How many teenage mothers are there in the community?) *Social impact assessments* look at the effects, both positive and negative, of some program or practice on the social and cultural environment of a community. (Does the reduction in teen pregnancy put additional demands on educational or social service systems?) *Social indicators* are an effort to devise quantitative measures of some social phenomena, such as the extent of poverty or crime. (How can we effectively measure the rate of teen pregnancy in a community?) *Cost-benefit analysis* involves the quantitative comparison of the costs and the benefits of a program or practice in order to make an assessment about whether the program should be changed or ended. (What are all the costs of running the program and are there less expensive ways to reduce teen pregnancies?)

A final point of contrast to be made between basic and applied research has to do with advocacy, which means that someone is pushing for a particular outcome of the research. Basic research tends to place more emphasis on discovery than on advocacy, at least in the ideal: The discovery of any new knowledge about human behavior is considered desirable, even if it contradicts previous knowledge or reflects unfavorably on existing social programs. The outcomes of applied research, on the other hand, are often used to decide whether to continue, change, or cancel programs. People's jobs may be on the line, or their pet projects at stake. Because of this, the clients who contract for applied research may have strong feelings about and a personal stake in the results, and they may advocate for certain outcomes in the research. They want to hear that their program works, not that its impact is equivocal or nonexistent. As a result, applied researchers can come under pressure to arrive at a predetermined outcome. Often, the clients simply do not understand the scientific importance of such procedures as control groups and replication. Because of the special salience of advocacy in applied research, the attempt to achieve objectivity, discussed earlier as a key characteristic of science, can become even more complicated and difficult. This issue is elaborated on in Chapter 7.

The Limitations of Science

Although the methods of science are very useful tools for acquiring valid knowledge about the physical and social worlds, science does have its limitations. One is that it cannot resolve fundamental moral issues for us. These are the major "should" issues: How should I lead my life? Should the nation go to war? Should I divorce my spouse? These are moral and ethical dilemmas whose resolution cannot be achieved through observation. To resolve them, we need to rely on basic values or religious or philosophical principles. Science may be able to inform us about the *consequences* of particular choices, and this could help us make a decision. However, the decision itself is still a fundamentally moral one.

Science also cannot help us with realities that are not observable. The spiritual or transcendent realities posited by many religions, for example, are beyond the realm of science. Science cannot tell us whether any gods or spirits exist or whether there is a heaven or hell. These matters involve a reality different from the physical reality that is available to us through our senses. Science can tell us how many people go to church or believe in God—these issues can be determined through observation—but not whether the spiritual beliefs of a church are correct or whether God exists.

So, it is important to be clear about the limitations of science: It can deal with issues that can be resolved through observation of the world available to us through our senses. Anything beyond that must be approached with other ways of knowing.

Separating Values and Opinions from Facts

Most of you reading this book will not become sociologists or conduct applied research. Nevertheless, you can "practice" applied sociology in your own lives by adopting a critical way of thinking about the world that parallels what sociologists do. **Critical thinking** refers to *a mode of assessment; it is a reflective process that can help people decide what to believe, what is accurate, and what actions are feasible in a situation.* At a general level, critical thinking skills would include the following (Browne and Keeley, 1986; Meyers, 1986; Browne and Litwin, 1987):

1. The ability to detect assumptions and values that underlie a position,
2. The ability to assess whether an argument is logical,
3. The ability to draw inferences from data or evidence,
4. The ability to evaluate whether evidence or data support a conclusion,
5. The ability to detect whether important information is missing or unavailable,
6. The ability to think up alternative inferences, assumptions, arguments, positions, or conclusions.

Being critical involves judgment and fault-finding. It implies that the truth is elusive, complex, and multifaceted. In fact, in most realms, to talk of a single truth may be a distortion of reality that gives us the sense that we understand the world better than we do (Paul, 1990).

Scientists have learned the value of critical thinking as a method of gaining knowledge about the world, and applied sociology uses these same methods. Glimpsing how scientists engage in critical thinking—which is what this book is about—can enhance your understanding of the scientific process as well as contribute to the development of critical thinking skills in your everyday life. I conclude each chapter of this book with a short assessment of how the content of that chapter can be translated into critical thinking skills.

In this chapter, I have addressed the issue of objectivity and its importance in scientific inquiry. Objectivity has to do with the impact of values on our opinions and judgments, and the line between values, opinions, and data can get blurred. Being clear on what these are and how they differ from one another is central to critical thinking. **Values** refer to *people's conceptions of what is good or bad, right or wrong, and they often serve as criteria for choosing goals or behaviors.* Values are people's preferences for what ought to be. Some groups in the United States believe that people should work and support themselves because work and accomplishment are indications of an individual's worth as a person. Values can derive from a cultural heritage or religious revelation. Or they might emerge out of a political or social philosophy. From a sociological perspective, values themselves are not right or wrong, although they do help people decide what is right or wrong for them.

An **opinion** is not as certain or as fundamental to one's way of life as a value. It is *a judgment, an appraisal, or a conclusion that a person draws based on some personal experiences, general knowledge, or intuition.* It could be my opinion that a particular football team will win its next game or that the death penalty for drug dealers will help stop drug trafficking. Opinions are not based entirely on solid evidence in the form of proven causal linkages between events. Instead, they are judgments arrived at from the subjective weighing of bits of information and filtered through personal biases and values. So, for example, it makes intuitive sense to some people that the threat of such a severe penalty as death would lead some drug dealers to consider other ways of making a living.

Opinions about human behavior are rife, and people sometimes state these opinions with such certainty and sincerity that it is easy to assume that they must be true. Yet, years of studying human social behavior have made me acutely aware that people can passionately and sincerely express opinions that are quite inaccurate, or at least so oversimplified as to be terribly misleading. When confronted with an opinion, it is critical to be skeptical and ask, Is this someone's judgment or is it a statement of fact supported by systematic observations?

The scientific approach rests on **data,** or *observations that have been made.* Data are based on seeing, feeling, touching, or recording some phenomenon. The scientific method, as described in this book, is a method for systematically collecting and analyzing data. A person's values and opinions might be based on data, but they are not the same thing. Data need to be interpreted and analyzed in order to give them meaning, and science offers some rules to guide such interpretation and analysis. This interpretation can also be influenced by people's values and opinions. But it is important to keep the notions of values, opinions, and data separate. In science, judgments are made and conclusions drawn on the basis of the analysis of data, not on values or opinions.

In terms of critical thinking skills, then, we can establish the following guidelines for assessing information or arguments:

1. How faithful is the argument to the five characteristics of science?
2. How much factual content is there in a discussion? How much data are presented? Are the data verifiable?
3. Does the discussion revolve around the interpretation of data or the data themselves? Are there alternative interpretations of the data that are logical and defensible?
4. Can you detect the values and opinions being presented and separate them from the facts?
5. Is the person presenting the argument an advocate for a particular position? What potential bias does this suggest?

Key Terms for Review _____

applied sociology
basic sociology
critical thinking
data
opinion

science
social science
social structure
sociology
values

For Further Inquiry _____

Linda H. Aiken and David Mechanic. *Applications of Social Science to Clinical Medicine and Health Policy.* New Brunswick, NJ: Rutgers University Press, 1986.

    This is an excellent volume summarizing some of the contributions that social science research has made in helping health care practitioners provide better services to clients and in developing health care policy.

Bernard Barber. *Effective Social Science: Eight Cases in Economics, Political Science, and Sociology.* New York: Russell Sage Foundation, 1987.

    This book contains interviews with eight social scientists who describe some of the ins and outs of their applied research. It is an informal look at how social science research is done and what the practitioners think of it.

Pauline Bart and Linda Frankel. *The Student Sociologist's Handbook,* 4th ed. New York: Random House, 1986.

    This book is not technically about social research, but it is an excellent resource for doing library research and writing in the social sciences. Any student planning to take more social science courses would be well advised to spend the money for this paperback: It will help you learn how to find information in the social sciences.

Howard E. Freeman, Russell R. Dynes, Peter H. Rossi, and William Foote Whyte (eds.). *Applied Sociology: Roles and Activities of Sociologists in Diverse Settings.* San Francisco: Jossey-Bass, 1983.

    This book contains 27 articles covering the complete range of applied research methods and applied settings in which sociologists work.

Garvin McCain and Ervin M. Segal. *The Game of Science,* 5th ed. Pacific Grove, CA: Brooks/Cole, 1988.

    These authors present an easy to read, yet complete overview of the enterprise of science, both natural and social. In addition to covering the basic logic of science, the book also gets into interesting issues such as the "culture" of the scientist.

Richard P. Nathan. *Social Science in Government: Uses and Misuses.* New York: Basic Books, 1988.

    Nathan, a political scientist, chronicles some of the major applied research that has been sponsored by the government and points out its benefits as well as its downside. He discusses research on welfare reform, job training programs, revenue sharing programs, and the like.

Marvin E. Olsen and Michael Micklin (eds.). *Handbook of Applied Sociology: Frontiers of Contemporary Research.* New York: Praeger, 1981.

This is an excellent compendium of articles reviewing the contribution of applied research in many areas, from the family to education and from health care to legal services.

Howard M. Rebach and John G. Bruhn (eds.). *Handbook of Clinical Sociology.* New York and London: Plenum, 1991.

This book provides a detailed overview of the fields of consulting and clinical sociology, as well as many illustrations of the specific kinds of work that applied sociologists do.

Exercises

1.1. Shortly before the Super Bowl was to be played in Miami in 1989, a riot erupted in one of Miami's neighborhoods. A man had been shot and killed by a police officer in the neighborhood, and in response some people in the neighborhood went on a rampage of destruction. What would be possible individualistic and structural explanations of this event? (To learn more details of this event, consult the *New York Times,* which your library should have on microfilm, or the *New York Times Index.* This newspaper is an excellent source of information about daily events at the national or international level.) What elements of the social structure might come into play in understanding this event? How systematic or objective was your knowledge of this event before you read about it? What about the newspaper accounts? Did they focus on the individualistic or structural level?

1.2. Find a social program that is currently in the news (scour the newspapers, magazines, and broadcast news). In all of the statements about the program from politicians, journalists, and others, can you determine how much of what is said is based on values and opinions and how much on data? From what you can tell, is support for it based on any systematic observations? What kinds of observations could be made in order to provide a scientific foundation for deciding whether to continue, change, or eliminate the program?

1.3. It is useful to explore your values and preferences to see how bias can enter into your own analysis of a problem. Select some problem or policy that is in the news. First, describe what you think would be a feasible solution to the problem. Next, explore with the class how your preferred solution might be influenced by your personal values. Have other students in the class suggest ways in which your recommendations might be biased.

The Elements of Science and Research

OUTLINE

At the foundation of the social scientific approach to problems is a certain logic or way of thinking, and the building blocks for that logic are presented in this chapter. This critical way of thinking can be focused on our most difficult and agonizing problems and can directly impact on people's lives, as the following case study illustrates.

Rick was a young, healthy schoolteacher in Brooklyn, New York, in the late 1970s. He lived in a brownstone on West 78th Street in Manhattan and enjoyed summers at the beach on Long Island. He was also gay. In the summer of 1980, he noticed some bumps behind his ear. His doctor was stunned when he diagnosed the malady as Kaposi's sarcoma, a rare form of skin cancer not often found in healthy young people. Adding to the doctor's surprise was the fact that there was another young man in a nearby hospital with the same rare disease. After some inquiry, the doctor realized, to his additional surprise, that Rick and the other man with Kaposi's had many mutual friends. After his diagnosis, Rick's condition deteriorated rapidly. He lost weight and felt tired all the time. He quit his job. Before the end of the year, Rick was dead, one of the first people in the United States to die of Acquired Immune Deficiency Syndrome (AIDS), although no one recognized the disease by that name in 1980. (This case is taken from Shilts, 1987.)

AIDS has certainly been one of the more tragic public health issues of recent years. In the United States, it has taken its heaviest toll on young, healthy people in the prime of their lives. The disease destroys their immune system, leaving them vulnerable to a host of infections that most of us brush off without noticing. The prognosis is grim: severe weight loss, blindness from infections that attack the optic nerve, repeated bouts of severe pneumonia as bacteria fill the lungs and inhibit breathing. The outcome is predictable: Most eventually die because there is currently no known cure. When public health investigators first noticed something unusual in the early 1980s, all they knew was that young, healthy people were dying of diseases like Kaposi's sarcoma and *pneumocystis carinii* pneumonia that had simply not been health problems for such people previously. In their search for a solution to this puzzle, one of the first clues was the distinctive life-styles of most of the early patients: They were either gay males or intravenous drug users. In a fashion that I describe later in this chapter, these clues were used by applied sociologists and other scientists to begin unraveling the mystery surrounding AIDS.

Before that, however, I present the basic logic that underlies the scientific method and sets the social sciences apart from the way most laypeople think about the world. There is nothing magical or mysterious about this logic. It is merely a systematic way of observing what occurs and analyzing what has been observed.

The Goals of Social Science Research _____

All social science research focuses on achieving one or more of the following goals: description, explanation, and prediction. **Description** refers to *discovering facts or describing reality*. It is a picture or account of what exists, often summarized in terms of numbers, percentages, or some other statistics. Descriptive research answers such questions as: How long do families stay on welfare? What are the attitudes of members of this community toward Asians, Latinos, or other minorities? or, Do the clients of this health center feel satisfied with the services they receive? Descriptive research focuses on presenting in a systematic and objective fashion what is happening in a particular social realm. Examples of descriptive research are *needs assessments* and *social indicators* (see Chapter 1). Before problems can be attacked, we often need to have answers to questions like, How much, How often, and How many? In the area of health policy, for example, statistics like infant mortality rates or overall death rates can be used as indicators of the health status of one group relative to another or to measure changes in health status over time. Needs assessment and social indicators research are discussed at length in Chapter 6.

Explanation focuses on *the determination of how or why something happened.* It goes beyond description to try to explain, or find the causes of, some phenomenon. Explanatory research would focus on slightly different questions than descriptive research: *Why* do some families find it more difficult to get free of welfare? or, *Why* is dissatisfaction high among some health center clients and not others? Traditionally, the explanatory research of most social scientists was basic research, as described in Chapter 1. Today, however, explanatory research has become an important tool in the arsenal of applied research. In a study of a teen parenting program, for example, the researchers wanted to know not only whether the program reduced repeat pregnancies among the program's clients but also why this happened (Henderschott and Norland, 1990). They wanted to know whether the program worked by changing the teens' levels of self-esteem or whether some other mechanism was involved. Such explanation is important because we often need to know why something happens in order to institute or evaluate a policy that will ameliorate the condition. This particular example of applied research was a *program evaluation.*

Prediction refers to *making projections about what will occur in the future or in some other place.* It uses our present knowledge to predict what we would expect to find in another situation. For example, prediction is a goal in some types of *social impact assessments.* If a river is to be dammed to produce electrical power, we can try to predict the social impacts this will have: Increased jobs lead to increased population, putting additional pressure on the school system; if the new workers are young and unmarried, crime rates may increase; and the newly created lake will provide enhanced recreational opportunities (Love, 1983). Social impact assessments, conducted by social scientists, are an attempt to predict the impacts on the social and cultural environment of establishing a program in order to decide whether the benefits outweigh the costs or to see how the costs can be reduced. It is often possible to predict something without explaining it. In fact, actuaries at insurance companies do this all the time by calculating risks and premium levels for insurance policies. From data on past automobile accidents, for example, they predict that young males will—for whatever reasons—have many more accidents than older people, and their insurance rates reflect this fact.

Although we can delineate each of these three goals of research separately, we should recognize that even a simple research project might pursue two or three of them simultaneously. In achieving these goals, applied researchers also focus on one additional overriding goal—*control,* the ability to shape social conditions so that a particular outcome occurs. If we can design a teen parenting program with features that actually do reduce repeat pregnancies among program clients, then we have been able to shape the program so that a desired outcome results. Through our ability to describe, explain, and predict, we can achieve some degree of control that permits us to shape social policy. As Chapter 6 shows, much applied research focuses on how to achieve such control and how to evaluate how much control we have achieved. Before getting into those details of applied sociology, however, we need to look at the basic building blocks of the scientific approach.

The Building Blocks _____

Scientists attempt to be much more precise in their thinking, language, and analysis than people usually are in their everyday lives. They do this in order to reduce the ambiguity, uncertainty, and confusion that can occur when people are not very clear and precise. The building blocks of this precise thinking are the concepts, variables, hypotheses, and theories that are used by scientists.

Concepts and Variables

Human beings conceptualize all the time; it is in our very nature. To *conceptualize* simply means to form an idea of something or to conceive of it mentally. When you get up in the morning, you conceptualize what your day will be like: where you will go, whom you will see, what you will do. You form a mental image of the day. Scientists also conceptualize about what they study. In fact, at the core of all scientific work are **concepts,** *mental images or ideas.* Each concept refers to a group of elements that are all presumed to possess some characteristics in common. Sociologist Jonathan Turner calls concepts the "basic building blocks of theory" (1974:5). *Crime, poverty, education,* and *social class* are examples of concepts used in the social sciences. We could define each of these concepts by specifying what all the elements identified by the particular concept share in common. So, all *crimes* involve some violation of a criminal code. If an act does not violate a criminal code, it is not included under the concept of *crime.*

Scientists try to be very precise and detailed in developing concepts so that they can make clear and precise statements about what they find in the world. This detail often sounds like minor quibbling to laypeople. But it is essential to be precise if science is to be accurate and cumulative. For example, if two separate researchers produce some findings on the relationship between social class and crime, we need to be sure that they both mean the same thing by social class and crime. If, by social class, one researcher is referring to people's level of education while the other is referring to their income level, then they are talking about two quite different, although related, phenomena. If their concepts have different meanings, then their research results are not directly comparable.

Some concepts have only a single category or value. The concept *universe,* for example, refers to the totality of all things that exist. There is, by definition, only one universe (ignoring the science fiction device of alternate time lines, each with its own universe), and it doesn't make sense to talk about degrees or amounts of universe. It either exists or it doesn't. Most scientific concepts, on the other hand, contain a number of categories or values, and these concepts are called **variables** because their *values can vary.* Age and gender are two important variables in social science research. Age can take on a whole range of values, such as 2 or 42 years, but gender can take on only two values, female or male.

Hypotheses

A central strategy in the scientific method is the development of **hypotheses,** which are *testable statements describing the relationship between two or more variables.* Hypotheses state what the researcher expects to find, and they are at the core of most research, with the exception of some descriptive research where they may not be necessary or may be implicit. In order to be useful, hypotheses must be testable; that is, they must involve statements of fact that can be decided by some empirical test. A hypothesis linking the variables of social class and crime might look like this: Lower-class people will commit more burglaries than people in the middle or upper classes. A statement that is not testable, and thus not a useful scientific hypothesis, is the following: Crime among the lower classes should be reduced. This is a statement of preference or value that cannot be resolved by empirical test.

In stating hypotheses, researchers usually distinguish between two types of variables. An **independent variable** is *a variable that brings about a change in another variable. The variable that is changed* is the

dependent variable; *its value is, in a sense, dependent on the value of the independent variable.* So, a hypothesis would typically take the following form: Independent variable *X* has a specified effect on a dependent variable *Y*. The hypothesis "Males commit more violent crimes than do females" links the independent variable *gender* with the dependent variable *violent crime.* It is important that the independent and dependent variables in hypotheses be clearly specified.

Theory Development and Verification

The ultimate goal of a science like sociology is to shape our knowledge into theories (Collins, 1989). A **theory** is *a set of logical and empirical statements that provides an explanation of some phenomenon.* Often, we not only want to know that something happened but also why it happened. It is interesting to know that social class is linked to crime, but is it far more valuable to know why: What social structures or social processes influence people in lower-class positions to commit more crimes, or at least more of certain types of crimes, than their middle-class counterparts? Theories provide this explanatory knowledge, and social science theories focus on social structure and social process (see Chapter 1) as the key independent variables that shape and explain people's behavior. Theories are broader and more encompassing than concepts and hypotheses. In fact, theories serve to link a variety of concepts and hypotheses into an elaborate, abstract explanatory network.

Theory verification is a primary goal of basic research and a secondary or implicit goal in much applied research. The process of theory verification is outlined in Figure 2.1. The figure shows that theories are very abstract because they describe general concepts rather than specific things or events; observations, on the other hand, are very concrete. An abstract concept would be the notion of *crime;* a concrete observation would be *Joe Smith robs a convenience store.* So, the first step in theory verification is to derive testable hypotheses from abstract theories. Then observations are made to see if the hypotheses are confirmed. These observations, along with any conclusions drawn from them, are the research findings. If the research findings confirm the hypotheses, they serve as support or verification for the theory.

Because theories are very abstract, a large number of hypotheses can be derived from any theory. In fact, more hypotheses can be derived than we could ever possibly test. As a result, theory verification is always a matter of degree because there are always hypotheses that have yet to be tested. However, if many hypotheses from a theory have

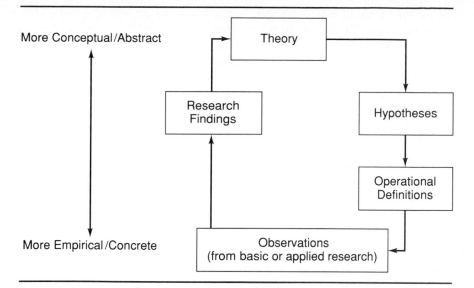

Figure 2.1 The Process of Theory Verification

been tested and confirmed, then we have confidence that the overall theory is an accurate explanation of reality. On the other hand, if only one or a few hypotheses derived from a theory have been tested, or if some hypotheses have been confirmed and others disconfirmed, then we would be cautious about considering the theory a completely accurate explanation. It may need revision before it can serve as an acceptable explanation.

In some people's minds, the term *theory* carries with it connotations of conjecture or speculation. They contrast unproven theory with proven fact, but this is a misunderstanding of theories as they are used in science. A theory is, first and foremost, an explanation. It may be well tested and well proven or not, but its level of verification is not what makes it a theory. For example, one thoroughly tested theory is Emile Durkheim's explanation of suicide based on the influence of social bonds and social regulation in people's lives (Durkheim, 1897/1951). Although we are still trying to assess which parts of social life these mechanisms affect, the basic proposition that fewer social bonds in people's lives increase the chances of suicide has been well established through research. On the other hand, there are a number of theories that point to early childhood experiences or labeling processes as determinants of sexual preference, but these have not yet been well proven. So, theories are not just speculations or conjecture; they are attempts to link concepts, hypotheses, and observations into a structure of explanation.

Theory development and verification are areas where basic and applied research diverge from one another, although the difference is more a matter of degree than of kind (Nafstad, 1982; Larson, 1990). Both types of research utilize theories. In basic research, theory development and verification are primary goals while they are less central in applied research. However, applied researchers use theories in a number of ways. First, existing theories may be used in developing research strategies and solutions to problems in applied research. For example, an environmental impact assessment of the effect of building a power plant in a rural area might address the following question: What would be the impact of the new jobs and additional people in the labor force (Love, 1983)? There are well-tested theories that can help answer this question: Theories of labor force participation and mobility in the workplace can help us assess the likely characteristics of these new workers; theories linking such variables as age, gender, and crime can tell us what kinds of crime might increase and by how much; theories of the life cycle can tell us what kinds of educational or health services these new workers and their families will need. Applied research often begins by turning to existing theories as a source of knowledge (see Figure 1.1).

A second place for theory in applied research is in explaining the outcome. If a needs assessment shows that certain kinds of people on welfare tend to be deficient in literacy and math skills, theories of poverty, subculture, and education may point to some of the reasons for this, and that knowledge could contribute to the shaping of an intervention plan. Once again, it is important to recognize that facts by themselves are sometimes not very enlightening, or at least not totally satisfying. Full understanding typically calls for an awareness of the social structures and social mechanisms that lie behind the observed facts and explain their occurrence.

Third, theories play a part in applied research because the research outcome can provide implicit, if not explicit, verification for some theory. A study of teen parenting programs was based on theories of the development of self-esteem and the effect of self-esteem on adolescent behavior (Henderschott and Norland, 1990). If the program works as predicted, then further confirmation for the theories of self-esteem on which it was based is provided. This verification may not have been the primary goal of the research, but it can still be an outcome. However, theory verification is not an inevitable by-product of applied research. If applied research is to serve this goal, procedures will have to be carefully planned and included in the research so that this goal can be achieved. Basically, programs would have to be designed so that some outcomes could be interpreted as confirmation for the theory while others could be interpreted as disconfirmation. In fact, some sociologists argue that applied sociologists should feel as much obligation toward providing theory verification as they do toward providing a product for their clients. This can be done by integrating theory, as much as possible, into applied research projects.

Types of Research Designs

With these building blocks in place, scientists can begin to consider specific **research designs,** which are *detailed plans that specify exactly how a research project will be conducted and what observations will be made.* Chapters 4 and 5 discuss in detail the four research designs most commonly used in applied research, but I introduce them here in order to begin fleshing out how scientists do their work. An *experiment* is a controlled type of observation in which the value of an independent variable is allowed to change in order to observe its effect on a dependent variable. Experiments allow more precision and control than some other research designs and are useful for assessing causal relationships. The term *surveys* refers to observational techniques in which people are asked questions and their answers serve as data. Surveys are a useful and inexpensive technique for reaching large numbers of people. *Qualitative research* attempts broad descriptions of people's personal experiences and interpretations through directly observing people going about their daily activities or through lengthy and broad-ranging interviews with them. Unlike surveys or experiments, which are more likely to quantify the human experience, qualitative research assumes that some fundamental aspect of human social conduct is missed when reduced to numbers. Finally, *available data* refers to observations that are derived from data collected by someone else, such as a government bureau or a private or professional organization. Many organizations and agencies collect such data as a part of their daily operations, and the data can be very usefully and inexpensively put to use in many research projects.

Underlying all of these research designs is the question of how to measure the variables being studied, and there is considerable debate about this issue.

Quantification and Measurement _____

In the social sciences, **quantitative methods** refer to *making observations that are numerical in nature and can be analyzed through various statistical procedures.* Problems are reduced to questions such as, How much? How many? and How long? In contrast are **qualitative methods,** which *focus on those aspects of the human experience whose meaning can't be captured by reduction to numbers or quantities.* Chapter 5 discusses the qualitative approach in some detail, especially as it is used in applied research. Much of applied research, however, deals with issues that seem amenable to quantitative analysis. For example, policy analysts in the criminal justice area have been concerned with the problem of *recidivism,* which occurs when an inmate released from prison commits another crime. Recidivism is a very serious problem: A 1989 study by the Bureau of Justice Statistics found that two of every three inmates released from state prisons in the United States are rearrested for a serious crime within three years. How do we begin to get a handle on this problem? One research project focused on which punishments work best against criminals, with the independent variable being the type of punishment the criminal received: a jail term, a fine, or probation (Wheeler and Hissong, 1988). Then, the issue can be readily reduced to numbers. If we assume that the "best" punishment is the one that deters people from committing future crimes, the dependent variable could be how many weeks, months, or years a released convict stays free of crime for each type of punishment. Certainly other variables could be introduced into this analysis, such as the type of crime committed or the number of previous convictions for crimes, but all of these variables can be quantified. This study, focusing on people who had committed a first-offense misdemeanor, found that probation was the most effective deterrent against future involvement in crime.

Such quantification, of course, simplifies the richness and the complexity of the human experience. We don't know exactly why probation was more effective; we don't know how the various punishments were perceived and experienced by the individuals; and we know nothing about the quality of the lives of these people either inside or outside prison. And all of these are legitimate issues that could influence crime, recidivism, or other relevant matters. However, from an applied perspective, we have learned one very important fact from this quantitative research: For 100 first offenders, over 90 will be crime-free after three years if given probation as compared to less than 70 of those sent to jail. As a basis for making policy decisions, this is powerful evidence that has implications for such very practical considerations as jail crowding and the cost of our criminal justice system.

In addition to its utility for some applied research, quantification is also valuable because it affords us precision. We can state in very exact fashion the differences between groups or how much improvement can be expected because of a program. In the previous example, we were able to specify precisely what percentage improvement can be expected from probation as compared to a jail sentence. This enables us to assess whether the improvement is significant. It also puts us in a better position to state whether the costs of a program are worth the benefits to be gained from it. This becomes very important in cost-benefit analysis (see Chapter 6).

So, quantification is central to applied social research. This does not mean that people can be reduced to numbers, as social scientists are sometimes accused of doing. No social scientist would ever claim that the numbers can define the totality of the human experience. In any situation, there are human qualities and emotions that surely transcend the limited meaning that can be collapsed into a set of numbers. The experience of love, or respect, or awe in the life of an individual is certainly something quite apart from the statistics that tell us how many men and women marry or the percentage of Americans who attend church. Yet, for developing social policy and assessing solutions to problems, the numbers can be very valuable. The key is to recognize their limits, and this brings us to the topic of measurement.

Measurement refers to *ways of determining the existence, value, level, or degree of some phenomenon*. It is the process of moving from an abstract level to a concrete level (Miller, 1991). Research normally begins with an abstract definition of the concepts of interest—a verbal description of the characteristics of the concept, much like the dictionary definition of words. However, this is much too imprecise for scientific work because concepts often describe very complex phenomena that can manifest themselves in any number of ways. For example, the concept of *crime* has many dimensions. Homicide and assault are crimes, but then so are speeding in an automobile and making false statements on your income tax return. Although they all fall under the abstract concept of *crime,* in reality they differ from one another in some marked ways. So, abstract concepts can be imprecise because they are so general. Abstract definitions are imprecise for another reason: They do not tell us exactly how the existence or value of some phenomenon will be determined. This is a problem even with a concept as seemingly simple and straightforward as gender. Traditionally, gender is determined by asking people what their sex is. In some research contexts, however, this method may not be available. In the Census Bureau's effort to include the homeless in the 1990 census, for example, it sent census takers out into the streets after midnight to look for people sleeping in public places (Edmondson, 1988). Without waking the person (to protect the privacy of the sleeping person and the safety of the census takers), they made an observational judgment of the person's gender, along with other characteristics.

Given the clothing and hairstyles of some homeless people, there were probably more errors in this type of measurement of gender than in the way it is traditionally done. But the point is that even with a concept as straightforward as gender, there is more than one way to determine its existence or value in a particular case, and most concepts in social research are far more complex to measure than gender.

So, as an important part of the process of measurement, researchers transform their conceptual definitions into operational definitions (see Figure 2.1). An **operational definition** specifies *the exact procedures, or operations, that are used in measuring a concept.* It makes the abstract concept very precise and is typically more limited in nature than the abstract concept because virtually any concept can be measured with more than one operational definition, some by a large number. Each operational definition, in turn, focuses on a slightly different aspect of reality. Figure 2.2 provides two examples of how the same concept can be measured with more than one operational definition. Because a research project will use only one operational definition, it will address only one of the many aspects of reality subsumed under the abstract concept.

Developing operational definitions is very important and can be exceedingly creative and complex. There are also many practical obstacles that are encountered. In the previously mentioned study of the effectiveness of various types of punishment, the researchers needed to operationalize the dependent variable, recidivism. The conceptual definition of a crime is that it is the violation of a criminal code. But what operations, or precise steps, would you follow to determine whether people had committed crimes during a three-year span? You could ask them at the end of the time period whether they had done so, but we know that some people shade the truth, especially when asked about sensitive topics. Another approach would be to have a team of researchers follow them around and observe any crimes they might commit. However, this would be far too costly for most research projects, and it also suffers from a problem called **reactivity:** *The idea that being observed can change the way people behave.* In this case, being followed by a researcher may so intimidate or otherwise influence people that they don't commit crimes that they would have committed if not observed. If this happens, it is the observation, rather than the type of punishment, that reduced criminal activity. Yet a third problem with this operational definition is a technical one: In our system of justice, a person is innocent until judged guilty in a court of law. We can conclude that a person committed a crime only when a court has judged him or her guilty. Researchers do not have (nor should they have) the societal authority to judge whether a person has committed a crime. This decision is often a matter of judgment and interpretation

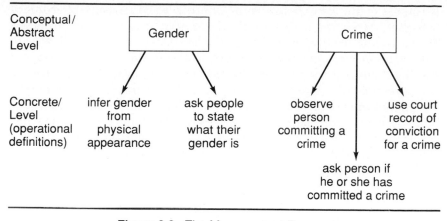

Figure 2.2 The Measurement Process

in the application of the law. Take the case of Bernhard Goetz who shot four men in a subway car. Did he commit felony assault or attempted murder? Or was his act one of self-defense, involving no crime? People understandably disagree about this, illustrating why it would be problematic to allow researchers or their assistants to assess whether a person has committed a crime. As noted in Chapter 1: Social reality is complex and based on the subjective meanings that people attach to actions and events. Goetz's actions are well known; it is their interpretation (attempted murder versus self-defense) that is under dispute. But that interpretation is crucial to how each of us reacts to Goetz and his actions. Science doesn't make reality any less complex, but it does force us to recognize the complexity and enables us to better appreciate it.

In the study of crime, researchers often rely on the courts to make the judgment of whether a person has committed a crime, and this was done in this study. They operationalized recidivism to mean "reconviction for any Class A or B misdemeanor or felony law violation" (Wheeler and Hissong, 1988:513). Then they examined the court records in the county where the people had been convicted of their first crime and the National Crime Information Center statistics. This operational definition has its weaknesses, of course, the main one being that many crimes never result in a court conviction. However, as with many choices among operational definitions, researchers select the definition that has the fewest problems and is the most accurate.

The accuracy of a measurement device is called its **validity,** and it is one of the major criteria used to assess measurement: Does an operational definition actually measure what we claim that it mea- sures? For example, a thermometer is a valid measure of temperature.

Is conviction for a crime in a court of law a valid measure of criminal behavior? Most sociologists would agree that it is a reasonably valid measure, although with some limitations. Another criterion used to evaluate measurement devices is **reliability:** *the ability of a measuring device to achieve consistent results each time it is used.* In other words, measurement results from one time to another should change only if the phenomenon being measured has changed. The specific techniques for assessing validity and reliability are complex and beyond the scope of this book, but it is important to recognize that there are sophisticated, although not foolproof, ways to evaluate the validity and reliability of measuring devices. Research in Action 2.1 discusses some aspects of operational definitions and validity.

RESEARCH IN ACTION 2.1 ══════════════════════════════════════

How Many Homeless People Are There?

Operational definitions have implications for the issues of advocacy and objectivity (see Chapter 1). Peter Rossi and his colleagues found this out in a needs assessment of homelessness they conducted in Chicago (Rossi, 1987; Rossi et al., 1987). Rossi and his colleagues' basic goal was to provide a solid foundation for estimating the number of homeless people in Chicago and determining some of their characteristics. The problem that arose was that their research estimate showed far fewer homeless people in Chicago than the various groups advocating for the homeless claimed existed. The latter said there were between 20,000 and 25,000 homeless, while Rossi and his colleagues, by their most generous estimate, could find no more than 7,000.

The advocates were outraged at this low estimate and responded by attacking the validity of Rossi's operational definition. The problem here is that there is no inherently or objectively "best" operational definition of homelessness. As Rossi and his colleagues (1987:1336) point out:

[T]here is a continuum running from the obviously domiciled to the obviously homeless, with many ambiguous cases to be encountered along the continuum. Any effort to draw a line across that continuum demarcating the homed from the homeless, is of necessity somewhat arbitrary and therefore potentially contentious.

This continuum is illustrated in Figure 2.3. Rossi and his colleagues had defined the homeless as people with no regular access to a conventional dwelling or residence. This excluded people who lived precariously in SRO (single-room-occupancy) hotels, double upped with other family members, or had a bed in a dormitory-type shelter. Advocates for the homeless thought that all these people ought to be included under the concept *homeless,* which would substantially increase the estimate of the number of homeless over that of the researchers.

In this case, values and interests play a part in the decisions about operational definitions in at least two ways. First, it is in the interest of the advocacy groups to stretch the operational definition in

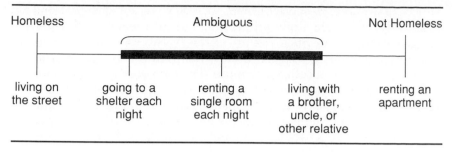

Figure 2.3 The Continuum of Homelessness

the direction of the domiciled end of the continuum, which will result in a larger estimate of the number of homeless. This will present the problem as more serious and widespread and increase the pressure on politicians and the public to devote resources toward alleviating the problem—a more beneficial outcome of the research as far as the advocates of the homeless are concerned. Second, as Rossi and his colleagues (1987:1336) point out, "A definition of homelessness is ... a statement as to what should constitute the floor of housing adequacy below which no member of society should be permitted to fall." Is it acceptable for people to live double upped with an uncle, brother, or other relative? If you think it is, then you will not see these people as homeless and will tend to restrict the definition of homelessness. A different political ideology might find such living accommodations unacceptable in late twentieth-century America on the grounds that our affluence should provide a home for every person or family. People who believe this will be inclined to expand the definition of homelessness. The point is that where you draw the line across that continuum is a function of political ideology, cultural values, and personal interest. There is no scientific way to decide that issue. And this is true of many operational definitions: There are no objective criteria that can be used to say which is best. The careful and critical stance is to be aware of the impact of values on decisions, even though the impact cannot be eliminated. In this way you can assess how much bias is created, and in what direction, by using a given operational definition. This research illustration reinforces a point made in Chapter 1: It is important to know in detail how a study is conducted. In this case, it is impossible to make a full assessment of Rossi and his colleagues' findings—to understand the true meaning of the numbers—without knowing how homelessness was operationally defined. Different operational definitions rest on different value bases.

Who to Observe? The Problem of Sampling

An important part of systematic research is deciding which people or groups will serve as a source of data. If the people we are interested in studying are few in number or we have unlimited resources with which to conduct research, then we could make observations on everybody. We could study all prisoners or all pregnant teenagers or all abusive spouses. Such luxury is rarely the case, however. More typically, we select *a number of elements from a larger population of elements,* and this is called a **sample.** The elements that make up the sample are often people, but they could also be households, groups, or organizations. Observations are made on the elements in the sample, and then what we find in the sample is used to draw conclusions about the population as a whole. Although we make observations on the sample, it is the population that we are really interested in learning about. The sample is only a practical vehicle for getting there, but choosing a proper sample is critical to drawing sound conclusions. So, researchers are very careful in choosing samples because poorly drawn samples are a major threat to objectivity and can lead to biased and inaccurate conclusions. In fact, poor sampling procedures can lead to biased samples even though the researcher is not aware of it and thinks the sampling is sound. For this reason, a great deal of thought and attention is put into sampling procedures.

The Importance of Representative Samples

A critical test that a sample must pass is to provide some assurance that it is representative of the population about which conclusions are to be drawn. Scientific sampling provides such assurances. The ideal in sampling would be to produce a *representative sample*—one that reflects the population on all relevant variables. If the population is 40 percent male, then a representative sample would be 40 percent male; if the mean annual income in the population is $27,000, then the sample would have the same mean income; and so on for all the variables relevant to a particular study. Conclusions drawn from such a sample can be safely generalized to the population as a whole. And this is the key issue in sampling: Can we draw inferences about the population from the sample?

A variety of sampling procedures are used in scientific research. The best of them are procedures that, in the long run, produce the most representative samples.

Sampling Strategies

The best *sampling strategies are those in which each element in the population has a chance of being selected for the sample.* These are called **probability samples** (Scheaffer, Mendenhall, and Ott, 1986). One of the major failings of sampling techniques is that they are often designed such that some people have little or no chance to appear in the sample. Probability sampling always begins with a *sampling frame,* which is a list of all the elements in a population that should have a chance to appear in the sample; the sample is then selected from the elements listed in the sampling frame. The basic issue is whether the sampling frame is complete: Do all of the elements in the population actually show up in the sampling frame? This problem can be illustrated in a needs assessment survey on which I worked that used households as the unit of analysis. A listing of all the households in a county (homes, apartments, and so on) was used as the sampling frame from which the sample was then drawn. If we had relied solely on telephone listings or voter registration lists to generate that sampling frame of all households in the county, it would have been incomplete and biased because households without a telephone or in which no one was registered to vote would be excluded. And it tends to be the poorer and less educated people who are without telephones and don't register to vote. So our sample would have been biased in favor of the more well-to-do and better educated. To avoid this problem, we supplemented these two listings of households with a list of all electricity hookups from the local electric company. Few Americans these days are without electricity, and these lists provided a fairly complete sampling frame from which to draw the actual sample.

The basic probability sample is called a **simple random sample** in which *each element in a population has an equal probability of appearing in the sample.* To illustrate this technique, you could write the names of each person in a group on separate, equal-sized pieces of paper and place them in a large bin. The bin is tumbled and a blindfolded person reaches in and selects a sheet of paper. The person removes his or her hand and retumbles the bin before selecting the next sheet of paper. This is done 100 times to select a sample size of 100. With such a procedure, most would agree that no slip of paper would have a greater probability of being selected than any other slip, as long as the person is blindfolded and the bin is repeatedly tumbled.

We can use the simple random sample to explain a little bit of the logic of all probability sampling, which is based on probability theory. *Probability theory* is based on the likelihood of certain phenomena happening. If I flip a coin, there is a 50 percent chance that it will turn up heads on any one flip. If I flip the coin 10 times, the most likely outcome will be 5 heads and 5 tails. However, it is possible, by chance, to get 4 heads and 6 tails or 3 heads and 7 tails. These last two outcomes are possible but less likely than the first. It is even possible to get 10 heads and no tails, but there would be a very small likelihood of this. With 10 flips, the odds are very good that, by chance, at least one of them will come up tails.

This same logic of probabilities is applied to sampling. If a random sample is chosen, the most likely outcome, by chance, is a sample that is representative of the population from which it was drawn. Somewhat less likely, but still very possible, is a slightly unrepresentative sample. A highly unrepresentative sample can occur, but the probability is very small. For example, the student body at my university consists of approximately 3,700 men and 3,700 women. If I selected a simple random sample of 200 students, I would like to have 100 men and 100 women in the sample. However, it would be likely, by pure chance, that the sample would differ from the population by a small amount, say 90 men and 110 women. It is possible that a sample with 190 women and 10 men could be picked, but the chances are very small. So random sampling procedures offer the greatest probability but not certainty that the sample is representative, because any sampling procedure has at least a small chance of producing a highly biased and thus unrepresentative sample. So, what probability sampling offers is not an unbiased sample but rather the *highest probability* that there is little or no bias in a sample.

Today, researchers don't use bins and blindfolds and pieces of paper to produce a simple random sample. In most cases, especially for large samples, computer technology is put to work. Each element in a sampling frame is numbered sequentially. So, 8,000 students would be numbered 1 through 8,000. Then, for a sample size of 200, a computer generates a list of 200 random numbers between 1 and 8,000. Then the elements in the population that were assigned those randomly selected numbers become the sample upon which observations are made. (For small samples, a table of random numbers might be used instead of the computer, but the logic is the same. See Monette, Sullivan, and DeJong, 1990, on the use of these tables.) The result is a sample in which there is no bias in the selection of elements and in which each element has the same chance of appearing in the sample.

Sometimes it is impractical or too expensive to use simple random sampling. An alternative (actually a variation on it) is **systematic sampling,** in which *every nth element in a sampling frame is selected for the sample.* So, with a population size of 8,000 and a sample size of 200, you would select every 8,000/200 or every fortieth element, beginning with a randomly selected starting point in the sampling frame. At the end of the sampling frame, you jump to the beginning and continue until you are back at the starting point.

Over the years, researchers have debated the relative merits of simple random versus systematic sampling. It seems that, in most cases, they produce nearly identical results in terms of unbiased samples. Because systematic samples are a little easier to do, they tend to be the preferred choice. There is one situation, however, where the utility of systematic samples needs to be assessed—where there is *periodicity* in the sampling frame or a cyclical pattern to the elements that might coincide with the sampling interval. Suppose we were sampling households in a large apartment building. The apartments are listed in the sampling frame by floor and apartment number (2A, 2B, 2C, 2D, 2E, 2F, 3A, 3B, and so on). Further, suppose that on each floor apartment F is a corner apartment with an extra bedroom and correspondingly higher rent than the other apartments on the floor. If we had a sampling interval of three and randomly chose to begin counting with apartment 2D, every F apartment would appear in the sample, which would mean that the sample is biased in favor of the more expensive apartments and thus the more affluent residents. So, when using systematic sampling techniques, the sampling frame needs to be carefully assessed for periodicity. This is only rarely a problem, however.

A third type of probability sample is a **stratified sample** in which a *population is divided into a number of groups, or strata, and then simple random or systematic samples are selected from each group.* In fact, this alternative might have occurred to you earlier when I mentioned that an unbiased sample of students at my university would contain 100 men and 100 women. Instead of selecting a simple random sample with a high but not certain probability that it will contain 100 men and 100 women, we could divide the population of students into two groups, one containing all male students and the other all female students. Then a simple random sample of 100 could be selected from each group. This provides certainty that the sample is unbiased as far as the variable of gender is concerned. Such stratifying is commonly done on variables that are important in a particular research project.

One benefit of stratified samples is that compared to simple random or systematic samples of the same size, they tend to be less biased. Another benefit is that one can select an extra large sample from a stratum that is relatively small in the population, thus ensuring that there are enough cases in that stratum for data analysis. For example, state and national opinion polls, which usually have a sample size of 1,200–1,500, typically include only 150–200 African-Americans, according to Howard Garrison (1981), who was a social science research analyst for the U.S. Commission on Civil Rights. Such a small sample of African-Americans is more likely to be biased than is a larger one. It also does not permit the sophisticated investigation of subgroups among African-Americans. There is substantial regional, religious, and socioeconomic variation among African-Americans, but once we start breaking the small sample down into all these subgroups, there will be too few cases in many of them to do an adequate statistical analysis. With a sample stratified by race, researchers can select disproportionately more African-Americans for the sample and can do a more sophisticated analysis of data on them, with more complex comparisons to other Americans.

The fourth type of probability sample is one with many applied research uses, such as public opinion polling. Called **multistage cluster sampling** or **area sampling,** it involves *sampling at a number of different stages, beginning by sampling clusters of people and later selecting the actual people within each cluster upon whom observations will be made.* It is called area sampling because the initial clusters are often selected by geographic areas, such as counties or congressional districts. Multistage cluster sampling is used when it is impractical or impossible to create a complete sampling frame of the population. For a statewide survey, for example, it is much more costly and time-consuming to create a list of all adults in the state than it is to do the same for a couple of counties. Research in Action 2.2 discusses an example of cluster sampling in applied research; it also illustrates once again how theories play a part in applied research.

RESEARCH IN ACTION 2.2 ▄▄▄▄▄▄▄▄▄▄▄▄▄▄▄▄▄▄▄▄▄▄▄▄▄▄▄▄▄

Controlling Delinquency

All social scientists develop an appreciation for the complexity of social reality. Chapter 1 reviewed research showing that the stronger response to a crime like spouse abuse (namely, arrest) tends to be more effective in preventing future episodes of abuse. Then, earlier in this chapter, we saw that probation was a more effective punishment for first-offense misdemeanors than was the seemingly stronger punishment of a jail term. So, which is it? Is a strong response to crime better? Or is the more lenient reaction better? Again, social reality is far more complex than we often think, as is shown in a study of juvenile delinquency (Palamara, Cullen, and Gersten, 1986).

Recall that the spouse abuse study described in Research in Action 1.1 was considered a test of specific deterrence theory as compared to labeling theory and that the predictions of labeling theory did not receive much support. This research on juvenile delinquency was also considered a test of labeling theory: Does the labeling of juveniles through police intervention increase their involvement in delinquency in the future, as labeling theory would predict? To test this, the researchers wanted a representative sample of juveniles between the ages of 6 and 18. They used a combination of sampling strategies, something that is often done in applied research. They combined cluster sampling with systematic and simple random sampling. First, for a large section of Manhattan, they listed all clusters of housing units containing eight dwellings or households. Systematic sampling was then used to select clusters of dwelling units: Beginning with a randomly selected cluster, every thirtieth cluster was chosen. Within each selected cluster, families were chosen if they contained a youth between 6 and 18 years of age. If there was more than one such youth in a family, one of the youths was randomly selected to be included in the study.

Over time, some youths in the sample came in contact with the police because of their delinquent activities, while others didn't. The researchers were interested in whether that contact produced an increase in subsequent delinquent behavior. After analyzing the results of their research, the investigators concluded that intervention by the police did not prevent future delinquency. Those who came to the attention of the police were more likely to be involved in future episodes of delinquency, which is what labeling theory would predict. So, unlike the spouse abusers, aggressive inter-vention seems detrimental with juveniles. This example shows the complexity of human behavior. The youths in this study—more likely to be runaways or truants than serious violent or property criminals—are in different circumstances than the spouse abusers. A unitary mode of intervention for all crimes is not likely to be effective with all offenders, illustrating again the value of careful assessment through observation to see whether interventions work the way we believe they will. This research study also illustrates how a variety of sampling strategies are often used together in a single research project.

There are a number of sampling strategies that involve **nonprobability samples,** in which *it is not known whether each population element has a chance of appearing in the sample.* In fact, with nonprobability samples, some elements may have *no chance at all* to appear in the sample, resulting in a biased sample. For example, a **convenience sample** is one in which *people are selected for the sample because they are convenient or available to the researcher.* Studies of the effectiveness of psychotherapy, for example, often use as samples the clients of a particular psychotherapist or mental health clinic. Psychotherapy clients who do not see that therapist or attend that clinic have no chance of appearing in the sample. Another example of a nonprobability sample is a **snowball sample,** in which *the early cases in a sample are used to help identify additional people to sample.* However, anyone who is not known by someone who is already in the sample has no chance of being selected for the sample.

Nonprobability samples are useful in situations where there is neither the time nor the resources to develop a complete sampling frame or where it is impossible to do so. Research in Action 2.3 illustrates this in the fight against AIDS. Nonprobability samples are also generally much less time-consuming and costly to construct. However, the major weakness with them is that we don't know what kind of bias they contain. Any nonprobability sample should lead to suspicion about bias, and we must be cautious about generalizing a population from such a sample.

RESEARCH IN ACTION 2.3 ━━━━━━━━━━━━━━━━━━━━━━━━━━━━━━━━━━━━━

The Fight Against AIDS

Scientists at the Centers for Disease Control (CDC) in Atlanta were among the first to look into the new disease afflicting people like Rick around 1980. A first step in attempting to understand a new disease is often to focus on the social characteristics and life-styles of people who contract the disease to see if some clues might be found regarding mode of transmission or potential genetic causes. Scientists at the CDC did this with the early cases of the then still mysterious disease. Participating in this investigation was William Darrow, a research sociologist with expertise in sexually transmitted diseases and the gay community. At the time, there was great controversy and confusion about the disease. Many thought it was relatively unimportant, while others thought it might be linked to inhalants that some gays used at the time to enhance sexual pleasure. Darrow, looking at the social characteristics and life-style patterns of the early patients, was alarmed. His conclusion: "It looks more like a sexually transmitted disease than syphilis" (Shilts, 1987:87).

In the first half of the 1980s, Darrow and other scientists at the CDC were attempting to test the hypothesis that AIDS was sexually transmitted. If it was, they could make some recommendations about curing, or at least controlling the spread of AIDS. As an important step in establishing that the disease was sexually transmitted, they needed to compare the sexual activities of gay men with the disease to those of gay men without it. One problem they faced was a sampling problem. A probability sample was out of the question because there would be no way to establish a sampling frame of all gay men without

the disease. Instead they used a combination of convenience and snowball sampling (Jaffe et al., 1983). They asked health departments, private clinics, and private physicians to provide names of gay men who would be willing to participate in the study. They also asked each person with AIDS to provide the name of a gay male friend who had not been his sexual partner. What Darrow and his colleagues found in this pioneering study was a link between sexual activities and AIDS: People with AIDS, compared to those free of the disease, were more likely to engage in what is now called "unsafe" sex; they had many more sexual partners; and they were more likely to find sex partners in bathhouses. In a later study of AIDS among prostitutes, they used a similar sampling procedure: recruiting prostitutes from among women in prison, from venereal disease clinics, and from methadone maintenance clinics. In these studies, they found that the prostitutes at greatest risk of contracting AIDS were those who were also intravenous drug users and never used condoms (Darrow et al., 1987).

The battle against AIDS is a good illustration of a situation where nonprobability samples are not only acceptable but required. Probability samples were out of the question, and the problem was too serious to be ignored. From research such as this, Darrow and other scientists were able to determine that AIDS was transmitted through contact with blood. Once this was established, they could make some critical public health recommendations aimed at controlling the spread of AIDS: Test the blood supply for antibodies to the AIDS virus, educate people about safe sex, close or closely regulate gay bath-houses and other settings conducive to multiple sex partners. If their research had not been systematically done—including the use of sound sampling procedures—the results would not have been accepted by the public health community and acted on by policymak-ers and politicians. As it was, even with sound research procedures, it was difficult to convince everyone that AIDS could be sexually transmitted. These recommendations were too late to help Rick, but they undoubtedly did save the lives of countless others.

CRITICAL THINKING

Clarity and Precision

I have spent considerable time talking about theories and hypotheses, measurement, and sampling because these are the major building blocks of the systematic approach of social science research. They are a part of the effort to be as careful and precise as possible in order to avoid misunderstanding and reduce the possibility of bias. An awareness of their importance and application to particular situations—whether in a research context or in everyday life—can enhance your ability to critically analyze information. In approaching a topic or situation, then, consider the following:

1. What explicit or implicit theories of human behavior underlie what a person is saying? What assumptions or values do these theories contain?
2. What level of precision is being used? Are the phenomena considered abstract or concrete? Could there be imprecision that is producing bias, error, or misunderstanding?
3. Are operational definitions being used? What values or interests might be served by these definitions as opposed to competing definitions? What bias might the operational definitions produce? Are there alternative operational definitions that could be used, and how would they change the meaning? Is there any question about the validity and reliability of the operational definitions?
4. Which people or groups are actually being observed? Are there people or groups who had little or no chance of appearing in the sample and what bias might this produce?
5. Are there alternative sampling procedures that might have produced different or better samples? Are the alternatives feasible?

Key Terms for Review

area sample
concept

convenience sample
dependent variable

description
explanation
hypothesis
independent variable
measurement
multistage cluster sample
nonprobability sample
operational definition
prediction
probability sample
qualitative methods
quantitative methods
reactivity
reliability
research designs
sample
simple random sample
snowball sample
stratified sample
systematic sample
theory
validity
variable

For Further Inquiry

Morton Hunt. *Profiles of Social Research: The Scientific Study of Human Interactions.* New York: Russell Sage Foundation, 1985.
> This is an excellent book, written by a professional writer rather than a social scientist, showing how social science is done and communicating the excitement and value of it. It focuses in detail on the work of five applied social scientists whose work had a substantial impact on public policy.

Abraham Kaplan. *The Conduct of Inquiry.* New York: Harper & Row, 1963
> This book contains a very good analysis of the logic of the social sciences, covering such topics as the development of concepts and theories and the role of values in research.

John G. Kemeny. *A Philosopher Looks at Science.* Princeton, NJ: D. Van Nostrand, 1959.
> To fully understand the scientific method, it is useful to have exposure to a field known as the *philosophy of science,* which focuses on the philosophical and logical underpinnings of our knowledge of the world. Kemeny's book is a classic statement on this.

Philip Kitcher and Wesley C. Salmon (eds.). *Scientific Explanation.* Minneapolis: University of Minnesota Press, 1990.
> This book also provides a perspective on the philosophy of science. Although it is not an easy read, it does provide some contemporary views on the topic.

D. C. Phillips. *Philosophy, Science, and Social Inquiry: Contemporary Methodological Controversies in Social Science and Related Applied Fields of Research.* Elmsford, NY: Pergamon, 1987.
> This is a challenging but excellent philosophical analysis of the issue of how closely applied research in the social sciences can follow the model established by the natural sciences.

Exercises

2.1 It can be useful to assess your personal experiences in terms of how closely they approximate good scientific sampling procedures. Start with some commonsense knowledge of your own. For example, based on the people you know, you have probably made some assessment of the likelihood that a marriage will end in divorce. Analyze the "sample" on which this knowledge is based. What are the characteristics of the people whose marriages you know personally? What kind of people are unlikely to appear in your sample? Do the same with other examples of commonsense knowledge.

2.2 Locate a recent issue of one of the major journals in sociology and find an article on a topic of interest to you. Identify the major concepts and variables, including the independent and dependent variables discussed in the article and any operational definitions given. What do the authors say about issues of validity and reliability in their measurement? What other possible operational definitions could have been used? Would these be more valid and reliable? Are there commonsense definitions of these concepts that are different from their sociological usage?

2.3 Suggest some possible operational definitions for the following concepts. Criticize each operational definition in terms of biases that it might contain.

child abuse	alcoholism
stress	marital satisfaction
socioeconomic status	race
educational level	poverty
welfare dependence	white collar crime

Find research studies in your library that utilize these concepts and compare your operational definitions with those in the study. Discuss issues of validity and reliability in relation to these operational definitions.

2.4 For the studies located in Exercises 2.2 and 2.3, describe the sampling techniques used. Criticize the sampling from the point of view of potential bias and suggest some better (even if more expensive and less practical) sampling procedures that could have been used.

CHAPTER 3

Analyzing Relationships Between Variables

Social science research sometimes focuses on a single variable. In needs assessment or other descriptive research, for example, interest could center on knowing how many people use illicit drugs or how many pregnant teens could use counseling services. More commonly, however, applied research focuses on the relationship between two or more variables—on how one or more variables impact on another variable. A **bivariate relationship** *involves two variables,* and a **multivariate relationship** *involves three or more variables.* In many cases, it may not be obvious, especially to the layperson unacquainted with the logic of social science analysis, which variables might be included in a particular research effort. Consider this rather harrowing case.

The problems of five-year-old David first came to light early in 1989 when a school social worker found bruises on him and filed a child abuse complaint (Kovanis, 1989). It was later learned that David lived in a rather troubled family. His father had abandoned him and his mother the previous year, and another man had moved into the trailer that was David's home. The man was, to put it mildly, a strict disciplinarian. When David disobeyed, he was forced to run many laps around the mobile home; if he ate too slowly, his head would be shoved into the metal tray of his high chair; when he didn't act sufficiently "tough," he would be humiliated by being forced to wear diapers. Another favored punishment was to take away the cassettes that had songs that David loved.

A second abuse complaint was filed when a family outreach counselor noticed a suspicious mark on David's forehead that might have been a cigarette burn. Once the child abuse complaints were filed, the situation could have been readily assessed and interventions put into effect. But that isn't what happened. The social worker assigned to the case had a difficult time meeting with David's mother. Because of staff shortages at the social service agency, personal illness of the social worker, and the work schedule of David's mother, they were unable to meet during the month and a half after the abuse complaints were made. At that point, a baby sitter noticed some bruises on David's neck that might have been caused by someone's choking him. She contacted a different social service agency but was told that there were no social workers available to handle the case. The baby sitter called the police, but the officer called out on the case decided that the most appropriate action was for the baby sitter to keep a close eye out for any further indications of abuse. The police apparently did not report the case of suspected child abuse to the department of social services as they were required to do.

On August 11, 1989, David was rushed to the hospital with severe head injuries. He died there the following day. The autopsy concluded that the head injuries were the result of an extremely severe shaking or his being shoved against a wall. The live-in companion of David's mother said that David was injured when he fell while brushing his teeth. The autopsy showed that David had suffered a broken arm two weeks before his death.

As David's case shows, child abuse, if ignored, can and does have tragic outcomes. In our society, social service agencies have at least some of the responsibility for detecting abuse and intervening to alleviate such problems. David's death was due in part to the fact that the social agencies contacted were inadequate to the task, particularly in terms of lacking sufficient staff to respond to all cases of suspected abuse. Social science research is one of the tools such agencies can use to help alleviate this problem by looking at multivariate relationships among variables. For example, the occurrence of child abuse can be related to such things as income, education, and poverty. Later in this chapter, we will see how knowledge of these multivariate relationships can help agencies deal with such problems as understaffing. First, however, we need to explore the notion of *causality* because interest often centers on whether one variable is the cause of changes in another variable.

Searching for Causes

Causality means that *one agent produces change or variation in another.* A baseball bat moving with a certain velocity causes the baseball to change direction and fly into the outfield; in the same fashion, poverty causes a pregnant woman to eat a poor diet and give birth to a premature baby. Causal statements about the natural world are often all-or-nothing propositions: A bat moving in the same direction with a given velocity will always hit the ball into the outfield. In the social sciences, however, causal statements are more likely to be probabilistic: The causal factor increases or decreases the *probability* that some event will happen. Poverty increases the likelihood that a pregnant woman will have a poor diet and neglect her health and thus give birth to a premature baby. This happens to some poor pregnant women but not others. The reason we can sometimes make absolute statements about the natural world is that we can more often specify all the factors that will influence an outcome. In the case of the baseball, the key factors influencing its flight are the direction and velocity with which the bat hits it, humidity, temperature, and prevailing winds. Knowing these few conditions, we can state with considerable certainty what will happen. With social phenomena, we do not typically know, or at least can't control, all of the factors that might influence an outcome. Whether a pregnant woman consumes a poor diet is influenced by a host of factors other than her poverty status: her educational level, the support networks available to her, her knowledge of nutrition, whether she has had previous children, whether she takes drugs, and so on. The causal factor of interest—in this case, the woman's poverty status—is only one of those factors, and it may act as the key factor during that time period in some women's lives but not in others'.

Although the concept of *causality* is a simple one, it is controversial because causality cannot be directly observed but rather must be inferred from observing other data. We do not see poverty directly *causing* premature births in the same way that a baseball fan sees the bat crash the ball into the outfield. Rather we observe that a poor woman has given birth to a premature infant; we don't actually see the poverty bring about the premature infant. However, by analyzing the conditions under which those two things occur, we can conclude that one caused the other. Because causality is based on inference, we need to specify the conditions that are necessary in order to confidently infer a causal relationship between variables. It is generally agreed that there are three such conditions (Hirschi and Selvin, 1967).

First, there must be an association or correlation between the two variables. This usually means that as the value of one variable changes, the value of the other also tends to change. Poor women are much more likely to have premature births than are nonpoor women, establishing the association between poverty and premature births and the first criterion necessary to infer a causal relationship. (How large such an association needs to be is a complicated issue that requires some knowledge of statistics to be fully comprehended.)

The second condition needed to infer causality is the proper temporal order of the variables: The causal (or independent) variable must precede in time the event that it causes (the dependent variable). Given our knowledge of how the world operates, it is illogical to say that A caused B to happen if A did not exist until after B had happened. Something that does not exist cannot cause something else to happen. In the study of premature births, the temporal sequence is easy to establish because we can determine that a woman is poor—the independent variable—while she is pregnant, and the premature birth—the dependent variable—naturally occurs after that. Thus the temporal sequence is appropriate for satisfying this criterion for inferring causality. In studies where both the independent and dependent variables are observed at the same time, however, it may be much more difficult to establish the time sequence. This is often true in surveys where we ask people about their thoughts, feelings, and behaviors. Suppose that we conducted a survey of teenagers, asking them about their delinquent actions and about their church-going behaviors, and found an association: Teenagers who report going to church also claim committing fewer delinquent acts than do those who do not go to church. Can we conclude that church-going reduces delinquency? Not with great confidence, because of the time sequence: Did the delinquency precede or follow the decline in church-going? It might be true that church-going leads people to be more law abiding, but it could also be true that delinquency arises first and leads a teen to drift away from religion. The point is that we cannot be sure unless there is some way to establish the time sequence. We could ask the teens which occurred first, but their memories may not be very reliable.

The third criterion for inferring causality is that the relationship between the independent and dependent variable does not disappear when the effects of other variables on each of them separately are taken into account. If the relationship does disappear, then it is called a *spurious* relationship—something like a false reading—that occurs only because both independent and dependent variables are related to the same third variable. For example, there is an association between the amount of ice cream consumed and the delinquency rate: As ice cream consumption increases in a community, so does the delinquency rate. Yet a little thought will suggest a third variable that independently influences each of these: the weather. Warm weather produces an increase in ice cream consumption, for obvious reasons; warm weather is also associated with increases in delinquency because juveniles are likely to be away from home and with their friends in warm weather and thus in an environment where delinquent actions are more likely to occur. The presumed causal relationship between ice cream consumption and delinquency is spurious—a false reading.

Assessing relationships for causality can be complicated, especially checking for spuriousness. Finding that a relationship between two variables is nonspurious when one additional variable, such as weather in the preceding example, is looked at increases our confidence in making causal inferences, but there may be other variables that would show the relationship to be spurious. In fact, even when many variables have been looked at, we cannot be completely confident of causal statements because we can never look at the effect of *all* possible variables. Nevertheless, sound research increases our confidence in causal inferences, and I will discuss how this is done a little later in this chapter.

Types of Relationships Between Variables _____

The important role of variables and hypotheses in research was discussed in Chapter 2. I want to build on that for the remainder of this chapter by looking at how applied researchers analyze the relationships between variables. The particular form of the relationship is stated in the hypothesis and specifies the precise way in which an independent variable affects a dependent variable.

An important step in analyzing the relationship between variables is to consider the way in which the variables are measured. One type of measurement is illustrated by the variable gender. Gender is measured by placing people into one of two categories, male or female. Gender is a *discrete variable* in that it can take on only a set number of separate values. A case is either male or female, and no one falls in between. Other variables, like age and income, are *continuous,* meaning that they can take on, at least theoretically, an infinite number of values. Age could be measured in terms of years, months, days, hours, or even smaller units. In social science research, we normally measure age in years because this provides sufficient precision for us to observe the effect of age on social behavior. However, it is always theoretically possible for a person to fall in between any two age categories because age can be divided into infinitely small units. Generally, when variables are discrete, sociologists analyze them through the use of contingency tables; when continuous, they use procedures known as scattergrams, correlation, and regression. There are a number of exceptions to this rule, but the overall point is that the type of measurement used—discrete versus continuous—influences the kind of analysis that can be done.

We can begin to grasp the logic of relationships between variables by looking at **scattergrams,** which are *diagrams that give a visual image of the relationship between two variables.* Suppose we were interested in the hypothesis that larger cities have higher crime rates than smaller cities—a bivariate relationship with two variables, city size and crime rate. Figure 3.1 contains a data set of 15 cities, along with their crime rates and population sizes in 1986. It also contains a scattergram of the variables crime rate and city size. Notice that the horizontal axis, called the X-axis, contains the values for city size, while the vertical axis, called the Y-axis, has the values for crime rate. Each city has been plotted onto the scattergram by first locating its population size on the horizontal axis and its crime rate on the vertical axis. Then a line is drawn straight up from that point on the X-axis and straight across from that point on the Y-axis; where the two lines cross is the location of that case in the scattergram. An asterisk indicates where each city falls. The asterisk in the lower-left corner of the scattergram, for example, represents Allentown, Pennsylvania, with a population of 104,000 people and a crime rate of 5,687.5 per 100,000 people. (The independent variable is always put on the X-axis. In this example, logic compels us to the conclusion that population size is the independent variable.) Once all the cases have been plotted, a visual impression of the relationship between the two variables is presented. In this case, as population size increases, the crime rate in the city also increases, shown by the asterisks tending to flow from the lower left to the upper right in the scattergram.

Positive Versus Negative Relationships

As the hypothetical scattergrams in Figure 3.2 illustrate, relationships between variables can take a number of forms. One way to specify the relationship is in terms of the *direction* of change of the values of each variable in relation to one another. A *positive relationship* is one in which there is a tendency for the values of both variables to change in the same direction; that is, as the value of one variable increases, the value of the other also tends to increase (see Figure

Case	Crime Rate[a]	Population	City
1	6,638.4	112,000	Abilene, TX
2	10,239.6	278,000	Birmingham, AL
3	12,487.9	372,000	Honolulu, HI
4	12,868.6	446,000	Oklahoma City, OK
5	10,268.8	554,000	New Orleans, LA
6	9,739.3	610,000	Jacksonville, FL
7	8,801.2	753,000	Baltimore, MD
8	9,997.1	894,000	Phoenix, AZ
9	10,963.8	914,000	San Antonio, TX
10	12,929.6	1,086,000	Detroit, MI
11	5,687.5	104,000	Allentown, PA
12	7,658.2	325,000	Buffalo, NY
13	13,938.3	486,000	Seattle, WA
14	9,932.0	653,000	Memphis, TN
15	15,331.3	1,004,000	Dallas, TX

[a]Rate per 100,000 population.

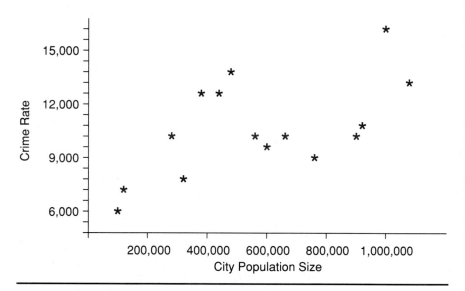

Figure 3.1 The Crime Rate and Population Size of Various Cities in the United States, per 100,000 people, 1986.
Source: Katherine M. Jamieson and Timothy J. Flanagan, eds., *Sourcebook of Criminal Justice Statistics - 1988.* U.S. Department of Justice, Bureau of Justice Statistics. Washington, DC: U.S. Government Printing Office, 1989, pp. 440-444; U.S. Bureau of the Census. *Statistical Abstract of the United States, 1988.* Washington, D.C.: U.S. Government Printing Office, 1988, pp. 33-35.

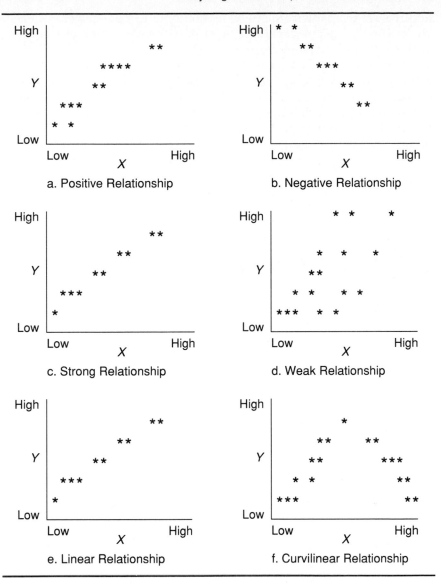

Figure 3.2 Types of Bivariate Relationships

3.2a). For example, there is a positive relationship between the variables education and lifetime earnings: As people's level of education increases, so does the amount of money they are likely to earn in their lives. A *negative* or *inverse relationship* is the opposite: As the value of one variable increases, the value of the other tends to decrease (see Figure 3.2b). There is an inverse relationship between education and family size: People with more education tend to have fewer children. So, as the variable of level of education rises, the value of the other variable (family size) decreases.

When we describe relationships in social science as positive or negative, we mean that there is a tendency for the two variables to change in the ways described. It does not necessarily happen in every case. If it did, we would have what is called a *perfect relationship:* The two variables change in the predicted direction on every case. In a perfect positive relationship, every case that is higher on one of the variables will also be higher on the other. If the relationship between level of education and income were perfect, every person who had a higher educational level than another person would also earn more income than that person. This doesn't always happen; we can find some people who have higher educational levels than others but lower incomes. The relationship is less than perfect, and in fact virtually all relationships between variables in the social sciences are less than perfect.

Strong Versus Weak Relationships

A second way of describing the relationship between two variables is in terms of the *strength* of the relationship. The strongest relationship is a perfect one, and the closer a relationship is to being perfect, the stronger it is. As Figures 3.2c and 3.2d illustrate, when the relationship between variables is strong, the cases in the scattergram tend to cluster around a roughly straight line, and they tend to scatter widely when the relationship is weak. There are a number of statistical techniques for assessing the strength of relationships, and they produce a number, or coefficient, that tells us how strong the relationship is. A perfect positive relationship would be indicated by most of these statistics with a coefficient of $+1.00$, while a perfect inverse relationship would have a coefficient of -1.00. If there were absolutely no relationship between two variables, the coefficient would be 0.00. Thus a relationship of $+.79$ is stronger than one of $+.34$, and relationships of $+.62$ and $-.62$ are equal in strength, although one is positive and the other inverse. As a general rule of thumb, a relationship between 0.00 and $+.30$ would be called weak, from $+.30$ to $+.70$ moderate, and above $+.70$ strong (Wright, 1986).

Linear Versus Nonlinear Relationships

A third way to describe a relationship between variables is whether it has the same direction and strength over the whole range of the independent variable values. A *linear relationship* is one that has approximately the same direction and strength whether the values of the independent variable are low, medium, or high (see Figure 3.2e). This is called a linear, or straight-line, relationship because statistical formulas can draw a straight line that best describes the relationship between the variables (more on this later in the chapter). In a *nonlinear* or *curvilinear relationship,* the strength and in some cases the direction of the relationship between the two variables change significantly for different values of the independent variable. Figure 3.2f shows a relationship that is positive when the independent variable values are low but then becomes negative at higher values of the independent variable. The relationship between age and death rates is curvilinear. During the first year of life, the death rate is fairly high, but it drops rapidly between 1 and 5 years of age (a negative relationship between age and death rate); between the ages of 5 and 50 there is only a weak relationship between the variables; after age 50, the death rate tends to increase with age (a positive relationship between age and the death rate).

This brief assessment of the types of relationships that can be found between variables will serve as a foundation for describing how sociologists investigate the bivariate and multivariate relationships between variables. With discrete variables, we typically conduct a contingency table analysis, described in the next section. With continuous variables, we use correlation, regression, and path analysis, which are described later in the chapter.

Analysis of Contingency Tables _____

A *contingency table* enables us to assess whether the value of one variable is *contingent* (depends) on the value of the other. This is also called the *crosstabulation* of the two variables. Contingency tables are easy to understand once the rules of constructing them are grasped.

Constructing Contingency Tables

Table 3.1a is a contingency table with two variables: the gender of prison inmates and whether or not those inmates have ever been convicted of a violent offense. Both of these variables are discrete, with two values: Gender can be either male or female, and inmates have either been or not been convicted of a violent offense. To properly construct a contingency table, first consider which variable is independent and which dependent. In our example, gender would clearly seem to be the independent variable because it is possible that gender might

TABLE 3.1   The Relationship Between Gender and Conviction for a Violent Offense, Among Prison Inmates in the United States, 1986

A.

	Gender	
	Male	*Female*
Percent ever convicted for violent crime	66.5% (284,332)	47% (9,220)
Percent never convicted for a violent crime	33.5% (143,235)	53% (10,397)
N	100% (427,567)	100% (19,617)

B.

	Gender	
	Male	*Female*
Percent ever convicted for violent crime	66.5%	47%
Percent never convicted for a violent crime	33.5%	53%
N	100% (427,567)	100% (19,617)

C.

	Gender	
	Male	*Female*
Percent ever convicted for violent crime	66.5%	47%
N	100% (427,567)	100% (19,617)

D.

		Percent ever convicted for a violent crime	*N*
Gender	*Male*	66.5%	100% (427,567)
	Female	47%	100% (19,617)

Source: Katherine M. Jamieson and Timothy J. Flanigan, (eds.). *Sourcebook of Criminal Justice Statistics—1988,* 621. U.S. Department of Justice, Bureau of Justice Statistics. Washington, DC: U.S. Government Printing Office, 1989.

influence the kinds of crimes a person commits. In fact, common sense might suggest that men in American culture are more likely than women to be socialized to be aggressive, leading them to commit more violent crimes. In addition, inferring a causal relationship requires that the independent variable must precede the dependent variable in time. People acquire their gender at conception—long before they have an opportunity to commit crimes. So, gender might affect whether people commit crimes, but the reverse is not possible. The hypothesis being tested in this table, then, is

Male prison inmates are more likely than female inmates to have been convicted for committing a violent crime.

In Table 3.1a, the categories of the independent variable have been placed in the columns while the categories of the dependent variable have been placed in the rows. This is a convention that I and many others use, but it is by no means a universal one. Some researchers use the independent variable as the row variable. Usually, the researcher's description of the table will make clear which variable is considered independent; if it doesn't, then you should be able to make that assessment either on the basis of logic or on the temporal order of the variables.

Each square in the table containing numbers and percentages is called a *cell*. The number of cases in a cell is called a *cell frequency* and the percentages are called *cell percentages*. Table 3.1a consists of two columns and two rows. The row containing the total number of cases (designated by *N* for *Number*) is called the *marginal* because it is at the margins of the table and is technically peripheral to the table: The key information is contained in the cells, and the marginals usually repeat what is in the cells. The marginals at the bottom of the columns show 100 percent of the cases. This shows how the percentages in the table were derived, and how to read the table: Cases are summed and percentages are read in the direction of the independent variable (in my example, cases are summed and percentages read down the columns). So, Table 3.1a would be read in the following way: 66.5 percent of all male prison inmates, as compared to 47 percent of all female inmates, have been convicted for committing a violent crime. This supports our hypothesis. An important point to keep in mind is that the percentages are calculated down the columns, but the comparisons that are used to test the effect of the independent variable are made between cells in the same row. We compare the percent of males convicted of violent crimes with the percent of females so convicted. That comparison gives us the information we want about the effect of gender on criminal behavior.

In a two-variable table like Table 3.1a, it would be possible to compute marginals either to the right of the table or at the bottom. However, marginals are typically computed only in the direction of the independent variable, as I have done in this example, because that is how the comparisons will be made. You need to know the total number of people in each category of the independent variable in order to compare percentages between the categories.

Two-variable tables are also often designated by the number of rows and columns they contain. So, Table 3.1a is called a 2 × 2 table (read "2 by 2"), and a table with 2 rows and 3 columns is called a 2 × 3 table. The number of rows is indicated by the first number, so a 2 × 3 table is not the same as a 3 × 2 table.

Tables can be constructed in many ways, but there are two overriding principles to follow. One is to accurately present the data to the reader. It is possible to "lie with statistics," but this is considered unethical by researchers. Instead, tables should provide all the information necessary to create an accurate portrayal of the information contained in the data. The second principle is to keep the table as simple as possible while being true to the first principle. In Table 3.1b, I have made Table 3.1a slightly simpler by removing the cell frequencies, which are actually redundant because they can be easily computed from the marginal totals and the cell percentages. In addition, comparisons to test hypotheses are usually clearer and more accurate using cell percentages rather than cell frequencies. The percentages tell us how many people were convicted of violent crimes in each category of the independent variable relative to the total number of people in each category. Because marginal totals will vary from one category of the independent variable to another, cell frequencies can be misleading. In fact, 30 times more male inmates than female inmates have been convicted of violent crimes, but this is because there are far more men in prison than women. Using cell percentages tells us how many male inmates have committed violent crimes relative to the total number of male inmates in prison.

This table could have been further simplified because there are only two categories for the dependent variable—cases that are not in one category of the dependent variable must be in the other. If an inmate does not fall into the "convicted of violent crime" category, then he or she must be in the "not convicted" category—those are the only two possibilities. So, Table 3.1c presents just the percentage who have been convicted of a violent crime. The number and percent who are not convicted of a violent crime can be reconstructed from the cell percentages and the marginal totals. (It is legitimate to delete a dependent variable row, but we cannot do this kind of simplification by deleting an independent variable column because it is precisely the independent variable categories that we need to compare as a test of our hypothesis.)

In deciding how much to simplify the presentation of a table, one guiding principle is that there should be enough information for readers to compute all of the cell frequencies and reconstruct the table if they believe that it is percentaged wrong. In Table 3.1c, each of the cell frequencies can be calculated. The lower-left cell, for example, would contain 33.5 percent of all the male inmates (100 percent $-$ 66.5 percent). Then using the marginal total, we can calculate the cell frequency by multiplying $427,567 \times 0.335 = 143,235$. Each cell frequency can be calculated in this fashion. Once we have the cell frequencies, we can reconstruct the table using either variable as the independent variable.

In Table 3.1d, I have violated the convention that I established earlier and recast the information in Table 3.1c with the independent variable as the *row* variable. Now you read the table across the rows. However, you should be clear that Tables 3.1c and 3.1d have the same information and come to the same conclusions. The only difference is the convention used for placing the independent and dependent variables in the table.

The Elaboration of Contingency Tables

The crosstabulation just described provides the basic foundation of data analysis, but virtually all research would go beyond this: Human social behavior is very complex, with many factors influencing a particular outcome. In some cases, the conclusions drawn from a bivariate crosstabulation turn out to be false once other variables are considered. More often, bivariate results turn out to be more complicated after further analysis. In either case, multivariate relationships are investigated, with variables other than the original independent and dependent ones included in the analysis. These additional variables are **control** or **test variables.** In some analyses, they allow us to see more clearly how the independent variable affects the dependent variable; in other analyses, they help explain *why* an independent variable has a certain effect on the dependent variable. Some test variables are called *antecedent variables* because they *precede* in time both the independent and dependent variables; other test variables are called *intervening variables* because they occur *between* the independent and dependent variables (see Figure 3.3).

The sort of multivariate analysis to be described here is called table elaboration or the **elaboration model** because it involves *elaborating a relationship between two variables by systematically introducing test variables into the analysis* (Rosenberg, 1968). In table elaboration,

Time Sequence of the Test Variable

a. Antecedent Test Variable

Test Variable → Original Independent Variable

Test Variable → Original Dependent Variable

b. Intervening Test Variable

Original Independent Variable → Test Variable → Original Dependent Variable

Outcomes of Partialling

Outcomes	Zero Order Table	Partial Tables[a]
a. No Effect	$X \xrightarrow{+} Y$	Z_1: $X \xrightarrow{+} Y$ Z_2: $X \xrightarrow{+} Y$
b. Split[b]	$X \xrightarrow{+} Y$	Z_1: $X \xrightarrow{+} Y$ Z_2: $X \xrightarrow{0} Y$
c. Relationship Reduced (spurious)	$X \xrightarrow{+} Y$	Z_1: $X \xrightarrow{0} Y$ Z_2: $X \xrightarrow{0} Y$
c. Relationship Reversed	$X \xrightarrow{+} Y$	Z_1: $X \xrightarrow{+} Y$ Z_2: $X \xrightarrow{-} Y$

[a] The test variable is designated by *Z*, with *X* being the independent variable and *Y* the dependent. This test variable has two values, Z_1 and Z_2.

[b] *Split* refers to a situation where one partial table continues to show a relationship between *X* and *Y* but the other does not.

Figure 3.3 Some Possible Outcomes in Table Elaboration

tables and the relationships they describe are labeled according to the number of test factors introduced. The original bivariate relationship is called a zero order relationship and the table that describes it is a zero order table. It is called zero because there is *no* test variable involved. When a test variable is introduced, a contingency table showing the relationship between independent and dependent variables is created for *each value* of the test variable. These tables are called *partial tables,* and the bivariate relationships they describe are *partial relationships*—partial because each table shows the relationship between independent and dependent variables for only part of the data: one value of the test factor. A table with one test variable is a first order partial table, a second order partial table includes two test variables, and so on. I discuss only first order partial tables because the goal is to understand the general logic of the procedure rather than achieve an in-depth introduction to it.

To learn more about a relationship, table elaboration looks for a number of possible outcomes when a test factor is introduced and partial tables created. One outcome is that the test factor has *no effect:* The relationship between the independent variable and dependent variable has approximately the same strength and direction in all partial tables (see Figure 3.3). This is a very informative outcome because it tells us that the relationship can be generalized to all conditions of the test variable. A second outcome is called a *split:* The zero order relationship remains in some partial tables but not others. This is shown in Table 3.2. The first part of the table shows the data from Table 3.1c. The results show, as many would expect, that male prisoners are more likely to have been convicted of a violent crime. However, the second part of the table introduces the variable of whether the inmates are in prison for a first offense or are repeat offenders. Here we see that among first offenders, there is almost no difference between men and women in involvement with violent crime, whereas with repeat offenders the difference between men and women is larger than in the zero order table. A simple statistic that can be used for analyzing differences found in tables is called the *percentage difference,* or %d. It is the difference in percentages between two cells in a table, and a higher %d means a stronger relationship between two variables. In the zero order table in Table 3.2, the %d is 66.5 percent − 47 percent = 19.5 percent. This tells us 19.5 percent more men than women were convicted of violent offenses. A useful rule of thumb is that a %d of less than 10 percent probably indicates that there is no relationship between two variables (Wright, 1986). The %d among first offenders is much smaller (6.7 percent), and it is larger among repeat offenders (26.5 percent). This tells us that when women are released from prison, they are much less likely than men to be

TABLE 3.2 The Relationship Among Gender, Conviction for a Violent Offense, and Recidivism Status for Prison Inmates in the United States, 1986

A. Zero Order Relationship

	Gender	
	Male	*Female*
Percent ever convicted for violent crime	66.5%	47%

$\%d$ 19.5

	Male	*Female*
	100%	100%
N	(427,567)	(19,617)

B. First Order Partial Relationship

	First Offenders		Repeat Offenders (Recidivists)	
	Gender		Gender	
	Male	*Female*	*Male*	*Female*
Percent ever con-victed for violent crime	71.7%	65%	65.5%	39%

$\%d$ 6.7   26.5

	Male	*Female*	*Male*	*Female*
	100%	100%	100%	100%
N	(76,744)	(6,047)	(350,823)	(13,570)

Source: Katherine M. Jamieson and Timothy J. Flanagan (eds.), *Sourcebook of Criminal Justice Statistics—1988,* 621. U.S. Department of Justice, Bureau of Justice Statistics. Washington, DC: U.S. Government Printing Office, 1989.

sent back for a violent crime. In other words, the relationship between gender and involvement in violent crime is true for recidivists but not for first offenders. This may mean that prison serves as an effective deterrent against violent crime for women but not men (although much more research would need to be done before drawing that conclusion with any certainty). So, a "split" outcome gives us information about which conditions of the test variable the original relationship can be generalized to. Both no effect and split outcomes enable us to specify more precisely the conditions under which the relationship between independent and dependent variables holds up, and this is very important information.

A third possible outcome in table elaboration is that introducing a third variable into the analysis has the effect of substantially reducing or eliminating the relationship found in the zero order table. All partial tables in this case show a weak or no relationship between the independent and dependent variables. What this means depends on the temporal order of the variables. If the test variable is an *antecedent test variable,* the relationship in the zero order table was *spurious:* The test factor is producing changes in both independent and dependent variables, making it appear that they are related when actually they are not. It is a false relationship. I illustrated this earlier with the relationship between ice cream sales and juvenile delinquency. On the other hand, if the test variable is an *intervening variable,* the independent variable is producing changes in the test factor that then bring about changes in the dependent variable. In other words, the independent variable produces change in the dependent variable only indirectly, by working through the test factor. The independent-dependent relationship is not false or spurious, but it is weaker when the test variable is not present.

A final possible outcome in table elaboration is that the relationship in some partial tables is the reverse of that in other partial tables. In other words, some partial tables show a positive relationship while others have a negative relationship. This again provides greater specification of exactly what the conditions are under which the independent variable changes the dependent variable.

There are other outcomes that can occur in table elaboration, but our discussion so far is sufficient to get across the logic of the approach. Applied social research typically involves a detailed search for possible antecedent and intervening test variables. Given the complexity of social behavior, a full understanding of relationships usually cannot be achieved by looking only at the bivariate relationship itself.

Correlation and Regression _____

With continuous variables, it is possible to use more precise and mathematically sophisticated statistical procedures than in crosstabulation. However, the logic of the analysis is very similar to table elaboration. We won't compute the statistics for these procedures, which are generally called correlation and regression, but we can begin to grasp their logic by returning to the scattergram in Figure 3.1, which has been reproduced in Figure 3.4. The scattergram shows that cities with larger populations also tend to have higher crime rates. For example, the four smallest cities have crime rates of 10,200 or less, and the three largest cities have crime rates of 10,900 or more. This illustrates what we described earlier as a positive relationship.

A statistic called the correlation coefficient is used to determine the strength and direction of the relationship in the scattergram. As Figure 3.4 shows, the correlation between city size and crime rate is $+.58$. Recall that statistics that measure the strength and direction of

Correlation coefficient: *r* = +.58
Regression equation: CRIMRATE = 7,635 + 0.005 (POPU)
Scattergram:

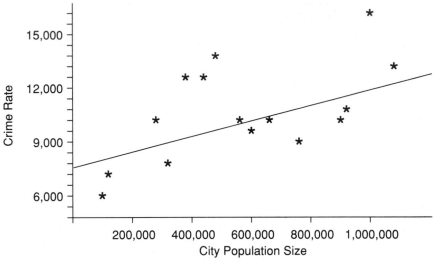

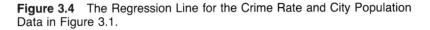

Figure 3.4 The Regression Line for the Crime Rate and City Population Data in Figure 3.1.

relationships between variables usually vary from +1.00 to −1.00. Using the convention discussed earlier, a correlation coefficient of +.58 is considered a moderate, positive relationship. An important point to remember is that all statistics are derived through mathematical formulas that are based on certain assumptions. The correlation coefficient is based on the assumption that the relationship between two variables is a linear one. If the relationship is actually curvilinear, then the correlation coefficient will make the relationship appear weaker than it actually is. This is one reason why researchers typically inspect the data in a scattergram: It is possible to see whether there is any curvilinearity in the relationship.

Researchers also conduct a type of analysis called linear regression. This provides a more detailed description of the relationship found in correlation analysis, and it allows us to infer or predict the most likely values of the dependent variable when we know what the independent variable is. It does this by computing the *regression line*. To understand the regression line, look at the scattergram in Figure 3.4. If we draw a straight line through the scattergram, as shown, then it is possible to measure the vertical distance of each case from that line. This distance is called the variance. If we do this for every case and sum up all those variances, we end up with the total variance between all the cases and that line.

It is possible, of course, to draw many lines through a scattergram. However, there is only one straight line that can be drawn that will have the minimum amount of total variance, and this is the regression line. Any other possible line that might be drawn will result in more total variance. So, the regression line is sometimes called the best-fitting line because it involves the least vertical distance between itself and all of the points in the scattergram. Without getting into the computation of it, regression analysis produces an equation that enables us to determine what that best-fitting line is for any two variables. The regression equation is as follows:

$$Y' = a + b(X).$$

The first element in the equation, Y' (pronounced "Y prime"), is the value of the dependent variable that we are trying to predict. The term a is the point where the regression line crosses the Y-axis; in other words, this is the point on the regression line where the value of the independent variable is zero. The term b is the regression coefficient, or the slope of the regression line; it shows the average change in the value of Y for each unit increase in the value of X. In other words, b shows how large an impact X has on Y. X is any value of the independent variable. (There are formulas for computing a and b, but we don't need to get into those in order to understand the logic of regression analysis.)

For the data in Figure 3.4, the regression equation is as follows:

CRIMRATE = 7,635 + 0.005 (POPU).

This regression equation tells us that among the 15 cities that are included in the analysis, when a city's population (POPU) increases by one person, the crime rate (CRIMRATE) increases by an average of 0.005 crimes (five one-thousandth of a crime). A population increase of 100,000 people would mean a predicted crime rate increase of 0.005 × 100,000, or 500. If a city anticipates that its population will grow by a certain amount, the regression outcome can be used for making projections regarding the need for additional police, judges, and other elements of the criminal justice system. What the city would be doing, essentially, is predicting that its crime increase due to population growth will be the average increase found in other cities as their populations increase.

With this regression formula, we can also determine the predicted crime rate for a city of any population size. The predicted crime rate in Buffalo, New York, with a population of 325,000 people could be calculated as follows: $9{,}260 = 7{,}635 + 0.005\,(325{,}000)$. Of course, not all cities of 325,000 will have crime rates of 9,260, but the regression equation offers us a best guess—based on the patterns seen in the actual relationship between the variables city size and crime rate in the data—as to how crime rate will change as population grows or shrinks. Policy decisions can be affected if a city's crime rate is significantly above or below that guess. Research in Action 3.1 describes a very sophisticated regression analysis that could be used to alleviate the problems that made it difficult for five-year-old David, whose case was discussed at the beginning of this chapter, to get assistance when he needed it.

RESEARCH IN ACTION 3.1 ━━━━━━━━━━━━━━━━━━━━━━━━━

How Much Child Abuse Is There in Your Community?

The system didn't work for David, partly because of insufficient staffing. This may not have been entirely the agencies' fault because it can be difficult for them to know exactly how many people need their services. This problem is not as great when clients themselves seek out the services. Schools, for example, can readily determine the need for teachers in a community because parents voluntarily bring their children to the schools. The need for other services, however, can be hard to detect accurately because the clients do not—or cannot—come forward voluntarily. This is often the case with child abuse. The abused child is often too confused, frightened, or immature to cry out; at the same time, the abuser either does not perceive his or her actions as abuse or does not want to be detected.

This hidden nature of child abuse confronts social agencies with a difficult staffing problem: They need some idea of how much abuse there is in order to decide how many case workers they need. However, if much of the abuse is hidden, how do they make this assessment? Do they staff on the basis of known cases? This would lead to understaffing if there are many hidden cases. What other criteria can they use? Regression analysis can provide some help in such cases.

To measure both the known and the hidden cases of abuse in a community can be expensive and difficult to do, certainly beyond the resources of most social service agencies. However, the U.S. Department of Health and Human Services (DHHS) has funded such projects in 26 counties across the country. These research projects gathered data on the amounts of abuse known to social service agencies and the amounts not officially reported, along with other information about the counties: income level, unemployment level, population size, crime rates, and so on. This data base can serve as a point of comparison for other counties to see whether the number of known cases of child abuse in their jurisdiction is comparable to that in other counties. If their case loads are low compared to other counties, then they may have lots of hidden cases that have not yet come to the attention of social service agencies.

Policy analyst Sheila Ards (1989) tested a number of different models for conducting this kind of analysis and found that a regression approach provided the most accurate estimate of the amounts of abuse in a community. Basically, what she did, using the DHHS data, was to create an elaborate regression equation that would show how much change in abuse rates (the dependent variable) would result from changes in a variety of independent variables. The independent variables were community characteristics such as crime rate, population density, racial composition of the community, and so on. Without presenting all of her results, which are quite complicated, we can illustrate some of them. The two factors that had the largest impact on rates of abuse were population density and arrest rates. Population density reflects the personal space that a person has in the family, and higher population densities may be a stressor that contributes to abuse. She measured population density as the percentage of homes or apartments in which there is more than one person per room. Through the regression equation, she determined that a 1 percent increase in the proportion of such living arrangements in the DHHS sample of communities translated into an increase in the abuse rate of 1.3 per 1,000 children. So, a community with 30 percent of its people with such living arrangements would have an abuse rate 6.5 per 1,000 cases higher than a community with 25 percent

of the living arrangements at that density (the 5 percent difference between communities in the number of people living with more than one person per room is multiplied by the 1.3 abuse rate to show 6.5 more cases per 1,000).

Arrest rates may reflect the certainty of arrest for an offense in a community. More arrests may mean that the likelihood of being arrested for committing a crime like child abuse is greater. Ards found that an increase of one arrest per 100 aggravated assaults committed in a community lowered the number of abused children by 6.8 per 1,000. A community with 12 arrests per 100 aggravated assaults would have 13.6 fewer abuse cases per 1,000 than would a community with 10 arrests per 100 aggravated assaults.

The outcome of this type of analysis is an elaborate regression equation which is called *multiple regression analysis* because it looks at the simultaneous impact of multiple independent variables on the dependent variable. This is a simplified version of the equation:

$$Y' = a + b_1(\text{DENSITY}) + b_2(\text{ARREST}) + b_3(\text{UNEMP}) + \ldots + b_n(\text{INC}).$$

The county simply enters its own values for the independent variables, such as DENSITY (number of people per room in households), ARREST (rate of arrest for aggravated assault), UNEMP (unemployment rate), INC (personal income per capita), and so on. Then the county can calculate what its projected abuse rate should be and if its rates are high or low in comparison to counties that are similar in terms of density, arrest rates, and so on. This data can then become one bit of information used in making policy decisions regarding staffing and other issues. If the known cases in a county are quite a bit below where the regression equation predicts they should be, then there may be many hidden cases. This may warrant some additional case worker staff and a more intensive effort to see if those hidden cases can be found. This might have benefited David. If the county in which he lived had many hidden cases, then a regression analysis might have uncovered this fact and more services might have been available. That could have translated into quicker action in responding to his case and possibly prevented his death.

There are a couple of things to keep in mind regarding the kind of regression analysis described here. First, it is not a foolproof method because it is based on certain assumptions. It assumes that one county is similar to all other counties in terms of the relationship between the independent variables and the dependent variable. This may not always be true. There may be counties where the abuse rate is much lower than would be predicted on the basis of arrest rates or levels of density because there is little hidden abuse. However, we would not know this because hidden abuse, by its nature, is unknown to us. This is why regression analysis is only one bit of information used in making policy decisions. If regression analysis tells us that there is much hidden abuse when in fact there isn't, then increasing staff may not help much but also wouldn't hurt (except for the additional expense of the staffing). On the other hand, ignoring a regression analysis that accurately tells us that there is much hidden abuse may result in some of those children, like David, not getting the help they need.

A second thing to remember about this regression analysis is that in looking at the relationship between independent and dependent variables, we are mainly concerned with predicting levels of the dependent variable, not with establishing causality. It may well be that some of the independent variables have a causal impact on the dependent variable. Density of living arrangements, for example, may put stress on families that increases the likelihood that a parent will abuse a child. However, we don't have to establish such causality in order for the regression analysis to be of use in this case because we are using the independent variables only to help us *predict* what the level of abuse should be in a particular county. Whether it is the density or something else that causes the high abuse rate is irrelevant because we don't plan to do anything about that. We plan to use the regression prediction to help us make decisions about staffing issues.

Path Analysis

Correlation and regression analysis are sometimes extended into **path analysis,** which is *a way of describing the causal interlinkages between many variables in multivariate analysis.* It is called *path* analysis because it traces causal paths through a network of relationships among variables. I have emphasized that social reality is complex, and a complete understanding of social phenomena can often be achieved only by considering a number of independent, intervening, and dependent variables at the same time. Path analysis shows how much of a direct impact each independent variable has on each dependent variable, and it also shows how much indirect effect the independent variables have as they work through intervening variables.

Path analysis enables researchers to describe a complex causal network among a number of variables. However, path analysis itself only provides the strength and direction of the relationships between variables; it is the researcher skilled in its use who must figure out the causal ordering of the variables in order to make sense of the outcomes of path analysis. An interesting use of path analysis is described in Research in Action 3.2.

RESEARCH IN ACTION 3.2 ═══════════════════════════════

Who Will Have the Longest Life?

My grandmother lived to be 84 years of age, but my mother reached only 75 and my father lived a short (by today's standards) life of 61 years. Could any of them have lived longer? What do I have to look forward to? And most importantly, is there anything I can do about it? As the number of older people in our society has increased over the past few decades, many researchers have turned their attention to studying the causes and consequences of aging. Many applied sociologists are working in the field of social gerontology, the study of social factors associated with aging. Sociologist Erdman Palmore, for one, has devoted his time to the study of the social factors associated with living a long life.

In one of his studies, he developed the path diagram shown in Figure 3.5, which presents the complicated ways in which a number of variables interrelate to influence how long people live (Palmore, 1982). The figure illustrates how an independent variable can have more than one type of effect on a dependent variable: It could directly affect the value of the dependent variable (parents' longevity and SES have this direct effect); the independent variable can also indirectly affect the dependent variable through its impact on an intervening variable (SES influences the activities that people engage in as well as their use of tobacco and alcohol, and activities/tobacco/alcohol influence longevity). Furthermore, an intervening variable might be influenced by two or more independent variables at the same time (satisfaction is influenced by activities, sexual relations, and tobacco and alcohol use). Finally, there might be a string of two or more intervening variables that come between an independent and a dependent variable (SES influences activities, which in turn influence satisfaction, which then impacts on health, which affects longevity). So you can see that this multivariate analysis can get

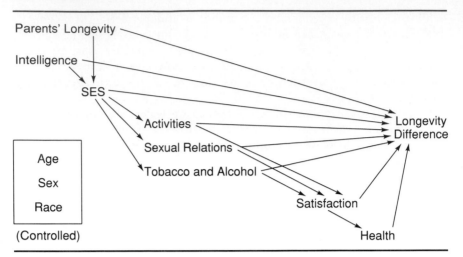

Figure 3.5 A Path Diagram of the Factors Affecting Longevity
Source: Erdman B. Palmore. 1982. "Predictors of the Longevity Difference: A 25-Year Follow-Up." *The Gerontologist,* 22 (no. 6), p. 514. Copyright © the Gerontological Society of America. Used with permission.

very complicated. The strength of each relationship between a pair of variables (independent-dependent, independent-intervening, and intervening-dependent) is calculated while holding the effects of all the other variables constant. This path coefficient is derived from the regression coefficient and shows how much one variable changes for each unit change in the other. So, one measure of health in this study was the person's self-rating of his or her satisfaction with his or her health, ranging from 0 (least satisfied) to 6 (most satisfied). Looking at the relationship between health and longevity, Palmore found no relationship among men but a regression coefficient of 2.20 among women. This means that for each one-point increase on the health satisfaction scale, women lived on average 2.2 years longer. Each relationship in a path analysis is somewhat analogous to partial relationships in the table elabora-

tion approach. However, unlike the correlation coefficient and other measures of the strength of relationship between variables, the regression coefficient can exceed $+1.00$ or -1.00.

Palmore's conclusions are too complex to summarize completely here, but they do suggest that there are things people can do to increase their longevity. Some are obvious, like not using tobacco, and Palmore's data showed this. However, he also found some less obvious relationships: Remaining active in clubs, neighborhood groups, and other organizations outside the family was a strong predictor of longevity, especially for women. Being satisfied with your work also leads to a longer life, especially for men. In fact, Palmore's analysis showed that a man with the most work satisfaction lived on average more than five years longer than a man with the least work satisfaction. Can I do anything about my longevity? Palmore's answer is, Maybe. If I don't smoke, find a job I enjoy, and stay active in groups outside the home, I may beat the grim reaper for a significantly longer time compared to someone who does the opposite. However, Palmore is cautious about claiming causality:

Controlled experiments are required to prove causation. However, these predictions do provide evidence that there *may* be a causal relationship between them and longevity. (1982:517)

In the next chapter, we will look at why controlled experiments are preferred for proving causality.

CRITICAL THINKING ———————————————————————

Assessing the Data Presented

I have emphasized that virtually all social science research involves bivariate analysis, and most is multivariate in nature. This is so because the complexity of social life leads us to recognize that feelings and behaviors are influenced by many social forces at the same time. In other words, multiple causation is routine in the social world. Not everyone feels equally comfortable dealing with such social complexity. In fact, it helps to have a characteristic called *cognitive flexibility,* or the ability to adapt one's thinking to new or changing circumstances. This is an open-minded approach to problem solving in which one can envision evidence on both sides of an argument and can see the "shades of gray" in reality rather than perceiving phenomena in terms of black and white, right or wrong. The cognitively flexible person can imagine multiple solutions to a problem and views problem solving as a complex series of steps. In applied social research, the cognitively flexible researcher is more likely to detect the depth and subtle nuances that underlie what is observed. The inflexible person will tend to stick with a rigid application of rules and standards and a favored way of coping with a problem. In assessing causal relationships or evaluating complex causal chains, the cognitively flexible person is able to consider many alternatives—various control, intervening, or test variables.

So the logic of social science propels us toward a constant search for control, test, intervening, and spurious variables. Critical thinking for the layperson can benefit from an analogous recognition of the complexity of social life and a consideration of the many factors that can come into play in any situation. This is the layperson's equivalent of multivariate analysis. Critical analysis would involve entertaining the following questions when confronted with an argument or presented with some data:

1. What causal relationships between variables are being stated or implied? Are they justified, given the conditions needed to infer causality? Are there alternative causal linkages that are plausible?
2. Is the relationship between the two variables adequately and correctly described in terms of the strength, direction, and shape of the relationship?

3. Are the contingency tables that present the data clear and accurate, or are they misleading?
4. Could understanding be improved or clarified by a multivariate analysis? Can you think of any control or test factors that might change the relationship and lead to different conclusions? Would they involve intervening variables or antecedent variables?
5. Can you diagram the stated and potential relationships in the form of a path diagram?

Key Terms for Review

bivariate relationships	multivariate relationships
causality	path analysis
control variable	scattergram
elaboration model	test variable

For Further Inquiry

Hubert Blalock, Jr. *Causal Inferences in Nonexperimental Research.* Chapel Hill: University of North Carolina Press, 1961.
    This is a challenging book that provides some rules for making inferences about causality in sociological research.

Travis Hirschi and Hanan C. Selvin. *Delinquency Research.* New York: Free Press, 1967.
    The authors present a classic exposition on the nature of causality using research in the field of juvenile delinquency to illustrate the points. You learn about causality and also about the problem of delinquency and its solution.

Darrell Huff. *How to Lie with Statistics.* New York: Norton, 1954.
    Huff's book is an informative and readable little book that agrees that you can lie with statistics—but only to the uninformed who lack the ability to think critically. Huff offers many ways to avoid being lied to by statistics.

Morris Rosenberg. *The Logic of Survey Analysis.* New York: Basic Books, 1968.
    This is the classic work on the logic of analyzing relationships between variables. It is very comprehensive and, although not an easy read, is worth the effort for someone who anticipates being involved in research and data analysis.

Hans Zeisel. *Say It with Figures,* 6th ed. New York: Harper & Row, 1984.
    Zeisel presents an excellent discussion of elementary data analysis and table construction that is very useful for those who wish to be more skilled at analyzing data that is presented to them.

Exercises _____

The following is a data set containing 20 cases and 5 variables. Each line contains information on a particular individual on each variable: age, gender, the number of automobile accidents, number of miles driven each week, and blood alcohol level at the time of the latest accident.

Age	Gender	# of Accidents	Miles/Week	Blood Alcohol
19	M	1	25	0.00
19	M	4	250	0.14
21	F	2	43	0.00
22	M	2	50	0.02
24	M	3	78	0.06
27	F	3	49	0.00
27	F	2	175	0.06
31	F	2	25	0.00
33	M	1	30	0.00
34	F	1	35	0.02
40	M	2	75	0.00
40	F	1	28	0.02
42	F	2	65	0.05
43	M	2	42	0.00
49	M	1	30	0.00
56	F	1	38	0.03
59	F	3	80	0.10
60	M	3	75	0.06
61	M	2	45	0.00
63	F	1	32	0.03

3.1 Using these variables, state three causal relationships that might be found among these variables. Justify your choice in terms of the criteria needed to assess causality. Justify why one variable is considered the independent variable and the other the dependent variable.

3.2 Construct a scattergram showing the relationship between the number of miles driven each week and number of accidents. Do the same for blood alcohol level and number of accidents.

3.3 For these same two relationships, construct scattergrams that control for the effect of sex. (Hint: You will end up with four scattergrams.)

3.4 Construct a first order partial table that relates the variables of sex and number of accidents, controlling for age. It should be a 3 × 2 table, with number of accidents being low, medium, or high and age being either young or old. Table cells should contain both frequencies and percents.

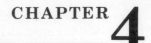

Experiments in Applied Research

The experiences of Lester, a 15-year-old from Miami, are, unfortunately, all too common (Gelber, 1988). Exuding an air of quiet self-assurance, he does not at first impress one as a "career criminal." Yet, his history suggests that he is headed in that direction. The first indication was his running away from home. By the time he was 11, he ran away so frequently that his mother sought help from the state. Repeatedly truant from school, he was caught by the police and placed in shelters or foster homes, from which he inevitably fled.

The first criminal charges filed against Lester were for shoplifting when he was 12. Shoplifting is often the first step for youngsters who are beginning to work their way into serious crime. Not long after, he was arrested for loitering and prowling. This was followed by three arrests for burglarizing houses, which put him behind bars for six months. His incarceration was supposed to encourage him to avoid future crimes. However, this was not to be. After release he didn't attend school as ordered and never went to see his counselor. He was rearrested very shortly and charged with a more serious felony, grand larceny.

To this point, Lester exhibits a pattern that is very common among criminals in the United States: rearrest after release from prison. How can this problem be reduced? What can be done to keep Lester from committing more crimes in the future? Some social experiments conducted by applied sociologists in the 1970s and 1980s have shed considerable light on these very complicated issues. To be able to critically assess the value of these experiments, however, we need to discuss what we mean by *social experiments* in applied research.

The first three chapters focused on the basic logic that underlies applied social research and data analysis. This chapter begins a more detailed discussion of specific research designs and strategies for gathering data that are used by applied sociologists (see Chapter 2). In other words, we begin to see exactly how applied researchers gather data and test hypotheses as a part of their work. This chapter explores one research design that is commonly used—the experiment—while the next chapter covers three others—surveys, qualitative research, and available data. These two chapters provide considerable substance to a major point of Chapter 1, namely that scientific research involves *systematic* observation. These research designs are a key part of making observation systematic.

I mentioned in Chapter 1 that some people are wary of the idea of scientifically studying human beings, especially when they hear about "experimenting" with people. Such talk brings to mind the possibility of manipulating people as well as images of test tubes, beakers, and possibly even the monstrous Baron Frankenstein. The idea of experimenting with people seems to imply, for many, that people are treated as unthinking objects with no free will, to be manipulated by others toward ends the people themselves have no control over. Yet none of this is involved in scientific experimentation. Experiments are nothing more than a logical way of making observations. As we will see, the strength of experiments is that they provide the most convincing demonstration of causality—that one factor brings about changes in another. Experiments can become very complicated, but we can begin to understand their logic by looking at the *classical* experiment, which provides the basic design for more complicated experiments.

The Classical Experiment

A key feature of all experiments is an **experimental stimulus,** or **experimental variable,** which is *one event or condition that is expected to have an influence on another*. In other words, the experimental stimulus is the independent variable that will change the dependent

Use of the Classical Experimental Design in Applied Settings

In the 1980s, California began a new welfare program called *workfare*. Basically, it required that most welfare recipients participate in job training programs and actively try to find work. The legislation also required that the program be evaluated in terms of whether it helps people find jobs. In order to make the most valid evaluation, the law stipulated that the research use a classical experimental design, with random assignment to experimental and control groups. So, 15 percent of the people eligible for the program were chosen at random and informed that they would continue to receive their welfare payments but would not be allowed to go through the job training program. They were the control group. The people who entered the program were the experimental group (Morgan, 1989).

Consider the logic of how the control group makes it possible to state causal influences with confidence. If a group of people receives the new job training services and a large proportion of them get a job by the end of a certain period, did the job training cause them to get the jobs? Possibly. But there could be factors other than the job training that produced the change. For example, the economy may have improved, resulting in more jobs, and this is what actually led to their success. With a control group of people who didn't receive the job training, we could assess these other possibilities. If the control group shows the same success in getting jobs as the treatment group did, then it is probably something other than the job training that is producing the change. On the other hand, if the control group shows no success in getting jobs and the treatment group shows success, then it is plausible to conclude that it was the job training experienced by the treatment group that made the difference. Finally, if the control group shows success at getting jobs, but not as much as the experimental group, then the job training is having an effect, but other factors are also at work. Without the control group, it is logically difficult to rule out these other possibilities as explanations for changes in the treatment group.

Creating a control group in this study seems simple enough, but it created two problems that illustrate some of the difficulties of using control groups in applied research. One problem was that the people selected for the control group were denied services that some of them would have preferred to have. Some of them would have liked the job training education, but they were denied it by chance—the random assignment to the control group. The second problem was in promoting the program. Because the control group people were to be kept out of the program, it was decided that the training and educational opportunities offered by the program should not be publicly promoted. Such promotion might antagonize those in the control group. But it also meant that some of the eligible people would not learn about the benefits of the program. As a consequence, fewer people applied for the program than expected.

variable, according to the hypothesis. In some experiments, the researcher actually manipulates this independent variable. So, in the study of spouse abuse described in Research in Action 1.1, the researchers made sure that different suspected abusers were exposed to different types of intervention: Some were arrested; some were counseled; some were separated from the victim. The researchers controlled the intervention by telling the police officers which one to use on each spouse abuse call. The mode of intervention was the experimental stimulus. In other experiments, changes in the value of the experimental variable occur independently of the researcher. For example, a study of ways to encourage people to reduce water consumption during droughts involved such an independent variable (Berk et al., 1980). Various communities responded to a severe drought by initiating a variety of conservation programs, but the programs differed across communities in the number, intensity, and duration of their efforts. These differing intensities of programs were considered the experimental treatment. These policy implementations were done independently by the communities and not for the benefit of the researchers. Yet the variation in policies over the communities could be used by the researchers as the experimental stimulus in an experimental design to see which approach worked best to reduce water consumption.

A group that is exposed to an experimental stimulus is called an **experimental group.** The classical experimental design also includes another group, called the **control group,** which is *comparable to the experimental group in all ways except that it is not exposed to the experimental variable*. The control group is essential in an experiment because it provides us with the confidence to say that changes in a dependent variable were caused by changes in an independent variable. The basic logic is as follows: If the dependent variable changes when the independent variable is present (the experimental condition) and the dependent variable does not change when the independent variable is absent (the control condition), then it is reasonable to conclude that the independent variable is producing the change in the dependent variable. Research in Action 4.1 offers an illustration of how this classical experimental design was used to assess the effect of a social policy and suggests how much weaker the argument is when there is no control group.

An important element of the classical experimental design, also illustrated in Research in Action 4.1, is the technique used for placing people into the experimental and control groups. It should be done by chance. *A selection process that is left completely to chance* is called **random assignment** and can be done by any procedure that ensures that chance determines which group a particular person goes into. (We discussed some of these procedures in Chapter 2 when we reviewed sampling.) Randomization is important because it influences the certainty with which we can make statements about causality. The ideal would be for experimental and control groups to be alike in all ways except that one gets the treatment and the other does not. However, two groups of people might differ in many ways: personality, social background, or personal experiences occurring during the course of the experiment. Randomization doesn't eliminate those differences, but it does reduce the likelihood that there will be a systematic difference between the two groups that might influence the dependent variable. For example, if we begin with a group of 50 people, 25 male and 25 female, then we would like both the experimental and control groups to have approximately half men and half women, assuming that gender is not a variable whose effect we are studying. If we use random assignment, there is a high probability that the two groups will be close to half male and half female. If we let people select for themselves which group they want to be in, it could be that people of one gender are more likely to choose to be in the experimental group, resulting in a disproportionate number of males in one group and females in the other. Then it becomes more difficult to conclude that differences between the two groups on the dependent variable are a result of the independent variable, because it could be the gender variation that is leading to the change. So, randomization increases our confidence that there are no systematic differences between experimental and control groups that might have an effect on the dependent variable.

The classical experimental design can be diagrammed in the following way:

		Pretest	Treatment	Posttest
Experimental Group:	R	O_1	X	O_2
Control Group:	R	O_3		O_4

In the diagram, R indicates that people were randomly assigned to groups, O indicates a measurement of the dependent variable (with the subscripts identifying a particular group measured at a particular time), and X indicates that the treatment or independent variable has been applied to a particular group. So, the diagram indicates that people were randomly assigned to experimental and control groups and that the experimental group received the treatment but the control group did not. It also indicates that the dependent variable was measured both before and after treatment with both groups. The key test of the hypothesis would be to see if there is more change in the dependent variable between O_1 and O_2 than between O_3 and O_4. If there is, then we can conclude that the treatment had an effect on the dependent variable.

As mentioned, one of the major advantages of experimental research designs is that they provide the strongest evidence for a causal relationship between variables. We can see how this is true by reviewing the criteria discussed in Chapter 2 for inferring causal relationships. The first criterion is to establish an association between two variables. This would be satisfied if the value of the dependent variable changes in the treatment condition but not in the control condition. The second criterion is that the relationship not be spurious. This is satisfied, in part, by the random assignment to conditions: If the treatment and control groups are alike—if they do not differ systematically from one another in any way—then there is no variable other than the independent variable that can account for differences in the dependent variable. However, recognizing that the groups could differ by chance, researchers sometimes use *matching* or *control variables.* With **matching,** *pairs of people are selected who are as much alike as possible on the indicated variables. Then one of them is randomly selected for the experimental group, and the other is placed in the control group.* Normally, matching is done on a number of variables, such as gender, age, or educational background, that are easy to measure and whose effect on the dependent variable is likely to be obvious. So, the experimental and control groups will be very similar to one another on the matched variables, and thus these variables are ruled out as possible causes of differences between experimental and control groups on the dependent variables.

One way to use a control variable is to make both experimental and control groups identical on that variable. Both groups could be made up of all females, and thus gender variation could not account for any differences between groups. Another way to use control variables is through statistical controls: The hypothesis can be tested separately for each value of the control variable. For example, the relationship between independent and dependent variables can be assessed among males alone and then among females alone. (This is the equivalent of the elaboration approach discussed in Chapter 3.) In short, both matching and control variables are a way to rule out other factors as causes of change in the dependent variable.

The third criterion for assessing causality is the time order: Changes in the independent variable (or the application of the treatment to the experimental group) must occur prior to changes in the dependent variable. As we noted in Chapter 2, this is often difficult to establish in some research methods, but it is readily established in experiments because the researcher controls the independent variable. The sequence in experiments is to measure the dependent variable (the pretest), expose the experimental group to the treatment (the independent variable), and then remeasure the dependent variable to see if there has been any change (the posttest). The proper time sequence is built into this procedure: The researcher knows that the independent variable occurred before the dependent variable changed.

Validity in Experiments

A key consideration in all research is validity, the extent to which researchers are actually measuring what they claim to be measuring (see Chapter 2). The same is true in experiments, although here the issue is called **internal validity:** *An experiment has internal validity when changes in the dependent variable are actually due to the independent variable and not to something else.* This is another way of describing the issue of causality. We can never be completely sure about causality, but we can design experiments in such a way as to increase our confidence that it was the independent variable that caused change in the dependent variable. *Change in the dependent variable that is produced by the independent variable* is called **experimental variability.** *Variation in the dependent variable produced by factors other than the independent variable* is **extraneous variability.** Good experiments are designed such that we can distinguish how much change in the dependent variable is experimental variability and how much is extraneous variability.

In order to grasp the importance of proper experimental design, let's consider some of the ways that change can be produced in the dependent variable, other than through the influence of the independent variable. These sources of change are called *threats* to internal validity because they threaten the certainty with which we can state that the independent variable produced change in the dependent variable (Campbell and Stanley, 1963).

A *history* threat to internal validity refers to the fact that something other than the manipulation of the treatment variable might occur between pretest and posttest that influences the value of the dependent variable. So, in the study of water conservation described earlier, if a huge rain and flooding had occurred between the initiation of the conservation policies and the measurement of water usage, people might have used water more freely, and we could not say whether any changes in water usage were due to the government policies or to the rain and flooding. Even if researchers are not aware of an event that produces a history threat, that event can still cause extraneous variation in the dependent variable.

A second threat to internal validity is *testing,* in which the pretest measurement of the dependent variable changes how people respond to the measurement device when the posttest measurement is made. For example, people may remember how they answered the questions in the pretest and modify their answers in the posttest. Sometimes people do this in order to be consistent from one time to the next, or they might be trying to trick the researcher. No matter why the testing effect occurs, it should be clear that changes in the dependent variable due to testing are not what the researcher is looking for.

A third threat to the internal validity of experiments is *reactivity* (see Chapter 2). Recall that reactivity means that some people change the way they behave when they know they are being observed. They may, for instance, be on their best behavior when their boss watches them; they are "reacting" to their boss's observance. The same may be true in any research, including experiments. This phenomenon was first noticed many years ago by researchers studying worker productivity at the Hawthorne Plant of the Western Electric Company near Chicago (Roethlisberger and Dickson, 1939). The researchers found that productivity increased when they made improvements in the work environment, such as better lighting or more rest periods. However, they also found that productivity increased when they reversed the improvements by dimming the lighting or taking away rest periods. Apparently, it was the attention the workers received by being a part of a research project, not the improvements in the work environment, that changed their work behavior. Such a phenomenon is now called the Hawthorne effect. In any experiment, the attention or special treatment that people receive by virtue of being in the experiment can produce changes in their behavior. Changes in the dependent variable due to the Hawthorne effect could be confused with actual experimental variation.

A fourth threat to internal validity is *experimental attrition:* As the experiment progresses, more people drop out of one group than the other. Some attrition is normal, especially in experiments that are long or require considerable effort on the part of participants. It becomes a problem, however, when the experimental and control groups end up being composed of different types of people. Then, it may be the variation in group composition, rather than the experimental treatment, that produces change in the dependent variable.

The point of good experimental design is not to eliminate extraneous variability but rather to distinguish between it and the experimental variability—variation due to the independent variable—that the researcher is studying. The classical experimental design can do this.

With regard to the threat of history, both experimental and control groups would experience such unanticipated events and both would be influenced by them. Thus, even if history produces change in the dependent variable, it would do so in both experimental and control groups, and we could still assess whether the independent variable produces additional change. If it does, then we can conclude that the independent variable is having an effect separate from the effect of history. The same logic applies to reactivity and testing because both groups can be expected to react to the attention of being studied and both will have been pretested. By comparing experimental and control groups we can assess whether the independent variable has an effect beyond that of either reactivity or testing. The classical design can also control some forms of experimental attrition, especially when it occurs because people move away, get sick, or die. These events are usually random as far as experimental and control groups are concerned and thus should occur almost equally in each group. Even if attrition is due to personal characteristics (maybe less educated or highly religious people are more likely to tire of experiments and drop out), these characteristics should be randomly distributed over experimental and control groups because of random assignment. However, attrition is difficult to control when it is produced by people's exposure to the independent variable. If the experimental treatment is difficult, unpleasant, or embarrassing, it might lead more people to drop out of the experimental condition than out of the control condition. The only thing that can be done if this occurs is to interpret the results carefully.

Other Experimental Designs

Pre-Experimental Designs

The classical experimental design serves as the standard for comparison. Some designs that, at first glance, seem similar to it are actually called pre-experimental designs because they lack randomization and control groups. The following design, for example, is one that many inexperienced researchers are tempted to use:

	Pretest	Treatment	Posttest
Experimental Group:	O_1	X	O_2

A pretest measure is taken, the group is exposed to the experimental stimulus, and then a posttest measure is used to assess whether the treatment produced a change. However, a little thought about the threats to internal validity should make clear that history, testing, reactivity, or attrition could be producing change in the posttest measure. With this design, there is no way to separate that extraneous variability from the effect of the treatment. As a result, this is considered a very weak experimental design in terms of its ability to establish confidence in causal relationships, and it is rarely used by serious social science researchers. However, I have seen numerous times in applied research when those unfamiliar with social science research methods have been tempted to use such a design without realizing what weaknesses it contains.

Here is another pre-experimental design:

	Pretest	Treatment	Posttest
Experimental Group:		X	O_1
Control Group:			O_2

The treatment is given to one group and that group is then compared to another group that has not been exposed to the treatment. The main problem with this design is that there is no random assignment to experimental and control groups. When random assignment cannot be done, which is sometimes the case in applied research, researchers often resort to finding a group that is similar to the experimental group to serve as a control group. For example, I recently participated in the assessment of a program to deliver social services to grade school children. Because some schools have the services and some don't and children could not be randomly assigned to schools, we used the schools without the services as the control group to compare to schools with the services. The problem, however, is that we couldn't use random assignment to give assurance that the two groups were comparable. Notice that testing is not a problem for this design because there is no pretest. Also, history is controlled by the assumption that extraneous events are as likely to influence people in the control group as in the experimental group. Likewise, the effect of reactivity could be assessed by comparing experimental and control groups.

True Experimental Designs

Pre-experimental designs have flaws that are avoided by true experimental designs like the classical design. True experimental designs use randomization, control groups, and other design features to control the threats to internal validity. Let's look at a few variations on the classical design.

One common variation, the *factorial design,* is used to investigate the simultaneous impact of two or more independent variables on a dependent variable. A common factorial design looks like this:

		Pretest	Treatment$_1$	Treatment$_2$	Posttest
Exper. Grp. 1:	R	O_1	X_1	X_2	O_2
Exper. Grp. 2:	R	O_3	X_1		O_4
Exper. Grp. 3:	R	O_5		X_2	O_6
Control Group:	R	O_7			O_8

Although this design may seem complicated, its simplicity can be recognized by looking at each element separately. Experimental group 2 and the control group describe the classical experimental design for the test of the effect of treatment 1; likewise, experimental group 3 and the control group are the classical design for the test of the impact of treatment 2. The only additional element to the design is experimental group 1, which tells us whether the *combined* effect of treatments 1 and 2 is different from the effect of separate treatments. This is an *interaction* effect: Two independent variables working in combination sometimes have a different effect than does either operating alone. Research in Action 4.2 describes a factorial design used to assess the effectiveness of policies intended to reduce criminal recidivism.

RESEARCH IN ACTION 4.2 ▰▰▰▰▰▰▰▰▰▰▰▰▰▰▰▰▰▰▰▰▰▰▰

Reducing Repeat Offenses Among Released Prison Inmates

Recidivism, shown clearly and dramatically in the life of Lester, is a serious problem in the United States. Currently, two out of every three former prison inmates end up being convicted of another felony. Concern over this issue rests, in part, on humanitarian grounds because we would like to help these people, many of whom, like Lester, have had a difficult time in life. Concern also arises from the recognition that 6 or 7 of every 10 prison inmates released into society will rob, assault, or rape again. The potential victims of people like Lester call out for us to do something.

There are many policies that could be developed to focus on reducing recidivism. One is to keep inmates in prison longer, but this only postpones the problem and may exacerbate it if inmates become more embittered about their plight. It is also a very expensive policy, and it violates a principal tenet of American justice: People are incarcerated for what they have done, not what they might do in the future. A more feasible approach is to look at the circumstances of inmates who are released for clues to why they continue to commit crimes. Released inmates tend to suffer economic hardship and high levels of unemployment. Few of them have job skills or many economic resources, and they are often not eligible for unemployment benefits upon release—such eligibility depends on how much a person has worked in the previous year or so. Given these conditions, it seems reasonable to conclude that some released inmates commit more crimes as a way to deal with this economic adversity. So, in the 1970s, sociologists designed a factorial experiment to assess whether social policies designed to improve the economic and employment opportunities of released inmates would reduce their rate of recidivism (Rossi, Berk, and Lenihan, 1980; Berk et al., 1985).

The LIFE (Living Insurance For Ex-offenders) experiment used two independent variables that were related to the economic and employment opportunities of released inmates: Financial assistance was provided to those who could not find employment and job placement services were available to all. There were three experimental groups (Figure 4.1): One received only financial assistance, the second only job placement services, and the third both. In addition, there was a control group that received neither financial assistance nor job placement services. Inmates were randomly assigned to these four conditions. The dependent variable was the level of criminal activity for two years after release. The researchers selected "high-risk" felons for the experiment—young males who had been convicted of multiple crimes and had at least one arrest for a property crime—because they had the greatest likelihood of becoming recidivists, and it would be difficult to tell which treatment most reduced recidivism if the rates of crime committed by the group as a whole were low.

When all the data were analyzed, the results were mixed but encouraging.

Receiving financial assistance did reduce recidivism, but only for property crimes. Also, those receiving financial assistance stayed out of prison for a longer period before being arrested and were less likely to ever return to prison. Crimes other than property crimes did not seem to be influenced by this variable. In addition, the job placement services did not seem to have an effect. It was the factorial design that enabled the researchers to separate out the effects of the two independent variables: The two groups that received financial assistance showed reduced recidivism for property crimes in comparison to the control group; the group receiving only job placement services did not. In addition, the group receiving both treatments showed the same reduced recidivism as the group receiving only financial aid; in other words, there was no interaction effect.

These same researchers also conducted a cost-benefit analysis of implementing the financial assistance program (see Chapter 6). They compared the cost of the program against the costs to the criminal justice system (police work, trial costs, and prison expenses) of the additional recidivism that would occur without the program. They concluded that every dollar spent on financial assistance would save a state $4.00 in criminal justice costs—a very cost-effective program .

After reviewing the results of this research on recidivism, social scientists, government officials, and criminal justice professionals recommended more research before making major social policy decisions. This led to a more ambitious experiment called TARP (Transitional Aid for Released Prisoners). It was designed much like the LIFE experiment, but its outcome was the opposite: Financial assistance did not reduce arrests for property

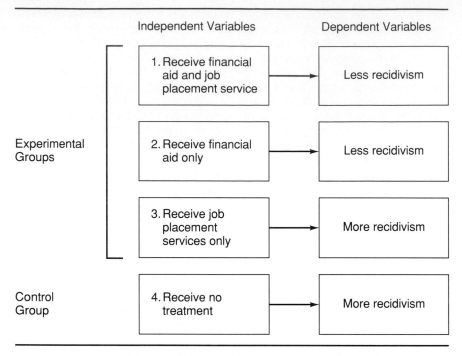

Independent Variables   Dependent Variables

Experimental Groups

1. Receive financial aid and job placement service → Less recidivism

2. Receive financial aid only → Less recidivism

3. Receive job placement services only → More recidivism

Control Group

4. Receive no treatment → More recidivism

Figure 4.1   The Baltimore LIFE Experimental Design

crimes. However, there were three key differences in the way TARP was designed that might explain its results. One was that the financial aid was administered by personnel in state unemployment offices rather than by a specially trained research staff. The trained staff might have provided some support or assistance, without realizing it, that the unemployment personnel did not provide. A second difference was that in the LIFE experiment, participants could earn some money and still receive most of their financial aid but in TARP this was not true. This seems to have caused the TARP participants to be less interested in working, and this unemployment may have increased their participation in crime. A third difference was that TARP was not limited to high-risk felons.

While the TARP experiment was being conducted, a California legislator heard of the LIFE experimental results and began an effort to start such a program in his state (Berk et al., 1985). Eventually legislation was passed setting up a program similar to the LIFE experiment, although in this case inmates actually applied for unemployment benefits when they were to be released from prison. The legislation provided that they would be eligible for unemployment benefits if they had worked enough hours in prison. The California program seems to have worked like the LIFE experiment: Those in the program had lower rates of recidivism than those not in the program. By a conservative estimate, California saved $2,000 for each inmate released into the program. However, one major difference in how the California program was run leads to caution in interpreting the results: Inmates were not randomly assigned to experimental and control groups. Those who worked sufficient hours in prison got into the program, and those who had not worked enough constituted the control group. It seems reasonable that there may be systematic differences between prison inmates who work a lot and those who do not. For example, the former may work more in prison in order to save the money they will need to successfully stay out of prison. This anticipation may lead them, once out of prison, to look for work more seriously and make more of an effort to keep any job that they get. In other words, those who are eligible for unemployment assistance—the experimental treatment—may also be better prospects for rehabilitation and less likely to commit crimes once released. The point is that without random assignment, we cannot confidently rule out these other explanations.

A second variation on the classical design is the *Solomon four-group design,* which looks like this:

	Pretest	Treatment	Posttest
Experimental Group 1: $\quad R$	O_1	X	O_2
Control Group 1: $\quad R$	O_3		O_4
Experimental Group 2: $\quad R$		X	O_5
Control Group 2: $\quad R$			O_6

The first experimental and control groups make up the classical experimental design, so this design protects against the same threats to internal validity that the classical design does. The additional experimental and control groups help researchers assess the extent of an interaction between the pretest measurement and the treatment. Being pretested and receiving a treatment may, in combination, produce different amounts of change than receiving the treatment alone or being pretested alone. This is called *pretest sensitization,* and it can make the results of the classical experiment difficult to interpret. The pretest can sensitize people to particular issues and in their sensitized state they react differently to the treatment from the way they would have had they not been sensitized. Remember that our sole concern is with the effect of the treatment on the posttest, and any other effects are extraneous variation.

With the Solomon design, we can assess these interaction effects. Experimental group 2 provides us with a measure of the impact of the treatment when there is no pretest and thus no possible pretest sensitization. If this group shows less change than experimental group

1, then there is probably a pretest/treatment interaction affecting the dependent variable. Control group 2 allows us to assess whether the passage of time alone would lead to posttest changes, even in the absence of a pretest.

A Solomon four-group design was used in a research project on the effect of public affairs television on political attitudes and behavior (Robinson, 1976). One of the major concerns was whether television shows that are critical of government activities might create a climate of cynicism and mistrust of the government. In particular, the researchers focused on a television documentary titled "The Selling of the Pentagon," which depicted efforts by the Department of Defense to manipulate public opinion regarding the military and defense issues. The pretest consisted of questions that tapped people's opinions regarding the behavior and credibility of various public officials and political institutions. The concern about a possible testing/treatment interaction here should be obvious: People who were just asked if they trusted government officials view a documentary that questions the trustworthiness of the Pentagon. It makes intuitive sense that these people might pick up on these themes more readily and thus express more cynicism in the posttest than would people who had not previously been asked about trust in government officials. The question is whether the treatment would have produced any change without the pretest. This cannot be determined without a group that receives the treatment but not the pretest, that is, the format used in the Solomon design.

The Solomon design is among the strongest experimental designs— it provides more information about the threats to internal validity than do the other designs. However, it also tends to be more expensive and time-consuming because of the need for two additional groups. When resources are scarce, as is often the case in applied research, researchers and their clients often decide that the additional certainty regarding causality is not worth the additional costs of the design.

When time or money are serious considerations, or when pretest sensitization is a concern, researchers sometimes turn to what is called a *posttest-only control group design:*

		Treatment	Posttest
Experimental Group 1:	R	X	O_1
Control Group 1:	R		O_2

This is the classical design without the pretests, and it is identical to the second experimental and control groups in the Solomon design. Some experts on research experiments argue that this design protects against the threats to validity as well as do any others as long as there is true random assignment to conditions (Campbell and Stanley, 1963). History should not be a problem because both the experimental and control groups would be exposed to the same intervening events; testing is not a problem because there is no pretest; reactivity can be assessed by comparing experimental and control groups; attrition should not be a problem if the posttest is given immediately after the treatment.

So far, we have been considering the independent variable as being either present or absent. In the recidivism study described in Research in Action 4.2, for example, the independent variable was financial assistance, and some inmates received it (the experimental group) while others did not (the control group). However, some independent variables are more complicated than this because they can be present to some degree or in some amount. In the recidivism study, it would have been possible to look not just at whether inmates received financial assistance but at how much they received. We could have hypothesized that there is some level of financial assistance that needs to be achieved in order for it to have an effect on recidivism. Or, there might be a negative linear relationship between financial assistance and recidivism: As financial assistance increases, recidivism declines. An experimental design to take into account such an independent variable would look like this:

		Pretest	Treatment	Posttest
Experimental Group 1:	R	O_1	X_1	O_2
Experimental Group 2:	R	O_3	X_2	O_4
Experimental Group 3:	R	O_5	X_3	O_6
Control Group:	R	O_7		O_8

Each experimental group combined with the control group constitutes the classical design. Each treatment is a different amount or degree of the independent variable. We can now assess what amount of the independent variable is necessary before it produces change in the dependent variable. Or it will tell us if the dependent variable continues to change as a greater amount of the treatment is given.

These are the major true experimental designs. There are some other variants, but those presented so far are sufficient for you to grasp the basic logic of experimentation. You should recognize the value in each of these designs in enabling you to assess with confidence the causal effect of an independent variable on a dependent variable. They provide the basic logic of causal analysis. They also provide further illustration of a theme in this book: what it means to use systematic observation as a foundation for drawing conclusions. The experimental designs show the extreme care that applied sociologists take in gathering data before drawing conclusions or making recommendations.

Quasi-Experimental Designs

There are times when it isn't possible to use the random assignment to experimental and control groups that is at the core of true experimental designs. Rather than forego research entirely, it is possible to use what are called quasi-experimental designs, which fall somewhere between true experiments and pre-experimental designs in terms of protecting against threats to internal validity. Although they don't have the controls of true experiments, they do utilize elements that provide more assurances than the pre-experiments regarding whether variation in the dependent variable was due to the experimental stimulus or to some other factor. However, the true experiments are definitely preferred when it is possible to use them.

Some quasi-experimental designs are based on one variation or another of a *time-series design*. As the name implies, these designs involve making a series of observations of a group over a period of time, both before and after introduction of the experimental stimulus:

$$O_1 \; O_2 \; O_3 \; O_4 \; O_5 \; X \; O_6 \; O_7 \; O_8 \; O_9 \; O_{10}$$

In this example, there are five pretest measures of the dependent variable and five posttest measures. The multiple measures of the dependent variable serve as quasi-control groups: If the value of the dependent variable changes at O_6, right after the introduction of the experimental stimulus, and not at any other time, then this is evidence that the change is due to the experimental stimulus. If changes in the dependent variable are due to reactivity or testing, then this should show up at some other of the measurement points and not just after introduction of the experimental stimulus. Even the impact of history can be evaluated to an extent. Assuming that an event that impacts on the dependent variable is equally likely to occur at any point during the time period that observations are made, the chance that it will occur such that it affects only O_6 is one out of 10. If only O_6 shows an effect, the researcher can argue that it is more likely that the effect is due to the experimental stimulus than to some other event. However, it should be clear that this design provides less protection against the threat of history than do the true experimental designs. In fact, some researchers maintain that history is the most serious threat to internal validity in the time-series designs. Research in Action 4.3 describes an applied research project that used a time-series quasi-experiment to assess a very important social policy that will affect most of our lives.

Assessing Policies on Mandatory Retirement

Social policy in the United States regarding mandatory retirement has changed over the years. Prior to the 1930s, it was a matter of individual and company choice: People retired when they wished, if they could afford it (most couldn't), or if their employer forced them to. The Social Security Act of 1935 established 65 as the mandatory retirement age. There were a number of benefits to this, including that retiring workers opened up jobs for younger workers. In fact, 65 came to be seen as the "normal" retirement age. However, many Americans believed that mandatory retirement based on age was discriminatory. So, the Age Discrimination in Employment Act (ADEA), as amended in 1978, raised the age at which most workers could be involuntarily retired to 70. The ADEA was further amended in 1986 to eliminate mandatory retirement entirely for most workers. We have come full circle in just over 50 years, from no mandatory retirement, to various age levels for retirement, and back to no mandatory retirement.

Mandatory retirement was eliminated largely because it was viewed as discriminatory. The objection was that people should be allowed to work if they are able, regardless of age. However, the policy has clear implications in a number of realms, especially for younger workers who might have difficulty finding jobs if older workers continue to work beyond age 65. Do older workers actually continue working beyond the "normal" retirement age when they are not forced to retire? To answer this question we need research to determine whether this policy change has an effect on people's decisions about whether to continue working or retire at age 65. However, given the nature of the phenomenon under consideration here, the use of a control group and random assignment is largely ruled out for both practical and ethical reasons: practically, the social policy was established for reasons that had nothing to do with younger workers and their plight; ethically, it would have been unfair to randomly let some workers continue working and force others to retire just to see what the side effects of the policy might be. There are some groups that could have been used as controls, such as workers in industries where mandatory retirement still existed, but these groups in all likelihood differ in significant ways from workers in other industries and would not make good control groups.

In the evaluation of policy outcomes such as this, it is often possible to use a time-series design, and this is what policy analyst Edward Lawlor (1986) did. Basically, the independent variable is the new social policy, in this case the raising of mandatory retirement from age 65 to age 70, which came into effect on January 1, 1979. The dependent

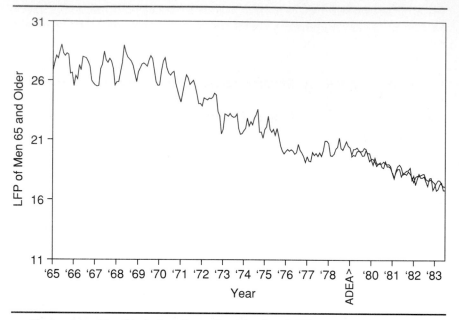

Figure 4.2 Monthly Labor-Force Participation (LFP) Rates of Men, 1965–1983.
Source: Edward F. Lawlor. 1986. "The Impact of Age Discrimination Legislation on the Labor Force Participation of Aged Men: A Time-Series Analysis." *Evaluation Review,* 10 (December), p. 801. Copyright © 1986 by Sage Publications, Inc. Reprinted by permission of Sage Publications, Inc.

variable is labor force participation of men aged 65 and older, which was measured each month. This allows for a series of observations before the introduction of the experimental stimulus (the raising of the retirement age) and a series of observations after. The pretest observations are labor force participation rates each month from 1965 to 1979, and posttest observations are the monthly labor force participation rates after 1979.

In analyzing the outcome of a time-series design, researchers look for changes in the *patterns* after the introduction of the experimental stimulus. With a series of observations, there are often random fluctuations from one observation to the next. In some cases, there may even be consistent variation

from one time period to another, and this was the case with the retirement rates between 1965 and 1983. As Figure 4.2 shows, there was fluctuation in rates from month to month, but the long-term trend was a gradual decline in the labor force participation of men 65 and older over the whole period. The decline is a little less rapid between 1965 and 1969 and then again between 1976 and 1979. But the striking outcome is that the whole period shows steady decline, and the decline does not become significantly steeper after the ADEA amendment comes into effect in 1979. Thus, although there is a change, or a decline, after the introduction of the experimental stimulus, the existence of a similar decline in the pretest observations suggests that it is not the experimental stimulus that is producing the posttest decline. If the decline had become significantly steeper during the posttest period, then that would be evidence of the effect of the experimental intervention.

Lawlor concluded from this time-series analysis that the social policy change initiated by the ADEA amendments of 1978 did not significantly affect the labor force participation of older men. For now, we can conclude that approximately the same proportion of men retire by age 65 whether there is mandatory retirement or not. Thus the impact of raising the age of mandatory retirement appears to be more symbolic than substantive. Whether this is also true for eliminating mandatory retirement in 1986 will have to be settled by future time-series, quasi-experimental research designs. In addition, it may be that our cultural conception of what is the "normal" time to retire might change during an era when there is no mandatory retirement. If more people begin to stay in the labor force after age 65, there may be more social pressure to postpone retirement. In other words, the effect of eliminating mandatory retirement may be indirect and delayed by a few years, or even decades. (Another policy change in the 1980s could put a new wrinkle in this: The age at which a worker can retire and receive full Social Security benefits was raised. Although it makes intuitive sense that this change might cause people to postpone retirement, it, too, needs to be studied empirically through a time-series or other type of quasi-experimental design.)

If it is possible to include a control group in the time-series design, then it would also be possible to assess the effect of history on the dependent variable. However, quasi-experimental designs are often chosen in situations, such as field settings, where the researcher has less control over people and events and may be unable to use random assignment to form experimental and control groups. If so, it might be possible to use as a control group an existing group that is similar to the experimental group in many ways (such as age, sex, socioeconomic status, and the like) but is not exposed to the treatment. This was done in a study of the impact of changing educational structures on adolescent development described in Research in Action 4.4. Although this study was not a time-series design, it does illustrate the use of a comparable existing group as a control rather than a group made up of randomly selected individuals.

RESEARCH IN ACTION 4.4

The Effect of Changing Schools on Adolescents

Adolescence is often characterized as a time of "storm and stress." Momentous physiological changes are occurring as puberty progresses; identity crises are not uncommon, as young people try to establish a sense of who they are; conflict with parents is frequent, as youngsters gradually assert their independence. Throughout this period, adolescents spend a good part of their time in school. What do the schools contribute to all of this? Can the schools be structured in a way that enhances positive outcomes of this transition? Some educational structures or processes might be studied in a laboratory setting, such as the impact of teaching styles on learning. However, the laboratory has little to offer in understanding the impact of many other structures. For example, by the 1990s, most school systems in the United States had established three levels: grade school (kindergarten through sixth grade, or K–6), middle school or junior high school (grades 7–9), and high school (grades 10–12). In earlier decades, most schools had two levels: grade school (K–8) and high school (grades 9–12). This change in organizational structure from two to three tiers produced two major changes for students. First, they must make two changes of schools as they grow up rather than one. Second, they make the first change at a younger age (about 11–12 rather than 13–14).

It would be impossible to mimic these differing educational structures and their impact on youngsters in a laboratory setting. However, sociologists Roberta Simmons and Dale Blyth (1987) found a setting in which to conduct a natural experiment on these issues. In the 1970s, the public school system in Milwaukee was making the transition from a two-tiered to a three-tiered school system. At the time of the study, some schools were still a part of the two-tiered system, and they served as the control group; other schools had changed to the three-tiered setup, and they were the experimental group. Here was a

real-life setting in which to see how the two educational structures affected adolescent development. This is not a true experimental design, however, because there was no random assignment of children to schools. Children went to the school in the district in which they happened to live. One danger with this type of design, of course, is that the students in the two different types of schools may be different from one another—one group might be poorer, less achievement oriented, or from more dysfunctional families. If these initial differences are substantial, they might account for differing experiences during the adolescent transition, and the schools may play no part. To investigate this possibility, Simmons and Blyth followed a common procedure for applied researchers: They compared children in the two school settings on a number of characteristics and behaviors, such as family income, achievement scores, quality of teachers in the schools, percent minority, and many others. Their conclusion was cautious but clear: "As in any natural experiment, one can neither control all extraneous variables nor claim that there are no initial differences. However, as far as we are able to determine, there are no major . . . differences between the . . . students" (Simmons and Blyth, 1987:29). The logic of experimental design makes them cautious about saying they are *certain* there is no extraneous variation. The same logic, however, lets them conclude that extraneous variables *probably* have little effect on the outcome because their search could find no differences between the groups.

Simmons and Blyth's findings have direct implications for the wisdom of going to a three-tiered educational structure and were translated into straightforward recommendations on educational policy. Among other things, they found that the transition from elementary to middle school, coming earlier than the elementary-to-high-school transition, was easier on children. The former is perceived as more gradual, and it coincides with fewer of the other changes of adolescence, such as the physiological changes of puberty. When the transition occurs after the eighth grade, as in the two-tiered system, it is more likely to be seen by both parents and students as part of the transition from childhood to adolescence. Consequently, there is more pressure on the child to relinquish old behaviors and adopt more mature ones. Another finding was that a number of changes occurring at once—for example, changing schools and entering adolescence—is more detrimental than spreading the changes over a period of time.

Although a great many students make the school transition quite well, Simmons and Blyth were able to identify those who are likely to be at risk of suffering some serious difficulties. For example, they found that female students, students who were experiencing many life changes simultaneously, those who had been treated poorly by their peers, had low self-esteem, and did not feel popular had more difficulty. With this information, teachers and school administrators could more readily locate children who may need more help during school transitions.

A major disadvantage of using a control group in a time-series design is that it doubles the number of observations that must be made. This is not a problem in most experimental designs because there is only one pretest and one posttest. Including the control group only increases the number of observations from two to four. In a time-series design, however, there is typically a *minimum* of three pretests and three posttests. Adding a control group increases the observations from 6 to 12. So, when deciding on whether to use a control group in a time-series design, researchers must weigh the importance of assessing the history threat to validity against the time and costs involved in using a control group.

Field Experiments

True experimental designs were first developed and used in the natural sciences where it was feasible to conduct research in a laboratory setting. Laboratories are artificial settings where the researcher can control all factors (light, temperature, the independent variable, and so on) that might have an impact on the dependent variable. This is the ideal setting for conducting experiments because the extensive control of the researcher gives the greatest confidence that the experimental and control groups are equivalent and that both experience precisely the same conditions during the course of the experiment. Laboratory experiments have been extensively used in research in psychology but less so in the other social sciences. Laboratory experiments are rarely used in applied research because the focus of the research is typically on some existing or future program or policy, and more can usually be learned by studying the program in the real world rather than in the laboratory.

So, applied research that uses experimental designs almost always involves **field experiments:** *experiments that are conducted in naturally occurring settings with people engaging in their normal daily routines with minimal interference from researchers.* Typically, the only interference from the researcher would be placing people into experimental and control groups (people may not even know they are in the experiment if observations can be made without talking to them) and introducing the experimental stimulus. Beyond that, people do as they would normally, often thinking little, if at all, about the experiment. In the study of recidivism described in Research in Action 4.2, for example, the only unusual event was that some inmates received employment services or payments at release and others didn't. Then the released prisoners were on their own and lived out their lives as they saw fit. The researchers made no further effort to interfere in their lives. Even measurement of the dependent variable—conviction for a later offense—could be done by looking at court records rather than directly contacting the participants. The study of retirement described in Research in Action 4.3 could also be accomplished without contacting anyone personally.

The major weakness of field experiments in contrast to laboratory experiments is the lack of control that researchers exercise during the course of the experiment. Laboratory researchers can claim that experimental and control groups are alike not only because of random assignment but also because the exact same treatment is given to both groups between the pretest and the posttest. They are exposed to the same physical conditions (the exact same lighting, heating, and people in the laboratory) as well as the precise same experimental conditions. For example, in a laboratory experiment, instructions to the subjects are never improvised or ad-libbed. Researchers read the same instructions from a script to each person going through the experiment. Field experimenters do not have nearly this degree of control. Some people in the control group might have very different life experiences between pretest and posttest than do some people in the experimental group. If these differences have an impact on the dependent variable, extraneous variation can result. The major way to control for this is through random assignment to experimental and control groups. With randomization, it can be assumed that life events that might influence the dependent variable would be as likely to occur to people in the experimental group as to those in the control group.

A major advantage of field experiments is that they have greater *external validity* than do laboratory experiments. **External validity** refers to *the ability to generalize conclusions from an experiment to the real world.* Laboratory experiments have been criticized on the grounds that they are so artificial that we learn little about the real world from them. The laboratory is such a faked setting that we cannot be sure that it is equivalent to real-life experiences where many factors impinge on a person at once and decisions have real and long-term consequences. Field experiments, on the other hand, are not artificial. They are conducted in the real world, often on the same people and in the same settings to which conclusions are to be generalized. All four Research in Action sections in this chapter, as well as those in many other chapters, illustrate the use of field experiments in applied sociology.

CRITICAL THINKING ─────────────────────────────

Is It a True Experimental Design?

People routinely make causal assessments in their everyday lives. We ask ourselves such questions as, Why was my spouse angry at me last night? Why is there so much crime in that neighborhood? Why did I do so poorly on this examination? However, these assessments tend to be done casually and are often based on few observations. This chapter provides the basic logic for making more systematic causal analyses. Not that we are often in a position in our daily lives to collect lots of observations or to compare experimental and control groups. However, experimental designs provide a model for organizing our thinking about information that we confront in the everyday world. A critical thinking approach would ask the following questions:

1. Is an argument based on information that approximates a true experimental or quasi-experimental design?
2. Is there a control group that can serve as a comparison point for assessing change? Was there random assignment to experimental and control groups?
3. Given the way in which the comparison/control group was selected, what kind of systematic differences might there be between it and the experimental group?
4. What alternative factors, other than the independent variable, could produce variation in the dependent variable? In other words, what sources of extraneous variability exist?
5. Given all of these considerations, how confident are you that you can infer a causal relationship? Why or why not?

One of the characteristics of the cognitive flexibility described in Chapter 3 is feeling comfortable with uncertainty—being able to reserve judgment and say that you are unsure about the veracity or accuracy of a conclusion. Even though you may not be in a position to make sufficient observations on an issue to constitute an experimental design, you can reserve judgment if the evidence presented does not justify making causal inferences with certainty. A cognitively flexible person would feel comfortable recognizing that there is insufficient information with which to draw a solid conclusion.

Key Terms for Review _____

control group
experimental group
experimental stimulus
experimental variability
experimental variable
external validity

extraneous variability
field experiment
internal validity
matching
random assignment

For Further Inquiry _____

P. Cutwright and F. S. Jaffe. *Impact of Family Planning Programs on Fertility: The U.S. Experience.* New York: Praeger, 1977.
>This study used a quasi-experimental design to study the impact of federally financed family planning clinics on counties. It illustrates the importance of control variables and also includes a cost-benefit analysis (see Chapter 6).

Evaluation Review: A Journal of Applied Social Research.
>This is one of the major journals in the field of applied social research. Every issue contains many articles that either use or analyze the use of true experiments and quasi-experiments in field settings.

George W. Fairweather and William S. Davidson. *An Introduction to Community Experimentation.* New York: McGraw-Hill, 1986.
>This book focuses on those wishing to evaluate the effectiveness of community action programs through field experimentation. It provides many examples of programs where this was done.

G. Kassebaum, D. Ward, and D. Wilner. *Prison Treatment and Parole Survival.* New York: John Wiley, 1971.
>The authors describe a randomized controlled experiment used to assess the effectiveness of a new counseling program introduced into a prison system in order to reduce behavior problems in prison and recidivism after release.

D. Kershaw and J. Fair. *The New Jersey Income-Maintenance Experiment.* New York: Academic Press, 1976.

This book describes the evaluation of a large-scale welfare program set up in New Jersey. It illustrates some of the political, ethical, and research problems that can arise in field experiments.

Exercises

There is a drug education program operating in all the schools in a school district. By teaching teenagers about how drugs work in the body and the damage that they can do, the program hopes to reduce a teenager's likelihood of using illegal drugs. You have been given the challenging task of designing a study that shows whether the program does, in fact, reduce drug usage. Because the program planners want to be able to show that it was the program that *caused* any declines in drug use, they want to use an experimental or quasi-experimental design.

4.1. What are the independent and dependent variables in this research? How could you measure them? Of the experimental designs discussed in this chapter, which would be most feasible? Which would be least feasible? Describe a true experiment and a quasi-experiment that could be used in this situation.

4.2. In a field project such as this, how would it be possible to create a true control group and random assignment to conditions? How would you assign people to experimental and control conditions?

4.3. Given what we know about the factors that produce drug abuse, can you think of any control variables that it might be useful to consider? How would these control variables help you in making inferences about what causes led to what results?

4.4. What are the major threats to internal and external validity in the experimental designs that you described earlier? How do the designs protect against those threats? Are there some threats to internal validity that cannot be eliminated in the evaluation of this program?

4.5. Locate a program in your college or community that is currently in operation. Using that program as an example, answer questions 4.1 to 4.4 again.

Strategies for Gathering Data

Early one morning in 1974 in Beaufort County, North Carolina, the body of the night jailer, a 64-year-old white male, was found in a locked cell in the women's section of the county jail. He had been stabbed with an ice pick and his pants and shoes were outside the cell. The person who had been incarcerated in that cell was Joan Little, a young, poor African-American. She had been sentenced to a 7–10-year term for breaking and entering and was awaiting transfer to the state women's prison. When the jailer's body was found, Little was gone, along with the keys to the cell and the jail.

Over the next few days, an extensive search failed to find Ms. Little. Authorities were on the verge of declaring her an "outlaw"—under the North Carolina statutes of that time, she could have been killed on sight by any citizen, whether or not she was resisting or attempting to flee. However, she turned herself in and was immediately charged with first degree murder. She eventually went to trial before a jury. Her future looked bleak for a number of reasons: She was accused of using sex to lure the jailer into her cell and then stabbing him to death as part of an escape attempt. Also, African-Americans accused of killing whites in North Carolina in the early 1970s were routinely convicted and were highly likely to receive the death penalty. Finally, there were no eyewitnesses, other than Ms. Little and the deceased jailer, to corroborate what actually happened in the jail cell that night. However, some applied social scientists were working on Ms. Little's defense team, and because of this, the outcome of her legal battle was different from what might have been expected. (The Little case and her trial are described in McConahay, Mullin, and Frederick, 1977.)

Before examining in detail the Joan Little case, we need to explore more of the research designs used in applied research. The first three chapters focus primarily on the *logic* of applied research, discussing such subjects as theory verification, hypothesis testing, sampling, and table elaboration. Chapter 4 began a discussion of precisely how applied researchers make observations and collect data by focusing on one type of research design, the experiment. This chapter explores the three other types of research designs and methods of collecting data: survey research, qualitative research, and available data. Applied researchers use a wide variety of data-gathering strategies, and often more than one in a single research project. The most appropriate strategy to use depends on the nature of the research problem, the types of variables and hypotheses being tested, and the resources available to conduct the research. The techniques all share the effort to make *systematic* observations and to collect valid and reliable data. After finishing Chapter 5, you should have a good idea of what constitutes systematic, valid, and reliable data gathering.

Survey Research

A **survey** is *a data-gathering strategy in which questions are asked and the answers serve as data.* Most often, we ask questions of individuals because the individual is the *unit of analysis:* We want to learn something about the characteristics, feelings, or behaviors of individuals. However, the unit of analysis could be something other than individuals, such as groups, organizations, or programs. If we were comparing one drug treatment program with another, the program itself might be the unit of analysis and we would collect data about the program. We could, for example, compare programs in terms of their rates of successfully getting people off drugs. (Obviously, individuals don't have rates of success—an individual is either off or on drugs.) However, even though the unit of analysis is the program or organization, a survey might still be sent to an individual. The director of the drug treatment program might fill out a survey that asks questions about the number of successes and other characteristics of the program and its clientele. So, the unit of analysis is what we want to collect data *about,* and this might be different from the actual *source* of the data.

Surveys are one of the oldest of the modern social science strategies and one of the most widely used. It is reported that Karl Marx conducted a survey in the 1800s (Babbie, 1990). Between the Civil War and World War I, many surveys were conducted in the United States to assess such things as economic productivity, the injury or exploitation of factory workers, and the extent of poverty and other problems in our rapidly growing cities (Turner and Turner, 1990). In this century, the use of surveys has grown at exponential rates. They are used in such disparate endeavors as basic social science research, public opinion polling, and product marketing. Surveys are conducted to help us understand human social behavior, sell beer and potato chips, and market political candidates. Even lawyers have used surveys conducted by applied social scientists to help them win cases in court, as Research in Action 5.1 illustrates. Despite their widespread use, it is easy to misuse surveys and collect data that has little validity or reliability. Rather than provide a complete overview of survey design and construction—books have been written on this—I will emphasize some of the major factors that can affect the validity and reliability of surveys.

RESEARCH IN ACTION 5.1 ━━━━━━━━━━━━━━━━━━━━━━━━

How to Choose a "Good" Jury

Joan Little's situation did not look good—an African-American woman accused of killing a white man, first degree murder charges. Her claim was that the jailer had attempted to rape her, and she killed him while defending herself. Fortunately for her, her case generated tremendous publicity and donations of money sufficient to hire a good team of attorneys. (Most poor defendants of color are not so fortunate.) Furthermore, her attorneys tried all the options available to them to select a good jury. A "good" jury, for the defense, is the one most likely to acquit the defendant.

The selection of a jury in a criminal trial is a very important and complicated process, and attorneys use a great deal of intuition, insight, and past experience to help them do it. Joan Little's attorneys also recruited applied social scientists for the defense team, and these researchers used survey techniques to assist in the jury selection.

There are three key steps in the jury selection process, and community surveys were used at every one by Little's defense team (see Kairys, Schulman, and Harring, 1975; and McConahay, Mullin, and Frederick, 1977). The first step is the matter of *venue,* or where the trial will be held. Juries are chosen from the community in which the trial is heard. Generally, the judge has the discretion of deciding where to hold a trial, but judges can be influenced if the defense attorney can argue that pretrial publicity or some other factor has prejudiced the members of the community against the defendant. In the Joan Little case, the social science researchers on the defense team conducted community surveys in many North Carolina counties, some rural like Beaufort, where the crime occurred, and one that was more urbanized and different in terms of prevailing values and attitudes. In all counties, a random sample of those eligible for jury duty was chosen and interviewed. They were asked many questions, including some about race, religion, politics, and other issues that might tap into possible prejudices. For example, they were asked whether they thought "black people were more violent than white people" and whether "black women have lower morals than white women." In Beaufort County, 63 percent of respondents agreed with both of these questions, compared to 35 percent in the more urban county. Survey respondents were also asked specific questions about the case to see what opinions or prejudices existed in the community. Thirty-eight percent of the Beaufort County respondents did not believe that Little killed the jailer in self-defense, compared to 18 percent in the more urban county. Little's attorneys were able to use evidence from these surveys and other sources to show that significant prejudices against their client existed in the trial community. The judge agreed and accepted their motion to move the trial to a less conservative, more urban community in North Carolina (although not the one the researchers had surveyed).

The second step in the jury selection process is the establishment of a jury panel from which the actual jurors will be chosen. The jury panel is selected from such sources as a list of all registered voters in the community and is supposed to be representative of the community in which the trial is to be held. Defense attorneys can make a *composition challenge* if they believe that the jury panel does not represent the community or that some groups are underrepresented. The community survey was used to assess this issue also. It showed that 30 percent of those eligible for jury duty in the community where the Little trial was originally to be held were African-American but only 13 percent of the jury panel were African-American, suggesting that the procedure for selecting the jury panel from the eligible jurors was biased in favor of selecting whites. Unfortunately for Little, the judge denied this composition challenge. However, it didn't matter in the end because the venue challenge was successful and the trial site was changed to another community.

The third step is selecting the jury itself from the jury panel. This is done through a process called *voir dire,* in which potential jurors are interviewed to determine if they are competent and impartial. After each juror is interviewed, defense counsel can challenge the juror either for a particular cause (which the judge must agree with) or for no reason (a peremptory challenge, which results in automatic dismissal of a juror). Community surveys were used during the *voir dire* to help Little's attorneys decide which potential jurors to challenge. The survey results helped to predict which demographic characteristics of the potential jurors (age, sex, income, education, race, and so on) were linked with negative attitudes toward the defendant. Because the survey was done in the same community that the jury panel was chosen from and the jury panel was supposed to represent the community from which it was drawn, the relationships discovered in the community survey should also hold for the jury panel. Sometimes, regression equations (see Chapter 3) were used to show which combinations of characteristics result in the most negative feelings toward the client. In the Little case, the social scientists developed a mathematical model of the "ideal" juror that the defense attorneys were then able to use as one element in a strategy of deciding which jurors to challenge.

These, then, are some of the ways in which applied social science research is used in the jury selection process. They helped Joan Little get a fairer trial than she would likely have gotten otherwise. After a five-week trial in 1975, she was found not guilty on all charges. Unfortunately for others, such techniques are very expensive and are thus normally available only to the fairly affluent.

Questionnaires Versus Interviews

Survey data can be collected in two different ways: with questionnaires or an interview schedule. A **questionnaire** is *given directly to the survey respondent who fills it out and returns it without any assistance from the researcher.* Questionnaires are sometimes sent through the mail or can be given directly to the respondents if that is feasible. An **interview** is *an instrument that is not given to the respondent but rather is filled in by an interviewer after questioning the respondent.* Interviews can be conducted either in person or over the telephone. In fact, telephone interviews have developed into a very fast and inexpensive method of conducting surveys. (The community survey described in Research in Action 5.1 was a telephone survey.) Sometimes, survey research uses a combination of questionnaire and interview formats in the same research, because some information is best gotten with one format rather than the other.

The choice of questionnaire versus interview format depends in part on the nature of the data to be collected. If the researchers know exactly what information they need and the questions can be understood without any assistance from an interviewer, then questionnaires are quite appropriate. Many attitudinal questions are of this nature, as are questions about demographic information such as gender or age. The questions are self-explanatory and easy to answer. However, questionnaires are inflexible: Questions or question wording cannot be changed as the person is filling it out. And there are situations where such flexibility is essential. In research on sensitive topics like sexual behavior, an interviewer can reword questions if the person feels uncomfortable or doesn't understand something. This is not possible with a questionnaire. For these reasons, the research on AIDS, by sociologist William Darrow and colleagues (1987) and described in Research in Action 2.3, utilized interviews. After all, the men being interviewed were asked very sensitive questions about their sexual behavior, the numbers and identities of their sexual partners, and their drug use. The possibility that the respondents might misunderstand a question or withhold information was very high. With interviewers, it was possible to watch for verbal and nonverbal cues that such misunderstanding or withholding was occurring and to probe for better information. Interviews are also preferred in exploratory research when we don't know much about the topic under study. It is then valuable for an interviewer to explore interesting lines of inquiry even though they don't appear on the interview schedule.

A second factor that comes into play in choosing between questionnaires and interviews is the feasibility of each. Generally, interviews are more expensive and time-consuming, and this has to be weighed against their benefits. When time and financial resources are limited, researchers sometimes choose questionnaires rather than forego data collection altogether.

Designing Survey Instruments

For astronomers, the telescope is an instrument for gathering data, and costly and painstaking steps are taken to be sure that a telescope has the proper focal length, materials, curvature of the lens, and so on to ensure that the best and most accurate images of the heavens are recorded. For survey researchers, the basic instrument for gathering data is the sequence of questions on the questionnaire or interview, and painstaking efforts are also made to be sure that the most accurate (valid) responses are collected by those questions (Babbie, 1990; Monette, Sullivan, and DeJong, 1990).

The questions on surveys can be either open ended or closed ended. *Open ended questions* are those in which no response alternatives are given and the person is expected to write out his or her own responses. *Closed ended questions* are those in which a fixed number of alternatives are provided. Closed ended questions are used when we know what all the possible responses to a question are and they are limited in number. For example, gender and marital status are two variables that would virtually always be measured by closed ended questions. Gender has only two possible responses (male, female), and marital status has a limited but fixed number of alternatives (single, married, separated, divorced, widowed). On the other hand, open ended questions are used when people could give many possible responses or when some of the responses are unknown, as in an exploratory study when we don't know enough about a topic to predict all the responses that might be given.

Once it is decided whether questions should be open ended or closed ended, the exact wording of the questions needs to be established. Many people believe that a reasonably intelligent person can design questions that will be properly understood by others. Nothing could be further from the truth. Words and phrases have a variety of meanings for different people, and some of those meanings are so subtle that we may not be completely aware of them. Researchers who design questions may attribute a different meaning to words and phrases than do the respondents who read them. Let me give one example of this. In a study of people's attitudes about social welfare policy in the United States, survey respondents were asked whether they believed we should spend more or less money on welfare (Smith, 1987). However, they were asked the question in three slightly different ways. One group was asked whether we were spending too much or too little on *welfare,* a second was asked about spending too much or too little on *assistance for the poor,* and a third was asked about money for *caring for the poor.* At first glance, all three questions would seem to have much the same meaning. Yet people's responses to them suggested something quite different. Basically, people responded much more negatively to the question with the word *welfare* in it than to the two questions with the word *poor* in them. People were much less willing to spend more money on welfare than they were to assist the poor: of the respondents 64.7 percent said that we were spending too little on assistance to the poor and only 19.3 percent said we were spending too little on welfare. This is a very dramatic change in opinion, caused by what might seem, at a glance, a minor difference in wording. Although the study didn't investigate why these differing responses occurred, it seems plausible to hypothesize that the word *welfare* raises in many people's minds images of laziness, waste, fraud, and bureaucracy. *Assisting the poor,* on the other hand, is more likely to be associated with giving and Judeo-Christian charitableness. So, these three questions were not all valid measures of the same thing; rather, the various versions of the question actually measured different attitudes or emotional reactions.

So, great care must be taken in the wording of questions, and in the design of survey instruments in general, to ensure their validity (Converse and Presser, 1986). The steps in developing survey instruments are summarized in Figure 5.1. First, researchers must obtain the items, or questions, that make up the survey. This can be done in a couple of ways. One valuable source of questions is previous surveys, especially those whose validity has been assessed. Over the

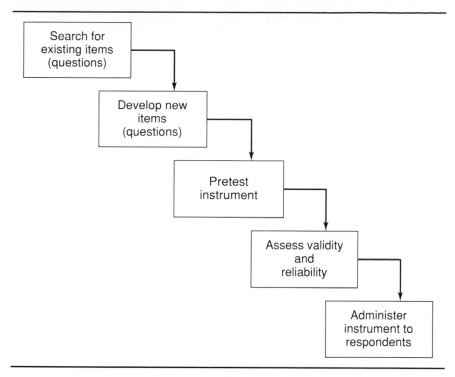

Figure 5.1 The Steps in Developing Survey Instruments

decades, social scientists have honed their skills at asking questions. Even simple questions that inquire about age, occupation, or marital status need to be worded carefully. Professional survey research organizations have been doing this for many years, and their experiences can be used in searching for ways to word questions. In addition to single questions about age or gender, applied researchers also ask complicated sets of questions called **scales,** *a series of questions whose responses can be combined into a single score.* An attitude scale, for example, would combine answers to a number of questions about an attitude into a single scale score on that attitude. A scale might consist of as few as two or three separate questions or as many as 30. Good scales are complicated and expensive to develop, but it is often possible to use an existing scale that has been developed by other researchers and tested for validity and reliability. (Many of these scales are protected by copyright and can be used only with permission.) So, researchers will always begin by finding out if someone else has developed a scale that will fit their purposes. These scales can be found in articles in research journals in the social sciences or in special anthologies containing many scales (for some examples, take a look at Lake, Miles, and Earle, 1973; and Corcoran and Fischer, 1987). Wherever a scale is found, its author will present information on how the scale was developed, whom it was tested on, and the results of reliability and validity tests.

If existing questions or scales cannot be used, which is often the case in applied research, then the researchers must develop new ones. Developing good survey questions, and especially scales, is complex and cannot be fully explained here. Basically, it involves having experts develop the questions, which are then refined until they are accurate measures of what they are intended to measure. Often, the only way to be sure that a question is valid is through a pretest, in which people respond to the questions to see if they are understood in the way the researchers intend. In fact, a good survey instrument is always pretested before it is actually used to collect data. A pretest is time-consuming, but it is also an opportunity to assess whether respondents interpret questions in the same way the researchers intend or whether some respondents have an unusual reaction to any of them. If a survey instrument is changed in any significant way after a pretest, the new version should be pretested again.

In addition to a pretest, all questions and scales should be assessed for validity and reliability (see Chapters 2 and 4). A complete discussion of how to test for validity and reliability is beyond the scope of this chapter (see Carmines and Zeller, 1979), but I will provide an illustration of how it is done to show the lengths to which researchers go in their efforts to be careful and systematic. Recall that validity involves how accurately an instrument measures what it claims to measure. One way to assess validity is to see if a measuring instrument draws the same response as another instrument that is known to be valid. To use a simple example, if we measure level of education by asking people how many grades in school they have completed, we could question whether they remember exactly how many grades they have completed or whether they are telling the truth (people who completed the eleventh grade may tend to round it up by saying they finished high school, or twelfth grade). We could assess the validity of our question by looking at the school records for the people in our sample. The school records are presumably accurate—they tell precisely which grades a person has completed. If our question produces the same results as the school records, then it is valid. In most cases, researchers will report not only whether a question or scale is valid but also how valid it is, expressed in a coefficient. Without validity checks of this sort, any question—and especially complicated ones involving scales—should be considered suspect. (In the previous example, you might ask why we didn't just use the school records to begin with and dispense with the question and the validity check. It might be feasible to check school records of the small sample of people who are being used in the validity check, but that approach would be far too expensive with a large sample, where the records of many different schools across the state or nation might have to be checked.)

Response Rates

A major concern in survey research is the **response rate,** *the proportion of people in a sample who actually complete the questionnaire or interview.* Some people inevitably refuse, because it is too much trouble or they prefer not to give particular information about themselves. Low response rates raise the issue of the representativeness of the sample (see Chapter 2). Recall that the goal of sampling is to ensure that a representative sample is obtained. This can be done, for example, by drawing a simple random sample. However, suppose that you mail out a questionnaire to a random sample, but only 50 percent of the sample return them. Your returned questionnaires are no longer a simple random sample of the population. Half of the sample *chose* not to respond. It is entirely possible that the people who refused are different in some significant way from those who returned their questionnaires. They may be more intelligent, more educated, or from a different social class. This significantly reduces the likelihood that the sample is representative, and it makes it more difficult to draw firm conclusions about the population from which the sample was drawn.

So, the response rate is a very important consideration in survey research. What is a good response rate? One hundred percent, of course! Anything below that begins to cast doubt on the representativeness of the sample. Realistically, however, the returns are never perfect, and most researchers would be quite pleased with a return rate of 80 percent or more. A return rate of less than 50 percent must be seriously questioned as to whether the sample is representative. I have seen surveys with return rates as low as 20 percent. Professional applied researchers would consider such a return rate unacceptably low and would have serious reservations about any conclusions drawn on the basis of such a response rate.

Given the importance of the return rate, researchers put substantial efforts into increasing it. Interviews typically have higher return rates than do mailed questionnaires, probably because people are more willing to throw away an anonymous questionnaire they receive in the mail than they are to refuse a face-to-face request for cooperation by an interviewer. So, interviews might be chosen over questionnaires if the return rate is a key issue. A way to increase return rates on mailed questionnaires is through aggressive follow-ups by mail or telephone. In good survey design, the original mailed questionnaire is followed within a week by a second questionnaire and an additional appeal to return it. If that is not successful, a telephone call is often made to urge cooperation. This strategy can increase the response rate by 15 to 20 percent (Heberlein and Baumgartner, 1978). Even if the initial response rate is fairly high, these follow-ups are done in order to push it as far toward that magical 100 percent mark as possible.

There are a number of other keys to increasing response rates: Provide a small payment for cooperation, keep the questionnaire or interview as short as possible, use competent and professional interviewers, and so on. The point is that good, systematic survey researchers make every effort to increase the response rate. All of the effort and resources put into developing questionnaires and interviews are wasted if the response rate is in the unacceptably low range of less than 50 percent.

The Logic of Survey Analysis

Sometimes the term *sample survey* is used to indicate that a survey is being conducted on a sample, or portion, of a population rather than on the whole population. Most surveys are, in fact, sample surveys—only rarely would we make observations on a whole population of people or organizations because it is usually too expensive to do so. Imagine using a population survey to study the attitudes of people in your state toward welfare. To survey all adults in my state would mean doing millions of surveys—far too expensive an undertaking for virtually all basic or applied research. Another reason to use sample surveys is that with good sampling procedures, sample statistics are an accurate reflection of population statistics, so the total population survey is not necessary.

Survey analysis begins with sampling. Sampling procedures were discussed in some detail in Chapter 2. Recall that you begin with a *sampling frame,* or a listing of all the elements (people, organizations, agencies, etc.) in the population that should have a chance to appear in the sample. Then elements are selected from that list in a random fashion and placed in the sample. With simple random samples, the random selection can be done through a table of random numbers or a computer-generated list of random numbers. With systematic samples, you begin at a randomly selected point in the sampling frame and select every *n*th case, *n* being determined by sample size and set to ensure that every element in the sampling frame has a chance to appear in the sample. In modern telephone surveys, a technique commonly used is *random digit dialing* (RDD), in which telephone numbers are selected randomly, either through a table of random numbers or a computer-generated list. A survey of households in a community, for example, would have a sampling frame that consists of all telephone numbers in that community. Then, every household whose phone number is selected through RDD is a part of the sample. (Phone numbers of businesses or other nonhouseholds would be ignored.) There is also equipment that can speed the process by selecting the numbers and doing the dialing automatically. The interviewer can even specify the telephone prefix in which the interviews are to take place and then the equipment randomly dials the last four digits in the phone number. With random digit dialing, then, every phone number has an equal chance of being selected for the sample, and there should be no bias in the sample.

The goal of all these sampling procedures is to ensure that every element in the population has a chance to appear in the sample. If these procedures are followed, there is a high probability of having a *representative sample*—one that is like the population in all significant respects. Recall from Chapter 2 that these procedures do not *guarantee* a representative sample, but they do make it highly probable. Then observations are made on the elements in the sample, and it is assumed that the sample results can be generalized to the population. Survey researchers use special statistical procedures, called inferential statistics, to assess their confidence that the sample results are true of the population.

Data analysis in survey research follows much the same logic as that described in earlier chapters, especially Chapters 3 and 4. The model is the randomized experiment with independent and dependent variables. The logical goal is that of the elaboration model: to assess the impact of an independent variable on a dependent variable while ruling out the effect of extraneous variables. If a political candidate is interested in assessing support for her candidacy among various racial groups, a survey could gather information about race and about probable voting choices. In this case, race would be the independent variable and voting preference the dependent variable. Using the analogy of the experiment, Anglo voters could be considered the control group; various racial groups could be the experimental groups. This allows for an assessment of the impact of race on the dependent variable and voting preference the dependent variable. Using the analogy of the experiment, Anglo voters could be considered the control group; various racial groups could be the experimental groups. males and females. Other extraneous variables would also likely be included in the analysis, with the overall goal of isolating the exact effect of race on voting preferences.

So, the logic of survey analysis is much like the experimental designs discussed in Chapter 4. The major difference is that the experimental and control groups might be naturally occurring groups rather than created by the researcher. The alternative to randomization and matching would be statistical manipulation of the data. Multivariate analysis would proceed following the logic of the elaboration model discussed in Chapter 3. Seen in this light, survey research involves a particular technique of making observations rather than a different logic of analysis.

Public Opinion Polling

One of the most widespread uses of applied survey research is in the field of public opinion polling, which uses surveys almost exclusively. In fact, commercial opinion polling firms have been among the major contributors to the development of modern survey research techniques (Babbie, 1990). The most widely known polling organizations were established by George Gallup, Elmo Roper, and Louis Harris, but today there are many others all across the country (Bradburn and Sudman, 1988). Some conduct polls at the city or state level while others conduct national opinion polls. Some conduct general opinion polls whose results are disseminated through the media while others are employed by political candidates to assess constituent opinions or the probability of success in a campaign. Special interest groups, such as abortion rights or right-to-life groups, also use opinion polling organizations to assess support for their positions. In addition, corporations hire polling organizations to assess attitudes and improve marketing techniques. All of these commercial polling organizations have been concerned with refining the various elements of survey research discussed in this book (sampling, questionnaire design, response rate, and so on) with the goal of enhancing the validity and reliability of the products they offer their clients.

So, survey research is conducted by researchers in universities, government, and commercial polling organizations. Despite the diverse settings in which they work, survey researchers communicate advances and new techniques in their field through a variety of professional organizations and journals. Among the organizations are the American Sociological Association, the American Marketing Association, and the American Political Science Association. Survey researchers have also formed their own organization, the American Association for Public Opinion Research, which publishes the very influential journal *Public Opinion Quarterly*.

Advantages of Surveys

One of the major advantages of surveys, especially mailed questionnaires, is that they are a relatively inexpensive and quick procedure for collecting data, especially from a large or geographically dispersed group of people or from a representative sample of a large group. However, their utility in collecting data from small groups of people should not be overlooked. In a program evaluation of a school social work program that I recently helped conduct, we surveyed a little more than 100 teachers. We used a survey approach because it was the most appropriate way of gathering the attitudinal data that we were after.

A disadvantage of surveys is that they depend on people to report their feelings and actions honestly and accurately, and, of course, it is possible for people to forget or misrepresent information. However, this can be counterbalanced, to an extent, by paying close attention to issues of validity and reliability. As I have emphasized, good sampling, careful question wording, and the like can produce more valid and reliable surveys.

Qualitative Research _____

Chapter 2 distinguished between quantitative and qualitative research. Quantitative research is based on reducing some phenomenon to a numerical form that can be added, subtracted, multiplied, divided, and in general *measured*. Survey research, for example, tends to be very quantitative in nature. Qualitative research, on the other hand, assumes that numbers miss some fundamental quality or essence of a social phenomenon. For the qualitative researcher, people's personal experiences and interpretations, the meanings they attach to things, and full descriptions of events must be taken into account to fully comprehend social phenomena. In reality, it is often difficult to draw a clear line between quantitative and qualitative research, as the continuum in Figure 5.2 suggests. They sometimes overlap and are often used together in the same research project. This was done, for example, in an evaluation of the effect of parental involvement with their children's schools (Smith and Robbins, 1982). When the federal government funds educational programs, it typically demands that parents be involved in the programs if school districts are to continue receiving the funding. For one series of federally funded programs, a research corporation was hired to conduct an evaluation of such parental involvement. The researchers administered a survey to parents that included a quantitative assessment of their involvement. However, the researchers also wanted to obtain direct observational evidence of parental involvement activities because there is much that is unknown about the nature of this involvement. For this part of the study, they used field researchers who would attend school meetings and events, conduct informal and unstructured interviews, and record what they observed at these events. This procedure provided a wealth

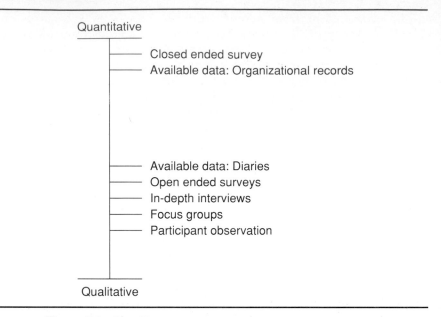

Quantitative

—— Closed ended survey
—— Available data: Organizational records

—— Available data: Diaries
—— Open ended surveys
—— In-depth interviews
—— Focus groups
—— Participant observation

Qualitative

Figure 5.2   The Placement of Research Techniques Along the Quantitative-Qualitative Dimension

of qualitative data to clarify and extend what was found in the surveys.

The choice between quantitative and qualitative research can be based on two considerations. The first has to do with the state of our knowledge about a particular phenomenon. When our knowledge is sketchy, as in the study just described, or when there is little existing theoretical understanding of the phenomenon, it may be difficult to develop the hypotheses and operational measures that are so necessary to quantitative research. In such situations, researchers often turn to qualitative research because it can be more exploratory. Rigid hypotheses and operational definitions are not necessary. In fact, research of this sort is likely to be very descriptive (see Chapter 1), and the outcome of the research may be to formulate hypotheses rather than to verify them. So, qualitative research techniques are not the best for research that is attempting to assess the causal effect of one clearly defined variable on another. Surveys or some sort of experimental research would be better in this case.

The second consideration in the choice of methods stems from a more fundamental controversy about human social behavior. Although it is a complex controversy, it basically involves two potentially opposing groups in social science: the positivists versus the subjectivists (Smart, 1976; Benton, 1977). A brief introduction to this controversy will help clarify the distinction between quantitative and qualitative research and provide some guidelines on when each is appropriate.

Positivists believe that the world exists independently of people's perceptions of it and that scientists can use objective techniques to discover what exists in the world (Durkheim, 1938; Halfpenny, 1982). Astronomers, for example, use telescopes to discover stars and galaxies, which exist whether or not we are aware of them. So, too, human beings can be studied in terms of behaviors that can be observed and recorded using some kind of objective techniques. Recording gender, age, height, weight, or socioeconomic position is a legitimate and objective measurement technique—the equivalent of the physicist's measuring the temperature, volume, or velocity of some liquid or solid. For the positivist, quantifying these measurements—assessing the *average* age of a group or looking at the percentage of a group who are male or female—is merely a precise way of describing and summarizing an objective reality. Such measurement provides a solid and objective foundation for understanding human social behavior.

Subjectivists (also called interactionists or followers of the *verstehen* approach) argue that these objective measures miss a very important part of the human experience: the subjective and very personal *meanings* that people attach to themselves and what they do (Glaser and Strauss, 1967; Wilson, 1970). Max Weber, an early proponent of this view, argued that we need to look not only at what people do but also at what they think and feel about what is happening to them (Weber, 1957). This meaning or feeling or interpretive dimension cannot be adequately captured through numbers. Researchers need to gain what Weber called *verstehen,* or a subjective understanding. They need to view and experience the situation from the perspective of the people themselves. To use a colloquialism, the researchers need "to walk a mile in their shoes." They need to talk to the people at length and to immerse themselves in their lives so they can experience the highs and lows, the joys and sorrows, the triumphs and the tragedies as seen from the perspective of the people being studied. Researchers need to see how the individuals experience and give meaning to what is happening to them. Qualitative research methods are an attempt to get access to that personal, subjective experience; for subjectivists, quantitative research, by its very nature, misses this very important dimension of social reality.

Although Weber was a subjectivist, he did believe that careful, qualitative research could produce objective, value-free knowledge of the social world. An extreme subjectivist position would go further than Weber by arguing that it is impossible to produce objective, universally true knowledge through the scientific enterprise. (We touched on this subject briefly in Chapter 1 when we discussed the objectivity of science.) Rather, all knowledge reflects, to an extent, the values and interests of those who produce the knowledge, whether they are scientists or laypeople. Those who take this extreme position argue that scientists do not just observe what exists but rather, by observing and measuring, help to create that reality. Science is not merely a process of *discovering* meaning but also of *creating* meaning. Scientific principles and laws about social behavior become another aspect of reality that can influence behavior. Even something as simple as computing an average age for a group creates a new reality: Instead of recognizing that some people in the group are 22 years old, others 34 years old, and still others 43 years old, we now say that the "average age of the group is 36.7 years." This summary statement gives the impression—creates the reality—that the group members share something in common in terms of age and that we know something very precise about their ages. But that sense of commonality or precision comes from the numbers, not from reality. In addition, even though the average appears very precise, it is actually less precise than listing all the ages of the group members.

This extreme subjectivist position does not view either quantitative or qualitative research as superior because both involve a subjective dimension. But it also clearly does not view quantitative research as the more objective or necessarily preferred technique. The positivist-subjectivist controversy is a long-standing one in the social sciences, and it does not have an easy solution. However, you need to be aware that there are these different views and that they influence an applied researcher's choice of data-gathering techniques. It seems to me that the most reasonable position to take on this issue is that both quantitative and qualitative approaches have their value and that we should be aware of the strengths and weaknesses of each. With some dimensions of social reality, quantitative techniques seem quite useful, but with the more subjective parts of social reality they may be less useful or even quite misleading. So, with this introduction, let's look at some of the types of qualitative research methods and their uses in applied research.

Observational Research

Surveys are based on what people say; observational research is based on the direct observation of behavior. The researcher actually sees people in action rather than asking them what they have done or intend to do. One of the most widely used types of observational research is called **participant observation,** in which *the researcher participates in the activities of the people being studied; he or she is a part of the lives of the people under investigation* (Burgess, 1984; Lofland and Lofland, 1984). From this vantage point, the researcher is in a unique position to perceive events as they are experienced by group members. The researcher actually has some of the same experiences as ordinary members of the group, enabling him or her to assess the situation from the perspective of the people involved.

To do participant observation, researchers must gain entry into the group being studied. In some cases, this can be relatively simple if the researcher is already a member of the group. A member of a racial minority group, for example, may not find it difficult to live in a minority neighborhood or join minority clubs and conduct a participant observation study. In other cases, however, it can be much more difficult to gain entry because the researcher will be recognized by group members as an outsider. When this happens, the researcher must gain the cooperation of the group members and explain why he or she is interested in studying the group. As you can well imagine, both efforts can fail. The likelihood of gaining cooperation can be increased if the researcher knows someone in the group or can catch the ear of some of its more influential members. This can be done through the use of *informants,* group members who are willing to bring the researcher to the group and provide information about the group. Cooperation can also be gained by explaining the purposes of the research in a way that is seen as reasonable and acceptable by group members and allows them to see themselves as benefiting from the research in some practical way. Cooperation is also enhanced by legitimizing the research—having it sponsored or supported by a group or organization that is viewed favorably by those under study.

Not all observational research is participant observation. In some research settings, participation is not necessary in order to get the desired data, and in other settings people might behave differently if they knew they were being observed. So, *nonparticipant observation* occurs when people are directly observed but without the observer's participating in their activities. Nonparticipant observation can be done if it is possible to observe a scene from a hidden location, with a hidden camera or through a one-way mirror. Or it might be possible to be present at a scene and observe it without the others being aware that an observer is present. For example, disguised observation has been used in studying the link between alcohol consumption and aggressive behavior in bars. The observers pretended to be patrons and used that status to make observations (Graham et al., 1980). In nonparticipant observation, problems arise because of the need to disguise the identities of observers at a setting. One problem is how to record observations without being discovered. In some cases, this calls for leaving the observational setting, at least briefly, to record observations. (There are special ethical considerations to take into account when using hidden or disguised observations, and these are discussed at length in Chapter 7.)

Data collection in observational research is quite different from that in quantitative research. A major mechanism of data collection are the field notes taken by an observer (Lofland and Lofland, 1984). *Field notes* are detailed descriptive accounts of what was observed in the field. The observer records as much as possible about what happened: Who was there, what they said and did, how they interacted with one another, and so on. Field notes would also include any analytical ideas or flashes of insight that occur to the researcher in the midst of observations. Obviously, no one can record everything that happens at a setting because too much is going on. So, observers are guided by the topic of their research as well as theoretical considerations that inform them about what elements in a situation might be important. However, they must also be open to the possibility that these guides may miss something important, so they need to be vigilant for other elements that might be important to understanding a particular social setting.

Whereas quantitative research culminates in a report that uses numbers and statistics to summarize what was found, observational researchers prepare a descriptive narrative of what they observed, the conclusions they drew from the observations, and the theoretical implications of those conclusions. The narrative is often more like a story than a scientific report because it describes some aspect of people's lives and activities in much detail. There may be some numbers and statistics in it, but the heart of the report is the description of what happened and how it was experienced by the people involved.

Because observational research deals in very subjective phenomena that are open to numerous interpretations, the possibility of misinterpretation and bias is taken very seriously. In participant observation, for example, the success of the research depends in good part on the rapport and trust that build up between the researcher and those under study. In fact, because of the close contact, personal and intimate relationships can develop. Although this is common, it is also something that researchers need to assess carefully because personal involvement can lead to the misinterpretation of data or an outright biased analysis. The data often take the form of descriptions by the researcher of what is happening and what is important in a situation and may include statements about what the researcher or others in the situation seemed to feel. It may involve judgments about what certain gestures, movements, or activities meant to the people involved. It often includes an interpretation of the meaning of certain words and phrases, including slang, that the researcher may not be thoroughly familiar with. Because of these problems, some participant observers keep a diary of their more personal feelings and reactions. For example, an observer who feels some animosity toward a group member would note this because it could influence the observer's interpretations of what that person says or does.

So, the possibility of misinterpretation and bias leads observational researchers to take steps to increase the validity of the measurements made. In fact, positivists favor more quantitative research precisely because of their claim (disputed by subjectivists) that quantitative techniques are more objective and less subject to bias. However, social scientists have developed procedures that can improve the validity of observational research. One such procedure is to be as thorough as possible in describing and interpreting situations. Observations that may seem unimportant at the time of data collection may be recognized as important by others who later review the data. Obviously, observers could never record everything that happens in a situation, but they try to err on the side of being too complete rather than too skimpy. A second procedure that enhances validity is for researchers to carefully assess their own desires, values, and expectations to see if these might bias their observations. If researchers expect something to happen, they will tend to see it as happening; so they must look especially rigorously for the opposite of what they expect and be critical if what they expect to happen actually seems to be happening. A third check on validity is to have other researchers observe the same group or setting to see if they come to the same conclusions. Fourth, validity can be assessed by comparing whether the results of observational research are consistent with the results of other research. If they are at wide variance, consider the possibility of validity problems in the data. Finally, the nature of behavior may give hints about its validity. If, while they know they are being observed, people do things that are dangerous, illegal, or stigmatized and risk punishment, then it is reasonable to assume that the behavior is not merely a performance for the researcher.

Systematic observational research needs to seriously consider the issue of validity. This can be difficult, but without it the data are less valuable. Research in Action 5.2 describes a research project in which participant observation was used because it provided much more valid data than a survey likely would have.

RESEARCH IN ACTION 5.2 ▬▬▬▬▬▬▬▬▬▬▬▬▬▬▬▬▬▬▬▬▬▬▬

Do Police Arrest Men Who Batter Women?

Research in Action 1.1 described an applied social science research project that was instrumental in changing how the police respond to spouse abusers in the United States. A major outcome of the research was that many police departments established new administrative policies that either required or strongly encouraged police officers to arrest men who batter women. The city of Phoenix did so in 1984, establishing arrest as the preferred police action in spouse abuse cases where there is probable cause that an assault has occurred. Presumably, the women of Phoenix had gained another layer of protection against assault. Indeed, the percentage of domestic violence calls that resulted in arrests in Phoenix doubled in the months after the new policy was initiated. Within six months, however, the arrest rate had dropped almost to where it had been before. What happened?

Sociologist Kathleen Ferraro (1989) tackled this problem with observational research. Because of the nature of the problem, questionnaires and interviews would probably not be of much help. To ask police officers if they followed the established policy of arrest would only invite them to shade the truth by casting their actions in words that would be acceptable to their superiors. In addition, it would be useful to see the interaction between the officer, the alleged abuser, and the abused woman in order to judge whether the officer's response was appropriate given the new arrest policy. So Ferraro and her colleagues conducted a participant observation study. Their initial approach to the Phoenix police department was met with some resistance—not an uncommon occurrence when doing such observational research—but intervention by university authorities helped gain the cooperation of the police. Ferraro and five colleagues rode with Phoenix police officers during their full 10-hour shifts, accompanying them on every aspect of their duties. They recorded what was said and done on all domestic disturbance calls and talked with the victim. The observers made no attempt to influence the officer's behavior, suggesting neither arrest nor nonarrest as options.

This applied research project points to some of the difficulties of conducting observational research in applied settings. One question that it raises is whether the observers influenced the officers' behavior. Would the officers have behaved differently if they were not being observed? This well may be the case, but it is difficult to imagine another strategy for gathering data that would have produced more valid results. It would be extremely difficult to observe the officers' behavior without riding with them. In addition, the officers' behavior suggested that they were not hiding a whole lot from the observers—once they got to know the observers, they behaved quite naturally. (This is a common finding in observational research.)

Ferraro and her observers found that for the most part, and despite established policy, the Phoenix police did not arrest men who batter women. Arrests occurred in only 18 percent of the cases that fell under the arrest policy. However, based on her own and others' research, Ferraro concluded that it is too simple to say that the officers were merely ignoring the arrest policy. The decision to arrest is a complicated one influenced by many factors in a situation. Officers on the scene have to interpret departmental policy as well as make judgments about such difficult legal issues as whether there is "probable cause" for an arrest. Probable cause means that the situation permits a reasonable conclusion that a crime has been committed. However, this conclusion is necessarily discretionary and judgmental. By seeing how the officers responded to victims and abusers in different settings, Ferraro and her colleagues were able to gain a better idea of how things looked from the officers' perspective. Most officers, for example, seemed to consider severe physical injuries or the use of weapons as sufficient for probable cause. However, minor injuries were not always considered sufficient. They observed one case where a woman had bruises on her neck from being choked by her husband, and she wanted to press charges against him. However, because the injuries were not serious enough—they did not require medical attention—and no weapon was present, the officer decided that a crime had not occurred. Phoenix's new "get tough on abusers" policy would seem to have called for arrest in this case, but the officer decided against it. In other cases, the observers could see that the couple's living arrangement seemed to influence the officers' decisions: An abuser who was not married to the victim was less likely to be arrested, even when the level of abuse was equivalent. This information would be hard to gather with other data-collection techniques, such as surveys, because the officers may not have even been aware that such factors were influencing their decisions.

Ferraro and her colleagues learned a lot about the attitudes and approaches of police officers by observing them interact with citizens on family dispute calls and talking to them during their long evenings on patrol. They learned, for example, that some officers believed that arrest of abusers would not work with Mexicans, Native Americans, and people in housing projects because arrest and violence were seen as routine

for such people and would have no deterrent value. With more "respectable" people, on the other hand, the officers thought arrest might work. Many officers also expressed the belief that women who call the police don't want their spouse arrested—they just want the police to get him out of the house for the night. If this is so, then the officers believe arrest is a waste of time because the women won't press charges the next day anyway. Ferraro's point is not whether these officers' beliefs are accurate or not, but rather that they tend to work against the strong arrest policy that the Phoenix police department had instituted.

Ferraro's research shows the value of observational techniques in applied research: We learn not only how often arrest is used but also about the situational factors that influence the likelihood of arrest and the thinking of the officers as they make a decision about whether to arrest. It would be impossible to find this out through after-the-fact questionnaires and probably even interviews because officers would tend to reconstruct their thoughts and actions in a way that makes them appear consistent with departmental policy. This research also shows the importance of continuous evaluation of social policy. Research had established that arrest works, but applied research is also necessary to determine whether the policy is carried out in the way it was intended.

In-Depth Interviews and Focus Groups

Most survey research is fairly standardized in that all respondents are usually asked the same questions in the same sequence. In fact, the questionnaires sent to various respondents would likely be identical. There are research situations, however, where such standardization is not appropriate and researchers need more flexibility in what they ask and how they ask it, especially when research questions cannot be formulated into precise hypotheses and knowledge of some phenomenon is too sketchy to allow precise measurement of variables. This is sometimes the case in market research where a company might be trying to determine what type of advertising campaign would be most effective or which groups to focus the advertising on. In such cases, in-depth interviews of a small number of people may be the best technique for gathering data. In **in-depth interviews,** *researchers follow a general interview schedule but are free to pursue other lines of inquiry that seem fruitful.* If the respondent raises a new topic that was not included on the interview schedule, the interviewer can ask further questions to elaborate on it. In fact, the in-depth interview resembles a conversation between interviewer and respondent, and researchers often tape-record the interviews in order to have a complete record of what was said. In-depth interviews are far more lengthy and less structured than the interviews in surveys discussed earlier.

In the least structured interview, the interviewer may have only a general topic area to serve as a guideline in asking questions. The interviewer must then use his or her knowledge of that topic area to ask questions that gather useful responses. For example, research on the conflicts between parents and their children might include the following instructions to interviewers:

> Discover the kinds of conflicts that the child has had with the parents. Conflicts should include disagreements, tensions due to past, present, and potential disagreements, outright arguments and physical conflicts. Be alert for as many categories and examples of conflicts and tensions as possible. (Gorden, 1987:45)

You can well imagine that it takes a skilled interviewer, with considerable knowledge of children and their parents, to conduct such an interview successfully. A slightly more structured interview on the same topic might provide the interviewer with some more specific questions and suggested probe questions. The interview schedule might say to ask each person whether he or she has had disagreements with his or her parents and to probe with questions such as, Do your parents make you angry? Do they understand you? and so on. It might even say to ask about concrete disagreements, such as those over dating, smoking, or drinking. But the interviewer is still free to probe into other disagreements and ask other questions.

The major advantage of in-depth interviews over observational research is that they are generally cheaper to do and don't involve such an extensive commitment of time by the researcher. Twenty-five lengthy interviews might be done by a researcher in a month, whereas participant observers might live in the field for months, possibly years. In addition, in-depth interviews can capture information about past events as well as those the researcher can't experience. For example in-depth interviews might be preferred over participant observation when studying riots because of the personal danger involved in going to the riot to make observations. The major advantages of in-depth interviews over surveys are that they are much more flexible, can be used more successfully in exploratory research, and enable the researcher to tap the more subjective dimensions of the human experience.

A strategy for gathering data that is related to the in-depth interview is the **focus group** or **group depth interview** (Greenbaum, 1988; Krueger, 1988). As the name implies, it is *an interview with a whole group of people at the same time.* Focus groups were originally used as a preliminary step in the research process to generate quantitative hypotheses and develop questionnaires and interview schedules, and they are still used this way, sometimes by survey researchers. However, focus groups are now used in their own right in applied research as a strategy for collecting data, especially when researchers are seeking people's subjective reactions and the many levels of meaning that are important to behavior. Today, tens of millions of dollars are spent each year on focus groups in marketing research alone.

A focus group usually consists of at least one moderator and up to 10 respondents and lasts for up to three hours. The moderator will have an interview guide that outlines the main topics of inquiry and the order in which they will be covered and possibly a variety of props, such as audiovisual cues, to prompt discussion and elicit reactions. The respondents will have been preselected for the focus groups using criteria relating to their usefulness in accomplishing the group goals. For example, if the focus group is to consider strategies for marketing high blood pressure medications to physicians, then the group would likely consist of physicians who have many patients with high blood pressure.

The moderator's job in a focus group is to initiate discussion and facilitate the flow of responses. Following an outline of topics to be covered, the moderator would ask questions, probe areas that are not clear, and pursue lines of inquiry that seem fruitful. However, a group depth interview is not just 10 in-depth interviews. Rather, the moderator uses a knowledge of group dynamics to elicit data that might not have been obtained in an in-depth interview. For example, a status structure emerges in all groups, including focus groups; some people become leaders and others followers. The moderator will use this dynamic by encouraging the emergence of leaders and using them to elicit responses, reactions, or information from other group members. Participants will often respond to other group members differently from how they respond to the researcher/moderator. In fact, in a well-run focus group, the members may interact among themselves as much as with the moderator.

Group moderators will also direct the discussion, usually from more general topics in the beginning to more specific issues toward the end (Krueger, 1988). In a focus group study of how to generate more support in a neighborhood for a community recreational and leisure center, the focus group session began with general questions about family leisure activities. Then the questions got gradually more specific by asking what the community center could do and what changes could be made. The general questions provide a foundation and a context without which the families might not be able to come up with useful answers to the more specific questions. Group moderators take great care in developing these sequences of questions. The moderator must also observe the characteristics of the participants to ensure the most effective participation by all members. So, a "rambler" who talks a lot but doesn't say much that is useful needs to be constrained, while those who tend to say little need to be encouraged to express themselves. In short, being a moderator of a focus group is a complex job that calls for an understanding of group dynamics as well as skills in understanding and working with people.

During a focus group, there is too much happening too fast to engage in any useful data analysis. The focus group is to produce the data, which would be preserved on videotape or a tape recording for later analysis. During the analysis, the researcher would make field notes from the recordings and then prepare a report summarizing the findings and presenting conclusions and implications. The data from a focus group are usually presented in one of three forms (Krueger, 1988). In the *raw data format,* the researcher presents all of the comments made by the participants about particular issues. This provides the client with the range of opinions that were expressed in the group. There is little interpretation by the researcher, unless there is some nonverbal interaction that needs to be interpreted or some nuance of meaning that could only be grasped by someone who was present at the group session. The second format is the *descriptive approach,* in which the researcher summarizes in narrative form the kinds of opinions expressed in the group, with some quotes from group members as illustrations. This calls for more summary on the part of the researcher, and the data are presented in a way that better conveys the meaning communicated in the group session. The third format is the *interpretive model,* which expands on the descriptive by providing more interpretation. The researcher provides his or her own interpretations of the group's mood, feelings, and reactions to questions. This may include the moderator's impression of the motivations and unexpressed desires of members of the group. The raw data model is the quickest manner of reporting results, but the interpretive model provides the greatest depth of information from the group sessions. Of course, the interpretive approach, because it does involve interpretation, is more likely to exhibit some bias or error.

A major advantage of focus groups over participant observation is that the former make it possible to observe more social interaction on a specific topic in a limited amount of time (Morgan, 1988). Moderators have some control over the amount of social interaction because they can direct discussion away from topics that are not fruitful, whereas in participant observation the observer must let the scene unfold naturally. However, this is also a disadvantage of focus groups in that they are fundamentally *unnatural* settings. In comparison to in-depth interviews, focus groups have the advantage of using the interaction between people as a way of stimulating ideas and encouraging group members to participate. In fact, well-run focus groups have very high levels of participation and thus elicit reactions that might not have been gotten in a one-on-one interview setting.

Available Data

In many cases, rather than collecting data themselves by administering surveys or making observations, applied researchers can use data that have already been collected by someone else. Such data are called **available data** or **existing data** because *the information is available for use by researchers even though it was collected by others with different purposes in mind.* Available data are collected by many corporations, private organizations, and government bureaus as a routine part of their daily operations. The American Medical Association, for example, might keep track of its members' names, medical specialties, incomes, and gender. Many research organizations, such as the Institute for Social Research at the University of Michigan and the National Opinion Research Center at the University of Chicago, collect data that can be used by others. In fact, Research in Action 5.3 describes a case where records kept as a routine part of operating our criminal justice system could be used in applied research. Organizational records are a rich source of existing data.

RESEARCH IN ACTION 5.3 ▬▬▬▬▬▬▬▬▬▬▬▬▬▬▬▬▬▬▬▬▬▬▬▬▬▬▬

Identifying "Good Risk" Prison Inmates

Chapter 4 presented the case of Lester, a juvenile who seemed to be spiraling into ever more serious crime. How should the criminal justice system handle offenders like this? With adult offenders, the system has two options. One is to make the punishment fit the crime: All people who commit a given offense are given the same sentence. There is something logical and fair about this approach; it avoids the possibility that inequity, bias, or prejudice might influence sentencing decisions. But it also ignores a very complex reality: All people who commit the same offense are not the same. As criminologists Marcia and Jan Chaiken (1984:195) put it: "There are many kinds of criminals, and to fix on any single punitive solution to the problem of crime is simplistic, unjust, and inefficient." The reality is that some criminals commit far more crimes than do other criminals. One criminal, for example, may commit 50 burglaries, 20 robberies, 10 assaults, and numerous drug violations during the span of a year. This person makes a very substantial contribution to the crime problem in comparison to another person whose only criminal activity consists of two burglaries during the year. In terms of controlling the crime problem, an effective criminal justice system would be one that sentences the former person to a longer jail term than the latter for the same crime. In other words, possibly the punishment should, to a degree, fit the criminal rather than the crime.

To do this, we need some valid way of separating offenders who are high risks for committing many additional crimes when released from offenders who are low risks. The Chaikens have been developing procedures for doing this based on data that are routinely collected by the criminal justice system. They began their work with survey data rather than available data. They conducted surveys of adult male offenders in three states, looking for the patterns of offenses among these people that would help them separate the high-risk offenders from the others. They first identified a group they called *omnifelons,* who reported committing a combination of robbery, assault, and drug offenses as well as a very high rate of property crimes like burglary and theft. They account for a very large proportion of the crimes committed in the United States. As Chaiken and Chaiken (1984:197) put it, these offenders are "deeply entrenched in a life of multiple drug use and violence, [and] constitute an important criminal threat to society."

So, how do we identify these people? Is Lester an omni-felon? The Chaikens found that omni-felons were different from other offenders in a number of ways: They committed violent crimes before reaching age 16; they abused hard drugs as juveniles; they had poor work records; and they committed numerous serious crimes as juveniles. The Chaikens' research shows that people who fit this mold are not good candidates for rehabilitation programs such as vocational training or drug rehabilitation or for early release from prison. When released, they tend to go back to a life of high-rate crime commission. Lester, however, doesn't fit this mold. His crimes were mostly minor and nonviolent and did not include abuse of hard drugs.

Information like that used by the Chaikens to identify omni-felons is a routine part of a prison record and is thus available data in the criminal justice system. It is available to judges, prosecutors, and juries to be used in making sentencing decisions: Give a long prison sentence to an omni-felon and send other offenders to alternate programs. Or it could be used to decide whether an offender might benefit from a vocational training or drug treatment program. The use of procedures such as this would replace the intuitive judgments that judges and juries currently make with more objective, valid, and defensible judgments.

So, if valid instruments to separate omni-felons from others can be developed, the criminal justice system contains the data to make these decisions. However, the Chaikens caution that their approach is far from perfect. Some classified by it as omni-felons actually commit relatively few crimes, and a few who were not so designated committed many crimes. The procedure needs to be refined if it is to be used in making very important decisions about people's lives. In addition, more research needs to be done to show whether the data available in the criminal justice system produces the same results as the Chaikens' survey data. Beyond these practical concerns, there are potential constitutional and ethical issues that need to be addressed. Some critics have argued that "making the punishment fit the criminal" is really a way of punishing someone for what he or she might do after release rather than what that individual has already done. This shows once again that public policy issues can be influenced by applied research, but that ethical and value considerations also typically enter into the policy process.

The government also collects an enormous amount of data on population trends, birth and death rates, health, unemployment, and so on. Many of these data sets are available to researchers. Some are in books or periodicals published by the government, but they are increasingly available on computer disk or CD-ROM. Some are available in libraries, especially those that serve as depositories for U.S. government documents. These data sets can be a rich source of information for applied researchers. For example, sociologists Brendan Maguire and William Faulkner (1990), in an assessment of the impact of state legislation requiring people to wear seat belts in automobiles, were able to use data on traffic accident fatalities collected each year by the Federal Highway Administration. Using these data, they were able to show that compulsory seat belt laws don't lead to a reduction in fatalities in traffic accidents. They then suggested that proponents of compulsory seat belt laws needed to look elsewhere for the rationale for such laws.

Another form of available data are documents, such as magazines, letters, diaries, and movies or other communication media. In fact, virtually anything that human beings produce as part of their social activities could be a potential source of available data. For example, sociologists Dennis Peck and Kimberley Folse (1990) were interested in the psychosocial condition of teenagers who commit suicide. Obviously, once a person commits suicide, it is too late to ask that person about his or her state of mind while contemplating suicide, and the state of mind of people who consider or attempt suicide but don't complete it may be quite different. So Peck and Folse analyzed the suicide notes left by teens who committed suicide as a way to measure their state of mind just prior to death. The notes were not created with any research purpose in mind—they were more of a last, desperate effort at communication by a troubled person—but they could be used as available data by the researchers to learn more about suicide.

In order to use available data, the researcher needs to access it and transform it into a form that is usable in the research. In some cases, this is a minor task, but in others it is a major job. For example, using organizational records will require gaining permission and cooperation from the organization and will call for someone to search through the organizational records for the appropriate information. Typically, researchers will use a coding sheet, which is merely a form that shows what information needs to be collected for each case. That information is usually only a small amount of the information in the organizational records, so researchers may have to filter through what is not wanted in order to gather what is needed.

Validity is a concern in available data research, as it is in all research: Are we actually measuring what we claim to measure? There are some new wrinkles on this problem with available data research because the data were not collected for the purposes of our research and thus may not be the best measure of the variables we are studying. To use a simple example that was mentioned in Chapter 2, if we measure the variable crime by looking at whether people have been convicted of an offense in a court of law, we will not have a completely valid measure of crime because many criminals are never caught and some of those caught are never convicted. Conviction of a crime is a part of the organizational records of the criminal justice system, and it is available for use for research purposes, but it does not include all crimes that people commit. Any time we use available data, we must carefully consider how completely and accurately they measure what we claim they measure. When the researcher designs the data collection instruments, these validity issues can be considered ahead of time, and the instruments designed to overcome many of them. With existing data research, however, this is not possible since the data have already been collected by the organization or agency.

Validity problems in existing data research can also occur when organizations change their methods of collecting data or if data is collected differently from one organization to another. Both problems arose in an applied research project that I conducted among elementary school students. One variable of interest was the students' grades in various courses. The problem was that the grading system and the report cards used changed from one grade to another and from one school to another. Younger students were graded on a satisfactory–unsatisfactory basis, and older students were evaluated with the traditional A–F grading system. The grade level at which the grading changed to the A–F system also varied from one school to another. So, in one school, second graders received the S–U grade, and in another they received A–F. In addition, some schools had courses on computers while others didn't, and this made the comparison of grades across schools difficult. The point is that each school used a grading system that best fit its educational needs, but it made the development of valid measures to make comparisons across grades or between schools much more difficult.

A major advantage of available data is that they are nonreactive in nature. Recall from Chapter 2 that if people know they are being observed, they may react by behaving differently from how they usually would. This is a problem because we want to know about their normal reactions to everyday situations—not their reactions to being observed. Surveys and in many cases participant observation are potentially reactive because people know that the researcher is observing them. Available data, on the other hand, are largely nonreactive because, when the data are collected or the documents produced, the people are not aware that they will be used for research purposes. Despite this advantage, a major disadvantage of available data is that measurement validity is often not adequate.

CRITICAL THINKING ⎯⎯⎯⎯⎯⎯⎯⎯⎯⎯⎯⎯⎯⎯⎯⎯⎯⎯⎯⎯⎯⎯⎯⎯⎯⎯

Is the Data Collection Strategy Appropriate?

The first four chapters of this book focused largely on the logic of applied research; this chapter is devoted to the actual process of collecting data or making observations. Although this overview has been brief, it is intended to sensitize you to the range of techniques that are used in making systematic and valid observations and to the strengths and weaknesses of the various data collection strategies used in applied research. These strategies are another element in scientists' efforts to conduct systematic, valid, and reliable observations, and they can also serve as an element in your efforts to think critically about issues. Basically, critical thinkers ask whether conclusions are based on observations that follow the procedures described in this chapter. They ask, What observations were made? How were questions asked? and, Was there a possibility of reactivity? The critical thinker also asks whether a particular data collection strategy is the most appropriate one, whether it provides the kind of observations that the researcher claims it does, and whether observations are being missed or distorted because of the strategy used. There is considerable sensitivity to the fact that distortion and misinterpretation are highly likely unless observation is done very carefully.

So, the materials presented in this chapter suggest that issues be approached with the following questions in mind:

1. Are conclusions based on observations that follow one of the standard strategies for data collection (surveys, participant observation, etc.)? Is the strategy used appropriate to the issue at hand?
2. What can be said about the data in terms of the positivist versus subjectivist debate? Does the data make assumptions, implicit or otherwise, regarding either position in this controversy?
3. Is the topic under consideration best addressed by what people say about their behavior (surveys) or by direct observation (participant observation)? Why?
4. What sort of reactivity could result from the type of research method that was used? Does the reactivity threaten the validity of the data?
5. How many different kinds of data collection strategies were used? Did they all come to the same conclusion?

Key Terms for Review _____

available data	participant observation
existing data	questionnaire
focus group	response rate
group depth interview	scale
in-depth interview	survey
interview	

For Further Inquiry _____

Earle Babbie. *Survey Research Methods,* 2d ed. Belmont, CA: Wadsworth, 1990.
> This is a standard text that covers all of the elements of conducting surveys in much more detail than was possible in this chapter.

William Sims Bainbridge. *Survey Research: A Computer-Assisted Introduction.* Belmont, CA: Wadsworth, 1989.

This is also a standard text on survey research, but it includes a computer disk with various programs and exercises that will run on an IBM or compatible microcomputer.

Bruce L. Berg. *Qualitative Research Methods for the Social Sciences*. Boston: Allyn & Bacon, 1989.

Berg provides details on the qualitative methods discussed in this chapter, as well as some others (e.g., ethnographies) that I have not included.

Norman M. Bradburn and Seymour Sudman. *Polls and Surveys: Understanding What They Tell Us*. San Francisco: Jossey-Bass, 1988.

This book, by two veteran survey researchers, focuses more on how to interpret and understand the results of surveys than on how to conduct them. It also discusses the history of surveys and their practical uses by polling organizations.

Don A. Dillman. *Mail and Telephone Surveys: The Total Design Method*. New York: Wiley, 1978.

This is a very good "how to" book with much practical advice on how to conduct surveys over the phone or through the mail.

John A. Lofland and Lynn H. Lofland. *Analyzing Social Settings: A Guide to Qualitative Observation and Analysis*. Belmont, CA: Wadsworth, 1984.

This is an excellent analysis of all of the steps in collecting and analyzing qualitative data.

Catherine Marshall and Gretchen B. Rossman. *Designing Qualitative Research*. Newbury Park, CA: Sage, 1989.

The authors provide a good introduction to qualitative research methods in applied research and policy analysis. Although it emphasizes educational research, the book includes many vignettes from other social science areas.

W. Lawrence Neuman. *Social Research Methods: Qualitative and Quantitative Approaches*. Boston: Allyn & Bacon, 1991.

This text covers all of the standard areas in sociological research methods, and it includes a thorough explication of the positivist-subjectivist controversy. This debate is weaved as a theme through the whole book.

Exercises _____

5.1. To grasp the difficulties of participant observation, it is useful to do it yourself. Choose a setting to observe and state some preliminary hypotheses about the kinds of things you are interested in studying in the situation. Then have at least two students make separate observations in that situation. Compare their "data."

5.2. Locate two separate research articles in social science journals that use different research methods (e.g., one uses surveys and the other uses participant observation). Describe each method and compare the kinds of quantitative and qualitative data that are produced. In what ways are either or both methods reactive? Is the reactivity a problem? How could the reactivity have been reduced or eliminated?

5.3. Locate an article in a newspaper or popular magazine that summarizes some research conducted on a problem. Does the article provide sufficient information about the research technique used to enable you to critically assess the information presented? What information is missing?

Applied Research Techniques

Until the 1950s, residents of the remote community of Arctic Bay, located on Baffin Island in far northern Canada, lived a relatively isolated, traditional existence. The settlement served as a base camp for the traditional food-gathering activities they still practiced in the twentieth century. Seal and whale hunting were especially important to them and were largely men's activities. Women's duties revolved around home, food preparation, and child rearing. The people lived in tight-knit families in which the children respected their parents. Elderly people were considered a valuable resource in the community. Arctic Bay was sufficiently small so that all the permanent residents knew one another well. Strangers did enter the community from time to time, however (Bowles, 1981).

Although their life was not idyllic, it did have considerable appeal to them. For one thing, it was the way of many generations of their ancestors, and this offered a sense of timelessness and meaning to their routines. Also, it was a very predictable, relaxed, orderly way of life with little stress or anxiety. There was a shared religion and value system and a great deal of consensus among the residents—at least about the important concerns, such as their spiritual life and how to be a good man or woman. There was little crime, alcoholism, or the many other problems that plague modern societies.

However, all of this was threatened when a lead-zinc mine was developed not far from Arctic Bay and offered work to the residents. At the mine, people would be paid an hourly wage to support themselves and their families; no longer would they have to pursue their traditional subsistence activities of hunting and fishing. In addition, permanent housing would be provided for them at the site of the mine, so they wouldn't have to make a long commute. However, this meant that either workers would be separated from their families for long periods of time or they would have to relocate their families in a strange community far from friends and relatives. Would such work be harmful for the people of Arctic Bay? Should they take the new jobs? How would their lives be changed if they do? Could the negative effects of such work be alleviated? There are types of applied social research that can help to answer these questions. It can help assess the impact of such major projects as a lead-zinc mine and help people decide whether they want such development in their lives and how the negative effects can be reduced. Applied social research does this by building on the logic of science and research that has been described in earlier chapters, but the research is designed in such a way that useful information is provided to those who need it, such as those planning the mining development near the community of Arctic Bay. This chapter will describe these major types of applied research.

Types of Applied Research

The first five chapters of this book analyzed the basic logic of research and the research designs that are used in both basic and applied research. However, applied researchers have developed a special set of techniques that involve an application of these research designs to make observations and recommendations that will be useful to program managers and policy analysts. These techniques are at the core of applied sociological research, and I focus on five of them: program evaluation, needs assessment, social impact assessment, social indicators, and cost-benefit analysis. There is often overlap in these activities, and one research project might include more than one of them. Taken together they encompass the activities in which most applied researchers in sociology are likely to be involved.

Program Evaluation

Over the years, many social programs have been established to help alleviate problems like poverty, unemployment, and child abuse. In addition, there are many social practices that people use to help them achieve goals. One example of such a social practice is the use of psychotherapy to alleviate mental distress. Another such practice is the use of physicians rather than nurse-midwives to deliver babies. With all policies and practices, the important questions are, Do they work? Do they achieve their goals? Do poverty programs reduce poverty? Does psychotherapy actually alleviate mental distress? Do physicians have fewer complications when delivering babies than do nurse-midwives? In short, we can ask about any social policy or practice questions about whether and how well they work. In fact, as federal and state governments have provided more funding for programs over the past 30 years, they have increasingly demanded an evaluation of their effectiveness (Weiss, 1987). Philanthropies, foundations, and international organizations that fund such programs also often demand such evaluations. There are a number of reasons for concern about whether programs and practices actually work. First, they are very costly, and no one wants to spend that kind of money if it is not accomplishing something useful. Second, if money is spent on a program that doesn't work, there are fewer funds available for programs that do work. Third, an ineffective program that continues to operate gives the illusion that a problem is being alleviated when it is not. This can lull people into the feeling that something is being done while the problem remains unsolved or gets worse.

.   To evaluate the effectiveness of programs and practices, applied researchers conduct **program evaluations:** *systematic observations to assess whether a social program or practice achieves its goals* (Rutman, 1984). These evaluations are one way of assessing whether society's investment in these programs is warranted and wise. In some cases, this evaluation focuses on a large program with many different elements. An example would be a delinquency prevention program that tries to keep youngsters in school, give them some job skills, and enhance their self-esteem all at the same time. In other cases, an evaluation might focus on a much more limited social practice that is not a part of an overall program. An example would be the provision of financial assistance to reduce recidivism that was discussed in Research in Action 4.2. In either case, scientific research techniques, incorporating some of the research designs discussed in Chapters 4 and 5, assess what the program or practice does and how well or poorly it does it.

A program evaluation would typically focus on one or more of the following issues (Rossi and Rosenbaum, 1981):

1. *Program design and planning:* Are the goals of the program clearly defined? Is the program based on existing social science knowledge of human social behavior? Is the program designed to achieve the stated goals?
2. *Program monitoring:* How well is the program run? Do the services or resources of the program reach those for whom they are intended?
3. *Outcome evaluation:* Does the program accomplish what it is intended to in terms of outcomes? Are there any unexpected outcomes, either beneficial or detrimental?
4. *Economic efficiency:* How much does the program cost? Is it worth it? Could it be done more efficiently?

Research Design. Program evaluations, like all research, strive for objectivity, validity, and reliability, and they use scientific research designs to do so. Outcome evaluations, for example, typically involve a *causal* analysis, with the program inputs as the independent variables and the program outcomes or goals as the dependent variables (Figure 6.1). In a job training program, for example, the program inputs might be such things as training sessions on how to dress and present oneself at a job interview and how to prepare a resume, as well as training in some job-related skills; the goals of the program might be to get a job or to become a permanent member of the work force. To see if the inputs have an effect on the goals, any of the true experimental designs discussed in Chapter 4 would be an appropriate research design. Experimental designs are especially useful for making causal inferences regarding the effect of independent variables on dependent variables. In most cases, a field experiment would be used in program evaluation. In other words, the program as it actually operates would be assessed. Some of the characteristics of a true experimental design may be difficult to achieve in the field. There may be resistance to randomization into experimental and control conditions. True randomization might call for giving some people—randomly chosen—access to a program or treatment and denying others such access. Program managers may be reluctant to deny access to some people, or they may be legislatively prohibited from doing so. Despite this resistance, program evaluators typically push for a true experimental design because of its superiority in inferring causality. And those who review these program evaluations, such as funding agencies or elected officials, have become increasingly knowledgeable about research design, and they are quick to point out the flaws in any design that is

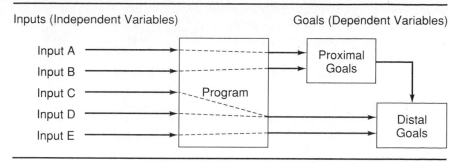

Figure 6.1 Linkage of Program Inputs and Program Goals

less than a true experiment. However, alternatives to the randomized experiment, such as quasi-experimental designs, are sometimes necessary (see Chapter 4).

The actual data collection in program evaluations is typically done through one of the techniques discussed in Chapter 5—surveys, interviews, focus groups, or the use of organizational records. Some qualitative techniques, such as participant observation, are used less often but still have utility, especially when qualitative data are required.

Program Inputs and Goals. A critical issue in program evaluation is the determination of whether a program or practice can be evaluated in a valid way. This is called an *evaluability assessment* (Rutman, 1984). One aspect of this assessment is to determine what the goals of the program are and whether their achievement can be measured. As surprising as it may seem, programs are often established and run without clearly delineating what the outcome should be. In other cases, the program goals are so broad that they are virtually worthless as criteria for evaluation. For example, the goal of the elimination of poverty is so broad that it is unlikely that one program will bring it about. Or, the goal of improved family functioning is so vague that it could mean any of a number of things. So, program evaluators typically begin by working with program administrators to specify the goals of the program or practice in as concrete a fashion as possible. As one program evaluator of considerable experience put it, the goals of a program should be "clear, specific, and measurable" (Weiss, 1972:26).

The next step in the evaluability assessment is to draw a link between program inputs or activities and the goals (see Figure 6.1). In other words, you need to specify which activities of a program will produce a particular outcome. This is especially important because programs typically do many different things at the same time. A social worker in an elementary school, for example, would likely do the following: one-on-one counseling with students, advising teachers on how to handle student problems, meeting with parents about their children's problems, linking parents with community agencies that can provide assistance, and giving talks to teachers' groups about how to identify problems. The expected outcomes of such a school social worker program might include goals such as enhanced student self-esteem, better academic performance, fewer behavior problems, lower rates of delinquency, and greater parental involvement in school affairs. If one or more of those outcomes occur, which of all of the social worker activities produced them? Was there some special combination that was important? Or were one or two of these activities the critical ones?

The point is that—in the ideal—a program should be able to specify that each input into the program will have a specified outcome. This is, essentially, the theory on which the program is based. Chapters 1 and 2 discussed the role of social science theories in both basic and applied research and pointed out that theories are important, but are used somewhat differently, in each. In program evaluations, theories are important in two ways. First of all, they are valuable in the design of programs to determine which inputs will produce desired outcomes. The school social worker program would be built on verified theories of socialization, child development, education, and self-concept development. Then, when the evaluation of the program finds success-ful achievement of goals in some areas but not others, it is possible to determine elements that are working well and those that need to be changed. This is impossible, however, if the link between inputs and outcomes is vague or nonexistent. When this delineation of inputs and goals is done, it is sometimes found that there are goals that no program elements are capable of achieving. The goals may have sounded lofty and noble during the development of the program, but then specific mechanisms to achieve the goals were either forgotten or eliminated for budgetary or other reasons. Obviously, if the program were evaluated against the goals for which no efforts were expended, it would probably be found wanting.

The second way in which theories enter into program evaluations is in deciding which outputs are both appropriate and feasible to use in evaluating a program. If an educational program were to focus on changes in self-concept as one of its outcomes, there is much verified theoretical work on self-concept development that could be reviewed. Existing theory and research tell us that self-concepts typically change slowly, often taking years to make significant changes. If measure-ments of self-concept change are made within a short period, say weeks or months, there may not be sufficient time for measurable change to occur, even if the program is having an effect. So, verified theory on self-concept development would inform us that self-concept change is probably not a feasible measure of the impact of a program over a short period of time, although it might be quite appropriate as a more long-term measure of the achievement of program goals.

Given the importance of clear-cut goals, inputs, and linkages, program evaluation is much easier and more valid when programs are designed with evaluation in mind. In fact, the ideal is to have applied researchers participate in the design of the program, and this is often done.

Measurement. Measurement is crucial to evaluation research, as it is in all research (see Chapter 2). However, in evaluation research, researchers often do not have the same degree of freedom as they do in basic research. The decision of what to measure and how to measure it can be limited because program inputs and goals, which are the independent and dependent variables in the research, are usually established by program managers and others. Once programs are established and operating, researchers must work with these inputs and goals even if they might prefer somewhat different ones. There is still some flexibility in the actual operational definitions that are used, but it is too late to make major theoretical or conceptual changes, even if warranted to improve the research. For example, in the recidivism experiment described in Research in Action 4.2, some inmates were given financial assistance and others were not. This independent variable took on two values, either present or absent. However, maybe there is some *level* of financial support below which recidivism is unaffected and above which recidivism begins to decline. If the program is designed to give all those receiving financial support the same amount, it is impossible to measure the independent variable in terms of the *degree* or *level* of such support. In this way, program inputs can limit the way in which the variables can be defined and measured. Of course, the program could be changed, but program inputs and goals are designed with many political, ethical, and practical considerations in mind, and program evaluation is only one of them. This is another reason to have applied researchers participate in designing programs.

Some program goals are so general that they can be achieved only after a long period of time—years or decades. These are called long-term or *distal* goals because their accomplishment is removed some distance in time from the program inputs that contribute to their achievement (see Figure 6.1). The intent of a job training program, for example, might be to help people become permanent members of the work force, which we may not be sure about for many years. As important as these distal goals are, evaluation of a program is often desired sooner. So, program evaluations often measure more short-term or *proximal* goals, which are closer to the point of program input and reflect intermediate outcomes that would presumably need to be achieved before the distal goals. For example, if a person is to get into the work force permanently, an intermediate step toward that goal might be success at getting job interviews or a first job. These proximate outcomes would reflect the extent to which the program is changing behaviors in the direction necessary to achieve the distal outcomes. In some cases, there may be a causal chain from inputs to proximate goals to distal goals: The job training program achieves the proximal goal of getting a first job, which in turn is a necessary step toward becoming a permanent member of the work force.

This example points to another important issue in measuring goals in program evaluation: whether to measure attitudes or behaviors. Today, most social scientists prefer to measure behavior over attitudes. One reason is that behavioral measures are generally more valid and reliable than attitudinal ones (Monette, Sullivan, and DeJong, 1990). Another reason is that the link between attitudes and behavior is much weaker than has often been thought. Our behavior is shaped by many factors, and our attitudes probably play only a minor role in many situations. None of this means that nonbehavioral measures should not be used, but it does strongly suggest that behavioral measures always be included where possible.

This brings us to another point relating to measurement in program evaluation: A number of different measures of outcomes are usually preferred. Program inputs are typically complex, and we can expect them to produce a number of outcomes. Each specific way of measuring an outcome is an approximation of the overall outcome of the program. For example, the major outcome of a driver training program is to produce good drivers, but the concept *good driver* is a very general one. We could measure it in a number of concrete ways: knowledge of traffic rules, score on the driver's exam, rating of driving abilities by some third party, or record of traffic violations. Each of these measures a part of what it means to be a good driver, so the preferred evaluation would include some or all of these measures. Using multiple measures might also enable us to specify the impact of the program more precisely. We might find, for example, that the driver education program increases knowledge of traffic laws but doesn't reduce the rate of traffic violations. This specificity can be useful in deciding whether to change some aspect of programs.

Utilization of Research. Program evaluation research is explicitly intended to have an effect by either documenting that a program works and should be kept running or suggesting areas where the program doesn't achieve its goals and should be changed or abandoned. Typically, the decision about what will be done with the results of a program evaluation is out of the hands of the researchers themselves. Funding agencies, program managers, or politicians may be the ones with the actual authority to change a program. Sometimes, the outcomes of program evaluations are ignored if they show that the program doesn't work. However, the program evaluators have a professional responsibility to prepare a valid, scientifically sound evaluation and a complete and objective report of the results, regardless of whether they cast the program and its managers in a positive or negative light. In some cases, the researcher may be contractually prohibited from publishing the results. If program managers decide not to act on the results of an evaluation, there is usually nothing more that researchers can do (see Chapter 7).

Another issue in the utilization of program evaluation results has to do with statistical versus substantive significance (Rossi and Rosenbaum, 1981). Although the concept of *statistical significance* is complicated and requires some knowledge of statistical analysis to be fully understood, it can be considered in a simplified way to mean that the program produces an effect that the researcher can reliably measure. It may be a very small effect, but it can be measured. The concept of *substantive significance* is quite different: It means that a program's effects are sufficiently large that it warrants the expenditure of time, money, or other resources to keep the program operating or to expand it. Statistical significance can be readily established, and with much consensus, by researchers using agreed upon statistical methods. Substantive significance involves far more judgment and the weighing of some expenditures of resources against others. For example, an employment program could produce a statistically significant reduction in recidivism; however, if the effect is small—say, 25 percent of those in the program become recidivists as opposed to 29 percent of those not in the program—it may be judged not sufficient to warrant the amount of money spent on the program. It does work, but the impact is too small to be worth continuing it. Statistical significance can influence judgments about substantive significance, but other factors also come into play in such judgments. So, a program evaluation outcome may be statistically significant but be judged not substantively significant.

Needs Assessment

Needs assessment research focuses on *collecting data for the purpose of determining how many people in a community will need particular services or products for a given period of time* (Dunham, 1983; McKillip, 1987). A corporation considering marketing a new product would need to know how many potential purchasers there are; a hospital considering expanding its obstetrical services would need to know how many pregnancies are likely to occur in its service area; and a school system would want to know how many students there will be at certain ages before building a new school. In all cases, a needs assessment could systematically determine the extent of need for a proposed service, program, or product. A needs assessment can ask not only how much need there is but also how much of that need is or could be filled by existing resources and personnel in the community. This is a *resource analysis*. Sometimes, organizations try to make an educated guess about existing needs and resources, but this is a very precarious foundation on which to base the expenditure of large amounts of money and other resources, especially because systematic needs assessments are often not that expensive to conduct.

In some cases, it is possible to assess need by interviewing key informants, people who have some sort of expertise or special knowledge about particular services or people. However, even expert knowledge may be based, at least in part, on intuition and speculation and thus show some bias. So, different perspectives on needs can be tapped by surveying the people in the community who would be likely to purchase the new products or receive the new services. If the recipients are not a well-defined group, it may be necessary to do a sample survey of a whole community—one of the more expensive forms of needs assessment that utilizes the techniques of survey design and sampling discussed in Chapters 2 and 5. In 1988, a needs assessment of this type was completed in Duluth, Minnesota (Anderson, Jesswein, and Fleischman, 1990). The goal of the research was to identify what the residents considered to be the major social problems in their city and to develop a plan of action to deal with them. The researchers surveyed a random sample of households in the city, but they also interviewed some key informants, particularly community leaders, who had some special knowledge of problems and services in Duluth.

Many needs assessment surveys, such as this one, ask people directly about problems or services. In other cases, however, people are not familiar with problems or are not aware that they need certain services or will need them in the future. For example, many people who are now mentally stable but who will experience some severe mental distress in the next few years will probably not respond positively when asked if they will need mental health services in the future. The potential recipients of services don't know about or can't anticipate their future needs. To measure this sort of need, a more indirect approach is required. Given what we know about the social patterns of people's lives, it is often possible to use social characteristics to predict fairly accurately what the future need for particular products or services will be. For example, the human life cycle follows some fairly predictable patterns. People are in grade school between the ages of 6 and 11; they attend college between the ages of 18 and 30 (although this is not as true as it once was); and most women have children when they are between the ages of 18 and 40. We can use this predictability to project into the future. If we know how many 10-year-old females there are in a community this year, we know the number who will enter their prime child-bearing years in another eight years. Based on the birth rate among 18-year-olds, we can project increases or decreases in the need for obstetrical services eight years from now. Obviously other information, such as migration into and out of the community, must be considered, and this kind of demographic analysis can become complex. But it can also be very accurate and useful if properly done.

Sometimes, data from surveys can be combined with a projection analysis to provide an estimate of needs. In human service planning, a sociological approach known as *social area analysis* has often been used (Johnson, 1983). Using community surveys, a city can be divided into a variety of social areas based on the socioeconomic status, family characteristics, ethnic group affiliation, and other demographic characteristics of the people in each area. Each area will contain people who tend to be similar in terms of these characteristics. Then we can look at existing research on the link between various social characteristics and some particular problem, such as mental disorder. We know, for example, that people with low socioeconomic standing tend to have higher rates of schizophrenia and thus more need for mental health services. In the planning process, then, those areas of a community whose members are characterized by low socioeconomic standing could be expected to have a greater need for mental health services and could be targeted for a greater expenditure of mental health dollars and other resources. Even though we have not measured the actual need for mental health services in the area, we have predicted that the needs would be higher in some areas than in others based on the social characteristics of the people living in those areas.

Chapter 1 discussed three goals of social research: description, explanation, and prediction. Needs assessment research is often highly descriptive in nature but provides some prediction in the form of projections. Explanation as a goal is less common in needs assessment research because it is often not necessary to know why something happens when trying to figure out how much of it there will be. It is not necessary to know why people of lower socioeconomic standing are more likely to be schizophrenic when the goal is to predict the level of need for mental health services in a community.

Social Impact Assessment

Politicians and policymakers have always considered the impact of their actions before initiating something new. It wouldn't be surprising, for example, if the Chinese rulers, before building the Great Wall, thought about whether it would disrupt trade routes or require the relocation of parts of villages. Likewise, the Egyptian Pharaohs may have chosen locations for their pyramids where the land was not good for agriculture. Today, such *impact assessment* is also done when new programs or projects are proposed, but the assessment is much more intensive, complete, and systematic (Dunning, 1985). There are a number of reasons why impact assessments are much more thorough today. One has to do with our understanding of the *systemic* nature of most things. The term *systemic* comes from the word *system,* and it reflects our recognition that physical, biological, and social environments are systems—they are made up of interrelated and interdependent parts. Each part is at least indirectly linked to all other parts of the system, and a change in one part can produce changes in many other parts, including unexpected and sometimes detrimental changes. This systemic understanding leads us to assume that new policies and projects will produce unplanned changes. Impact assessment is an effort to predict or measure the nature and extent of as many of the planned and unplanned changes as possible.

A second reason for the growth in impact assessment is the National Environmental Protection Act (NEPA) of 1969. NEPA requires that environmental impact statements (EISs) be prepared for all actions of the federal government that significantly affect the environment. Although NEPA originally emphasized the physical and biological environment, it now includes social conditions. So, **social impact assessment** (SIA) refers to *making an estimate of "the likely consequences of proposed programs and projects on individuals, groups, neighborhoods, communities, regions, institutions, and other social units"* (Finsterbusch, 1981:24). Sociologists typically work with economists, anthropologists, and other social scientists on social impact assessments because the consequences of major projects can be widespread.

With NEPA, the assessment of the impact of programs and projects has become institutionalized in law and government bureaucracy. This provides a mechanism through which the public can learn how it might be affected by a project and can have input into the decision making on that project. It also means that the courts can be used when grievances arise, and the courts have generally insisted on strict and substantive compliance with NEPA regulations in order to alert the public to the consequences of programs and projects (Liroff, 1978).

If program evaluations also assess the impact of programs, what is the difference between them and social impact assessment? They can overlap to an extent, but most SIAs assess the *expected* impact of a *proposed* action and program evaluation measures the actual impact of currently operating programs. In addition, the term *social impact assessment* is used when there is a project or major program whose initiation will have ramifications for many if not most members of some particular community (Bowles, 1981). By contrast, most social programs directly affect only those for whom they are intended. For example, placing social workers in elementary schools has direct effects on the children and families who become their clients. However, the teachers and other students will probably be largely unaware that the program is in operation, and most community members will not notice it at all. If they do benefit, it will be only very indirectly, and the program will probably have no negative impact on them (other than a minuscule increase in their taxes to support the program). On the other hand, a project to dam a river can have a severe impact on the lives of many, possibly all, people living in the area. Houses and sometimes whole towns have to be moved, roads may have to be relocated, and the recreational activities on the resulting lake may tax the transportation network in the area. Social impact assessment is used to evaluate the impact of such projects, and some of the techniques that are used are quite different from the techniques used in program evaluation.

The process of social impact assessment can be divided into three stages: impact estimation, response estimation, and policy or program modification (Figure 6.2). For the first two stages, a distinction can be made between *preimpact assessments* and *postimpact assessments*. Preimpact assessments are done during the planning stages of a project with the goal of shaping the project based on the information gathered in the assessment. Postimpact assessments, which might sometimes look like program evaluations, are done after a project is completed in order to assess what changes were brought about by the project. Of course, when a project is already completed and operating, much of the harm it causes cannot be undone, but the postimpact assessment is still valuable as a guide to future projects that are similar to it. Preimpact assessments are much more difficult to do, much less precise, and much more speculative than the postimpact assessments, which can be much more precise and quantitative because they can measure how many people actually were affected, to what extent, and in what way. Research in Action 6.1 describes a preimpact and a postimpact assessment.

A first step in a preimpact assessment is to use information from existing postimpact assessments: Impacts that occurred during earlier, similar projects might also occur in the current one. This means

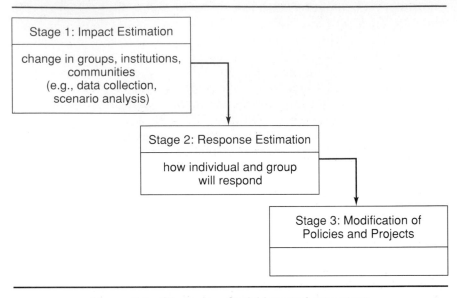

Figure 6.2 Stages in a Social Impact Assessment

Preventing Community Decline During Resource Development

When the construction of a gas pipeline was being considered in northern Canada in the 1970s, there was some concern about its impact on small native communities in the area. A preimpact assessment of the Kutchin community of Old Crow was conducted (Bowles, 1981). As with most SIAs, this assessment included a description of the geographical setting and physical structure of the community, the demographic characteristics of its members, their social patterns and life-style (family life, voluntary organizations, leisure pursuits, etc.), and their political and economic systems. It described the past and the present, including changes that were occurring in the community before the gas pipeline. Finally, a projection was made about the impact of the gas pipeline on such things as family life, traditional activities, and community affairs.

To give one illustration of the kinds of projections that were made, we can look at the projected impact on the family. The relatively high wages paid to work on the pipeline would likely attract workers from the Kutchin community. The relocation of these workers, usually male, to the new areas should make it more difficult for husbands and wives to maintain mutually supportive ties with one another. The absentee father should also tend to lose some degree of authority over his children. When the whole family moves to the new community, it loses ties with friends and relatives—that elaborate network of social support that helped it cope with problems and difficulties. The wage work that draws people to resource development should also contribute to the weakening of familial ties. In traditional communities, the parents and elders pass on knowledge and skills that are necessary for traditional subsistence activities such as hunting and fishing, giving parents and elders an important role in the lives of the young and encouraging dependence on and respect for them. Wage work, on the other hand, enables the young to earn sizable incomes independently of their parents and elders, contributing to the erosion of family authority. Given all of these social impacts, if the Kutchin community is not given any planning or support, it should experience considerable social disintegration. Problems like alcoholism, crime, and mental distress should increase. In short, economic development can bring about permanent changes in the social fabric of the community. The new project does not merely develop natural resources; it also changes a way of life. In this SIA, the researchers were able to project different levels of impact depending on where the gas pipeline was placed. This information then became one element in deciding whether and where to build the pipeline.

When, as described in the opening of this chapter, the development of the lead-zinc mine was planned in the vicinity of Arctic Bay, the community residents were able to benefit from social impact assessments of other communities that had experienced similar development. After all, many communities, like Kutchin, have had to cope with pipelines, mining developments, or other intrusions as a result of the development of natural resources. Based on what had happened in other communities, the Arctic Bay residents argued against the establishment of a permanent community to house the workers at the work site. They feared this relocation would create too much disruption of family life and traditional subsistence activities. Instead, they preferred a rotational system that allowed the workers to spend a week or two in their native communities after a period of working at the mine site. However, a lengthy period of absence can still create stresses for families. The experience of other communities where workers were recruited to work on oil-drilling crews showed that short absences, such as one week at home after working only two weeks at the drilling site, were least detrimental to the family.

In cases where it was necessary to move a whole community to provide a supply of workers, SIAs have demonstrated preferred ways to relocate: Move all members of the community together, move them to an area with which they are familiar (rather than, say, from a rural to an urban setting), and move them to an area where they have relatives. If done in this fashion, the relocation is far less disruptive of family and community life and creates far fewer social problems like crime and alcoholism.

Social impact assessments are based on certain assumptions, chief among them that it is desirable to minimize the negative impacts on people's lives that result when economic development or other programs are implemented. How to do so can become a very heated and controversial issue because it involves balancing the benefits to one group against the disadvantages to another. The findings of SIAs are sometimes used by both sides. Very often, the debate comes down to a matter of values: Maintaining some element of a traditional way of life is viewed as less (or more) important than providing additional natural resources that will enable others to maintain their way of life. Sometimes, the outcome is a matter of power relations: The group with more economic and political clout (usually the developers) gets its way while making some concessions to the less powerful groups. So, as has been emphasized repeatedly, the policy-making process is not guided solely by the observations of applied research, but the research does make a valuable contribution to the outcome.

---

gathering observations about what is happening in the present and has happened in the past and drawing some conclusions about an uncertain future. Then, as with the assessment of the Kutchin community described in Research in Action 6.1, a preimpact assessment would provide a detailed description of the past and present circumstances of the community. This data would be gathered using some or all of the research methods described in Chapter 5. Surveys, observational techniques, and existing records would come into play in most SIAs. Then a projection is made regarding how things will change as a result of the project. Projections could focus on a number of different levels of society (Finsterbusch and Motz, 1980):

1. The individual or household level (e.g., how do individuals and their families adapt if unemployment rises),
2. Groups or organizations (e.g., what business organizations will emerge or decline because of the development),
3. Community (e.g., are patterns of neighbor visitation disrupted in a neighborhood), and
4. Societal institutions (e.g., are traditional patterns of authority in the family changed on a widespread basis).

You can see from this list that the focus of social impact assessments can be very broad, often covering all dimensions of social life.

SIAs vary considerably in how precise and detailed they are in forecasting the future (Bowles, 1981). Some merely extend past trends into the future (e.g., if current birth rates continue, the population in the United States in the future will be X), while others predict that something new will happen at some time in the future. The most complete and useful SIA is a *forecast,* which projects a range of possible outcomes, specifies when and under what conditions each will occur, and elaborates the causal model that underlies the predictions. Many SIAs fall considerably short of this goal.

As with many other types of applied social research, SIA is guided by the *knowledge in use* criterion: The outcome of the research is judged in terms of its utility to decision makers (Bowles, 1981). Does the research alert the policymakers to the significant factors in a project or program? Are the results sufficiently clear and unambiguous that decision makers can weigh these factors? Although SIA research must be guided by the standard principles of social science research discussed in this book, it is also guided by the criterion of *relevance,* which may make some procedures more useful than in basic or other types of applied research. For example, in program evaluation, random samples are usually preferred, because a representative assessment of the overall outcome of a program is needed to determine how *everyone* might react to the intervention. With SIA, on the other hand, decision makers may want to know if there is a "significant" amount of opposition to a project, no matter what the source. They don't need to know how everyone reacts, only whether there is any opposition from anywhere. This need might be satisfied by a convenience or snowball sample (see Chapter 2), which are considered to be quite inferior to a random sample for most uses. If a convenience sample shows considerable opposition, the decision makers may not need to know how representative it is of all people in the community; they only need to know that this level of opposition exists in order to make policy decisions about the program. Knowing that the opposition was representative would not contribute anything more to their ability to make a decision.

When SIAs make predictions about the future, subjective elements can be a factor. In fact, some SIAs are almost completely subjective in nature, making some SIA research quite different from other types of applied research. Although much quantitative data may be gathered through such techniques as postimpact assessments, these will often be combined with the opinions of experts, commonsense assumptions, intuition, and speculation to make projections (Finsterbusch, 1981). In *scenario analysis,* several scenarios of future developments might be projected based on existing relationships between variables along with some intuition and speculation about what may happen in the future. One projection of population growth, for example, uses current birth rates while other scenarios might assume that the rate will rise or fall substantially in the future. Another subjective technique used in some SIAs is the *delphi method,* which involves several rounds of interviews with experts on what they believe will be the future extent and impact of various changes. After each round, the experts receive feedback on the more popular responses among the other experts. Those with divergent views can then reconsider their positions in the light of other expert opinions. In some cases, the experts are also given detailed criticisms of their own views for consideration in deciding whether they want to change their projections. The final report includes a statement of the most popular scenarios, along with some of the less popular ones as an indication of how much consensus there was in the group.

What I have described thus far is mostly the impact estimation stage of an SIA (see Figure 6.2). The second stage is to assess the likely responses of the affected individuals and groups to the changes projected in the preimpact assessment: Do they move, fight against them, or leave their families? This stage is also conjectural because the project and its consequent changes have not yet happened. It can be based on our existing knowledge of how groups have responded to similar projects or equivalent changes in their communities. Or it might be based on surveys, interviews, or observational studies of samples of the affected population regarding how they *might* respond if the project is initiated in the future.

The third stage in an SIA is the modification of projects and policies in order to minimize the negative impact and maximize the positive. This brings us back into the policy-making process, which tends to be guided more by politicians and project managers than by applied researchers. However, the applied researchers, using SIAs, provide the clear articulation of possible outcomes that are then used by policymakers in making decisions.

Social Indicators

Many disciplines use summary quantitative measures to describe the condition of some large structure or process. In the economic realm, for example, financial analysts use the Dow Jones average as an indicator of the overall condition of the stock market. In the criminal justice field, the Federal Bureau of Investigation uses the annual crime rate as an indicator not only of the extent of crime but also of the effectiveness of law enforcement or even the quality of life in the United States. The social sciences have also developed such measures and call them **social indicators:** *quantitative measures of significant social phenomena* (de Neufville, 1981). The term *social* implies that the focus is on the status of and change in social behavior, groups, institutions, or larger social systems. So, the divorce rate would be one way to measure change in the social institution of the family over time. As such, the Dow Jones average and the crime rate are also social indicators. The former has been used primarily by economists, and the latter by many sociologists.

The central issue in social indicators research is measurement (see Chapter 2). What social phenomenon, at what level of abstraction, does a social indicator measure? At one level, a social indicator is concrete data. The crime rate tells us exactly how many crimes were reported to the police in a particular jurisdiction. However, in social indicators research, the indicators are also abstractions from reality; they are assumed to stand for some broader aspect of social reality based on a theory that links the measurement with reality. For example, based on the theory that crime, as a form of social violence, is produced in part by alienation and social disorganization, the crime rate can be considered an indicator of the extent of alienation and social disorganization in society. So, social indicators are operational definitions (see Chapter 2). The crime rate is one operational definition of the measurement of alienation. However, what sets social indicators apart from most operational definitions is the effort to establish measures that can be used by a variety of researchers, monitored over a period of time, and incorporated into the policy-making process. In other research, operational definitions may be somewhat unique to a particular research project.

The basic logic of social indicators research parallels the development of operational definitions. The first step is to clearly define at the conceptual level what is to be measured. For example, we could begin with the concept of *community health*. In Table 6.1, this concept is defined at the conceptual level in two different ways. The first definition is based on the assumption that a healthier community is one with less disease. The second definition assumes that some disease will always exist in a community and that the healthier community is the one that can cope effectively with the disease that exists. The next step is to find some factors that can be measured quantitatively to represent these two notions of community health. Alternative ways of measuring each concept are listed in Table 6.1. Some of these measures, such as data on death rates, are readily available and routinely collected by government or other agencies. In other cases, it may be necessary to conduct a community survey to collect the necessary data to construct the indicators. Social indicators by

TABLE 6.1 Moving from Concept to Measurement in Social Indicators Research

Conceptual Level	Measurement
Community health = Amount of disease in a community	Rates of various diseases Death rates Days lost to work due to illness Life expectancy
Community health = Health resources available to assist people in coping with disease	Number of hospital beds in community Number of doctors of various specialities in community Number of people with health insurance

themselves tend to be descriptive in nature: They are intended to describe the state of some social phenomenon but usually not to explain or evaluate it.

Another important consideration in designing social indicators is which comparisons are to be made. All indicators involve some comparison, even if the comparison is implicit. When a death rate or crime rate is presented, for example, an implicit comparison is made with the death rates or crime rates of previous years. After all, the reason for presenting such rates is typically to see whether they have changed over time. Sometimes, a single indicator by itself can have some policy relevance. We might say that the poverty rate is 14 percent, and that is unacceptably high for an affluent society such as our own. However, there are often implicit comparisons that are used to justify this statement: "The poverty rate was lower than that 20 years ago" or "Other industrial nations have lower poverty rates." The value assumptions behind these statements are, respectively, "The poverty rate should go down as society becomes more affluent," and "The United States should have a poverty rate comparable with other industrial nations." So, creating a measurable indicator is only part of social indicator research; an equally important part is to indicate which comparisons will give the most appropriate or effective *meaning* to the indicator.

It typically takes considerable resources to create valid social indicators and to collect the necessary data. As a result, social indicators research is often done by large organizations that have considerable financial and human resources. Three types of organizations do most of this research in the United States. First, federal or state government agencies produce most of the social indicators. The Federal Bureau of Investigation produces crime indicators; the Bureau of the Census produces a vast array of indicators on health, commerce, birth rates, and the like; the Bureau of Labor Statistics publishes indicators of unemployment, earnings, labor union membership, and so on. Second, private, profit-making organizations like the Gallup organization publish indicators based mostly on the public's attitudes toward a variety of issues. The Gallup organization collects data on people's attitudes toward the schools their children attend, and this serves as an indicator of how good a job the nation's schools are doing in the eyes of the public. Because Gallup collects this same data over the years, there is a running record of fluctuations in these indicators. Third, university-based or nonprofit organizations, such as the Survey Research Center at the University of Michigan or the American Medical Association, collect data that can be used to develop social indicators.

Because they measure the status of some social behavior, group, or social institution, social indicators have played a key role in developing and changing social policy for many years. They serve to inform both the public and the policymakers about key issues such as the well-being of society and the extent of change in various aspects of the social structure. As far back as the nineteenth century, social surveys were conducted on the living conditions and health status of working people as a way of getting an indication of the kinds of reforms that might be needed (Turner and Turner, 1990). More recently, the poverty rate has been routinely used as evidence in the debate over the need for various social programs. When the poverty rate goes down, some argue that such programs are no longer necessary; when it goes up, others claim that the government must do more. Of course, the poverty rate is only one small aspect of the overall problem of poverty, employment, and the distribution of wealth in society. Applied social scientists and many policymakers are aware of this, and consider the poverty rate (or any social indicator) in the context of many other issues. Research in Action 6.2 illustrates the development of fairly complex social indicators that incorporate many different kinds of information in order to get a more complete view of reality. However, there is always the danger that social indicators will be viewed in an oversimplified and possibly distorted fashion.

RESEARCH IN ACTION 6.2 ===

What Is the State of Our Nation's Social Well-Being?

Are Americans better off in the 1990s than they were in the 1970s or 1980s? Some individuals are better off, of course, while others are not. But overall, has life in our society gotten better or worse? One approach to answering this question would be to establish some quantitative social indicators that could be compared year after year. This would certainly be more objective and less biased than the judgments that individuals are likely to make based on the limited information of their own personal experience.

This is what the Fordham Institute for Innovation in Social Policy has been doing for almost 20 years. It has created Indexes of Social Health that monitor the social well-being of our society (Miringoff, 1989). These indexes are based on quantitative information about how our nation performs in dealing with a variety of social problems. For example, the Index of Social Health for Children and Youth provides a composite score that combines data on a number of problems relevant to the quality of life for young people. Data included in this index are

infant mortality
child abuse
children living in poverty
teen suicide
drug abuse
high school drop-outs

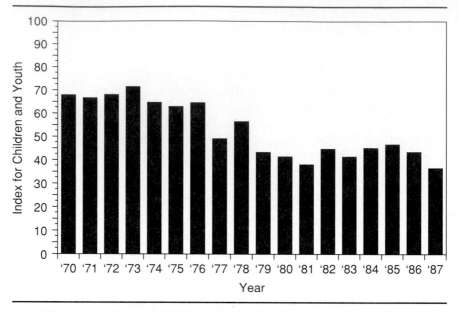

Figure 6.3 Index of Social Health for Children and Youth, 1970–1987. *Source:* Marc L. Miringoff. 1989. *The Index of Social Health, 1989: Measuring the Social Well-Being of the Nation,* p. 6. Tarrytown, N.Y.: Fordham Institute for Innovation in Social Policy.

Clearly, an increase in any of these problems would seem to indicate that life has become worse for young people. Most of the data are collected by one government agency or another, and the Institute combines them into indexes.

As far as the social well-being of our youth is concerned, it has declined dramatically in the past 20 years. There is more abuse, poverty, and suicide among our children and teenagers. In fact, according to the index, 1987, the last year for which data are available, was the worst year since 1970. In 1970, the index stood at 68, with a higher score indicating greater social health; by 1987, it had plummeted to 37 (Figure 6.3). On the whole, life for our children and teenagers appears to have gotten demonstrably worse over the years.

Although an indicator of this sort does not identify the causes of the problems, it can be very useful in the policy-making process by calling attention to their existence and depth. It offers a very dramatic portrayal of changes in the problem over time that can serve as an important motivation to encourage policy discussions about the issue. The indicator can also serve as a general way of measuring the state or condition of some major realm or institution of society. In this case, the Index of Social Health for Children and Youth can be considered a general assessment of how well American society treats its young people. And it seems to tell us that we aren't doing as good a job as we once did!

Despite the dangers of distortion, social indicators are important in a democratic society such as ours. As the chair of the Council of Professional Associations of Federal Statistics pointed out:

> These social indicators . . . absolutely must be made available to any interested citizen with a minimum expense and difficulty because an informed electorate is an absolute requirement of a working democracy. (Woolsey, 1986:3)

Social indicators are also used by policymakers to make decisions about the allocation of resources. Thus indicators can be used to establish past trends, and then, using regression techniques (see Chapter 3), projections can be made about future conditions or for locating the greatest need for resources. This was done in one effort to figure out how to most effectively allocate funds for programs to reduce infant mortality (Ferriss, 1988). Past trends were used to establish links between infant mortality and such community characteristics as educational level, access to health care, and economic well-being. With these indicators, communities at high risk for infant mortality could be identified and funds channeled toward them.

Cost-Benefit Analysis

When applied research is used to evaluate programs and policies, it is sometimes possible to list all of the benefits of the program as well as all of the costs. *Comparing the benefits of a program with the costs* is called **cost-benefit analysis,** and it is sometimes a part of program evaluations and social impact assessments. It enables program managers and policymakers to weigh whether the benefits are warranted given the costs. An example is described in Research in Action 6.3.

Despite its seeming quantitative precision and its precise weighing of costs and benefits, cost-benefit analysis has limitations. A major one is the difficulty of precisely measuring the costs and benefits of a program. Direct costs and benefits are often easy to measure in monetary terms, such as how much government money is needed to run a workfare program for a year. It is much more difficult to place a dollar value on such things as a reduction in the crime rate because people are employed. The costs to the criminal justice system to control crime can be estimated, but what about the reduction in fear and improvements in the quality of life that result from a lower crime rate? These are difficult to measure in any quantitative way. Another limitation of cost-benefit analysis is that much of the measurement is based on assumptions whose accuracy may be difficult to assess with any certainty. Projections about how much the crime rate will drop are based on assumptions about how many people with particular

Do Welfare Programs Help People Find Work?

For people who have been fortunate enough to have a job to support themselves and their families, it is hard to imagine what it is like to take welfare—to be on the public dole. But Oscar knows what it's like. He had a good job as a window washer until he hurt himself at work and couldn't do it anymore. For him, welfare meant being sent on many useless job interviews—jobs that he knew had already been promised to someone else. The interviews often meant a long bus or subway ride, but to refuse to go would mean a loss of welfare benefits. Adam also knows about welfare. For him it meant having to come to the welfare office to get benefits and then being treated "like a dog" and talked to "like I'm a child." Judy, Paula, and Kathy also experienced welfare. They didn't get a job from welfare, but they were forced to come into the welfare office (even if they were sick), sit for hours, and be interviewed in what they perceived as a rather futile and demeaning dance whose choreography helped them get their welfare benefits but not a job. (These cases are described in Goodwin, 1983.)

For these people, welfare was an unwanted, demeaning necessity. In some cases, it was a virtual assault on their sense of dignity and self-worth. For all, work was far preferred over welfare. For decades, politicians and policymakers have struggled with the issue of welfare dependency: Does giving people welfare make them more dependent and less willing to work? Critics of welfare have argued that those who are on welfare, especially for a long time, are in danger of losing the social and personal skills that might enable

them to support themselves and find a job. These skills and qualities range from the sense to dress appropriately for a job interview to the organization needed to be prompt, from the desire to get ahead to the basic sense of self-worth that can enable them to tackle new challenges.

To cope with some of these problems, welfare in the United States has gradually been changed to what has been called *workfare:* Benefits are contingent on receiving job training and seriously looking for work. This has been done in a variety of ways in different jurisdictions, and all raise the same question: Does it work? or, How *well* does it work? The Manpower Demonstration Research Corporation has addressed this question in a number of applied research projects, including a cost-benefit analysis of a workfare program in Virginia (Riccio, 1987). This program provided participants with some education and job training services as well as child-care payments that helped them put their children in day-care. The benefit-cost ledger for this program looked like the one shown in the accompanying table.

Notice in this ledger that whether something is a cost or a benefit depends on whose perspective is used. When people get jobs, they pay taxes; this is a benefit for the government, which receives more tax revenues, but a cost to the worker who did not have to pay taxes before becoming employed.

Because we can attach a monetary value to each of the costs and benefits described in the ledger, we can compute a quantitative assessment of whether, from both the recipient's and the government's perspective, the benefits outweigh the costs, and by how much. For the participants in this program, the benefits outweighed the costs by $700 to $900 per participant. The government also showed a clear gain: benefits between $150 and $300 greater than the costs per participant. In other words, for each dollar the government spent on the program, the government received between $1.38 and $1.82 from the various benefits. These data provide policymakers with some very solid information to incorporate into their decision making about programs that will influence—hopefully for the better—the lives of people like Oscar, Adam, Judy, Paula, and Kathy.

Benefits	Costs
To Participants	*To Participants*
Increased earnings if people get jobs	Higher taxes paid
Increased fringe benefits	Reduced welfare and other public
Increased child-care payments from the program	assistance if they get a job
To Government (Society)	*To Government (Society)*
Increased tax payments if people get jobs	Public funds to operate workfare program
Reduced welfare and other public assistance	Public funds for education and training services and day-care

characteristics (age, sex, socioeconomic status) would be likely to be unemployed and commit crimes had they not gone through a workfare program. Although these projections can be made, they are no better than the assumptions on which they rest, and widely different projections could be made with different assumptions. Despite these limitations, researchers do engage in cost-benefit analysis, and attach a monetary value to various costs and benefits. However, it is a very complex process, and the researchers are aware of the extent to which it requires assumptions and value judgments. Cost-benefit analysis should never be accepted at face value without careful scrutiny of those assumptions and values. In addition, researchers are aware that this type of analysis has most validity where program costs and benefits are most clearly and unambiguously measurable in a quantitative way.

CRITICAL THINKING

Is There Systematic Evaluation?

This chapter emphasizes, even more directly than the others, the importance of evaluating social policies and programs through systematic observation. With many policies, there is a tendency to rely on intuition—or even wishful thinking—in assessing how well they work. Especially if a policy has been in operation for a long time, we presume that it is achieving its goals, and it is typically not hard to find anecdotal evidence in favor of it. Anecdotal evidence involves pointing to one or a few cases that reflect a positive outcome of a policy. The problem is that this is not *systematic*—we are likely to miss or ignore the cases that don't show the positive effect. In other words, especially when we have a vested interest in seeing a program work, there is a strong tendency for an anecdotal approach to miss contrary evidence. In critical thinking, it is assumed that this selective assessment of data can and will happen, and that we may well be unaware of it when it does occur.

To practice critical thinking, then, consider the following:

1. Has any effort been made to evaluate policies or judgments through systematic observation?
2. What goals are being sought in a program or policy? Are there any implicit goals that are not stated? Are the links between program inputs and goals clear?
3. How are the goals being measured? On what implicit or explicit assumptions or values are the measurements based? What alternative ways of measuring could have been used and how would that have changed the inferences drawn?
4. To what extent are statements based on conjecture, speculation, or subjective assessment as opposed to more objective methods of assessment? Do those arguing in favor of the program have a vested interest in seeing it perpetuated? Could this be biasing their judgment?
5. If quantitative data are presented to support an argument, is the measurement legitimate? Are the numbers accurate representations of what is being claimed at the conceptual level? What are the value assumptions that seem to influence the way in which measurement is done? If data had been measured differently, might a different outcome have occurred?

Key Terms for Review _____

cost-benefit analysis
needs assessment
program evaluation

social impact assessment
social indicators

For Further Inquiry _____

Kristi Branch, Douglas A. Hooper, James Thompson, and James Creighton. *Guide to Social Assessment: A Framework for Assessing Social Change.* Boulder, CO and London: Westview Press, 1984.

> This is a comprehensive overview of how to do a social impact assessment. It can serve as a guide for actually carrying out an SIA.

Daniel Glaser, with Edna Erez. *Evaluation Research and Decision Guidance: For Correctional, Addiction-Treatment, Mental Health, and Other People-Changing Agencies.* New Brunswick, NJ: Transaction Books, 1988.

The authors provide a thorough review of how to assess the effectiveness of organizations or agencies whose goal is to change people in some fashion—make them drug free, law abiding, mentally healthy, or educated. Studying the effectiveness of these organizations is different and more difficult than studying organizations that produce products like cars or pizzas. And it is at the core of most applied social research.

Egon G. Guba and Yvonna S. Lincoln. *Fourth Generation Evaluation.* Newbury Park, CA: Sage Publications, 1989.

This book focuses mostly on evaluation in educational settings. It challenges conventional ways of thinking in that it takes an interpretive approach, viewing all knowledge as a social construction. Even scientific knowledge is seen as socially constructed, as only one version of reality.

William Millsap (ed.). *Applied Social Science for Environmental Planning.* Boulder, CO: Westview Press, 1984.

This book of readings focuses on using applied research, particularly social impact assessments, for making decisions on environmental impacts. Written by various social scientists, the readings illustrate a wide range of SIAs that were conducted prior to doing environmental planning.

William R. Shadish, Jr., Thomas D. Cook, and Laura C. Leviton. *Foundations of Program Evaluation.* Newbury Park, CA: Sage, 1991.

This volume looks back at the origins of program evaluation and at the accumulated experiences of experienced program evaluators to provide an insightful discussion of the development of the field and of key issues that are relevant today.

Heather B. Weiss and Francine H. Jacobs (eds.). *Evaluating Family Programs.* New York: Aldine de Gruyter, 1988.

This book provides an interesting summary of the kinds of research evaluations that have relevance for the family as a social institution. Many programs are evaluated and numerous methodological issues are discussed. This is a very good resource.

Exercises _____

6.1. Locate in your library a volume titled *Health, United States, 1988,* published by the U.S. Department of Health and Human Services. It presents many social indicators of health status, such as birth rates, death rates, and rates of various diseases. Identify three or four of these indicators. What comparisons are being made in order to give meaning to the indicator? What assumptions underlie these comparisons?

6.2. Review the costs and benefits listed in Research in Action 6.3. For each one, describe the assumptions or values that underlie the conclusion that it is a cost or a benefit for a particular group. Are there other costs and benefits—based on different assumptions and values—that you can think of?

6.3. Find a program operating in your university or community. Design an evaluation of it using one of the types of applied research described in this chapter. Include a consideration of such factors as program goals, operational definitions, and sampling.

Ethics, Objectivity, and Social Policy

When we use applied social research, we touch people's lives, possibly changing them, maybe making them better. But we can also make people worse off, and that is one of the main concerns of this chapter. Consider this case. John worked for a large corporation in Louisiana. He was a conscientious worker, doing his job faithfully and rarely missing days because of illness. He had a family to support and his job paid well and was fulfilling. John also liked to use cocaine occasionally—sometimes on weekends and every so often after work on weekdays. But he was careful never to use cocaine or be under its influence while at work. John's boss had no complaints about his work performance.

With the rising concern about drug use in the 1980s, the corporation John worked for established a policy of random drug testing of all employees. The professed reason was to increase employee productivity and cut losses due to accidents and absenteeism. Employees who tested positive would be given assistance to help them stop using drugs. A second positive test would lead to dismissal. Shortly after the policy was established, John was chosen randomly for testing. Needless to say, he tested positive because he had used cocaine three days earlier on a Saturday afternoon. John was very upset because he felt that he worked very hard at his job and that his recreational use of cocaine did not affect his job performance and was his own business. Nevertheless, he faced a serious dilemma: If he continued to use cocaine and was retested, he would be fired. If that happened, he would probably find it difficult to obtain another job as good as the one he had. His ability to support his family and maintain his life-style at its current level would be seriously affected.

Because drug abuse is considered a serious social and health problem, medical sociologists were brought in to help design the program of drug testing at John's company and to evaluate how well it worked. With their expertise on the social and psychological causes of such problems, along with their knowledge of research design and evaluation research, medical sociologists would seem to be in a good position to make a positive contribution to such a program. Applied research of this type, however, raises a number of serious ethical issues that this chapter discusses. (John's story is a composite case based on personal knowledge and information in Barrows, 1990.)

So, we could use applied research to change John's life, but should we? To understand the ethical issues that arise in situations like this, we first need to discuss some of the uses to which applied research can be put in society. A major theme of this book has been that applied sociology affects people's lives; therefore, we need to consider very carefully what we do and how we do it. In this chapter, we analyze some of the very controversial issues this raises. Central to this discussion is the topic of **ethics,** which deals with *what behavior is proper or improper, with respect to issues of moral duty and obligation.* A number of important and controversial ethical issues are central to applied sociological research.

The Uses of Applied Research

Applied social research is used in both the public policy area and the private sector by businesses and corporations. However, it has been used more extensively in developing public policy over the years, so the issue of the uses to which sociology should be put have been more clearly developed there. So, this discussion of the role of applied research in society begins by focusing on the public policy realm.

Public Policy Uses

We use applied social research to attack some of our most vexing social problems, in the hope of contributing to a better life for people (Lee, 1991). But solutions to problems don't just magically appear. Rather, they arise out of a complex process in which many groups play a part. The outcome of this process is called **public policy:** *the course of action defined by the laws, administrative procedures, judicial rulings, and other formal and informal practices of government in relation to a particular social problem* (Bullock, Anderson, and Brady, 1983; Tatalovich and Daynes, 1988). The groups involved in this process often have clashing sets of values, and public policy is typically controversial. After all, policy-making is about making choices. It involves conflict, bargaining, and compromise. Public policy can also be contradictory. In one arena, public policy may work toward one solution to a problem and in another arena toward an opposite solution; in yet a third arena that particular problem may be ignored.

The role of applied social research in this public policy process is to provide systematic data with which to assess policy alternatives (Brownstein, 1991). This can occur at three points: problem formulation, policy formulation, and policy implementation. At the level of *problem formulation,* sociological data can be used to make a judgment about whether a condition should be considered a social problem worthy of public attention. For example, if a needs assessment showed that poverty affected relatively few Americans and was on the decline, many people might conclude that we need not bother with special programs to combat it. Actually, research over the past 20 years has documented that poverty is widespread and that it is especially common among those least equipped to help themselves, such as children. This research finding has led many Americans to conclude that poverty is a problem and that we need a public policy regarding it. However, there are two things to keep in mind about the role of sociological data in problem formulation. First, the data *alone* do not produce the conclusion that poverty is a problem; people must still make judgments, based on the data as well as on their personal values and political beliefs, about *how much* poverty is acceptable or unacceptable. Second, the data do not necessarily point toward a particular solution to the problem.

At the stage of *policy formulation,* we use applied research in deciding what might be feasible or measurable solutions to a problem. Based on previous research, such as program evaluations, it is sometimes possible to see what has worked well in other settings and use that information to shape a current policy. Actually, basic research can be used as well as applied research at this stage of the policy-making process to provide evidence and support for the development of a particular policy to politicians or policymakers. In addition, programs and policies are often shaped by considerations of whether their goals can be measured. If we can't measure whether the goal has been achieved, it may need to be modified or abandoned.

Finally, at the stage of *policy implementation,* applied research is one of the key tools for assessing how well a policy achieves its goals as well as any other impacts—positive and negative, intended and unintended—it might be having. At this stage, applied research often takes the form of program evaluations or cost-benefit analyses that are designed and conducted explicitly to assess a particular policy. It provides a quantitative measure of how well a policy achieves its goals and helps policymakers decide whether and how to modify programs.

So, one of the major motivations for doing applied research—whether in sociology or chemistry—is to contribute to the development of social policy and thus make people's lives better. But what do we mean by *better*? In answering this question, we begin to see that the role of applied research in society is much more complicated—and controversial—than it at first appears.

Social Betterment

The social sciences focus on numerous issues about which people understandably become impassioned: crime, spouse abuse, homelessness, and the like. Earlier chapters described some of the applied research that has been conducted in an effort to alleviate some of these problems. So, applied social research is directed at the betterment of society, or some part of it. In fact, historically social reformers have been prominent in sociology—many sociologists have wanted to change and improve society rather than merely understand it (Turner and Turner, 1990). This was true of many of the founders of American sociology, such as Lester Ward, and it remains true of the many contemporary sociologists discussed in this book.

A simplistic view of the role of sociological research in social betterment is that the insights about society and social behavior that it provides translate into improvements in society. It is somewhat analogous to our view of knowledge of the physical world: The more knowledge we have about physics and chemistry, the better able we are to improve the physical world in which we live. We can build better shelters, design central heating, and grow more nutritious foods. Knowledge of anatomy and physiology translates into better health and health care. By analogy, some people argue, knowledge and insight regarding the social world can be put directly to use to improve our social environment. Hence, problems like crime, violence, and racism can be reduced once we know their social origins and nature.

Implicit in this analogy is a *technocratic* view of social problems. In this view, problems are seen as objective conditions about which there is consensus that improvement or change is needed. Deciding what is a problem is not, in this view, a matter of judgment or values. Just as there is consensus that cancer is an evil to be eradicated, so presumably there is agreement that crime, poverty, and alcoholism should be eliminated. In this view, the applied researcher is merely a technician who uses his or her tools to find the most efficient and least expensive solutions to these problems (Brownstein, 1991). So, medical sociologists working with a drug testing program for a corporation are merely directing the tools of their trade toward solving the problem of drug abuse, which would presumably benefit everyone. In addition, this technocratic view assumes that all people are, at least potentially, hurt by a problem and all benefit, at some level, from its solution.

Although this approach has some intuitive appeal, there are other more complicated and controversial ones. Sociologist James Rule presents a very different view, which characterizes social problems as

> contests over the control of desirable resources, including wealth, privilege, and, above all, political power. These issues turn on clashes of interest and thus represent *political* conflicts. (1978:12–13)

In other words, social problems are not objectively determined evils but rather matters of opposition, often bitter, between competing groups. Some groups benefit and others are hurt when some condition, like drug use, is defined as a social problem. Who benefits by defining drug use as a problem? The bureaucracies who fight the drug wars gain because they get more resources and their voices take on more importance; those groups who find drug use morally or religiously offensive also benefit because their way of life is given societal legitimation. Who suffers when drugs are illegal? Those who make a living from selling drugs suffer, as well as people like John who, for whatever reason, include drug use as a part of their life-style.

Poverty is another example. Just about everybody professes to want to eradicate it. Yet, do we all suffer by its existence? Certainly families whose incomes are below the poverty level suffer. Yet do most other Americans? Not really. In fact, many Americans benefit from the persistence of poverty. Our fruits and vegetables would be much more expensive were it not for the many poorly paid migrant farm workers, most of whom survive at or near the poverty level. Hotel and motel rooms would cost more were it not for the poverty-level wages paid to the people who clean them. So, the life-style of affluent Americans rests on the backs of people who have no other choice but to work for poverty-level wages. Those who benefit from a condition like poverty might not be inclined to define it as a problem or to direct significant societal resources toward its alleviation.

Solutions to problems also involve opposition between groups because some solutions may be unacceptable to one of them. After all, we could eliminate poverty today through a redistribution of wealth in the United States: Raise everyone's taxes and give the money to the poor, who would then no longer be poor. However, most Americans would find this unacceptable, especially if it meant a decline in their own standard of living.

So, social problems are not objectively defined conditions that can be resolved merely through the application of technical expertise. Rather, they are political issues that involve opposition, subjectivity, and judgment. Social betterment is also not an objective condition but rather a judgment based on some group's vision of what society ought to be like. Furthermore, the power structure of society comes into play here because it is the groups in positions of power that will be better able to impose their judgments of what society ought to be like. When applied social research is used to "better" society, then, the research can become a part of this political process—a part of the exercise of power by oppositional groups. In an age that admires science and technology, the social "sciences" have symbolic value as a weapon that can be used by one group or another to foster certain outcomes. At times, the issue of opposition is ignored or buried—nobody talks about it—and a problem is treated as if there were consensus about it. In this atmosphere, the debate turns into one of technique—how to most efficiently achieve an outcome—rather than one of fundamental values and judgment. But social betterment is not an objective condition—it is a judgment. It involves conflicting values and interests and opposition between groups with varying amounts of power. Sociologists who conduct applied research get pulled into this conflict, and thus the values of the discipline and its relationship to the power structure become important issues to consider.

The Power Structure and Applied Research _____

Scientists are people, and scientific work is as much a social activity as going to a Christmas party, marrying a loved one, or fighting in battle. Science is a social activity in the sense that it is embedded in a particular sociocultural and social structural context, as these terms were defined in Chapter 1, and it has outcomes for society and for people's lives. Cultural values and personal interests shape how and why people do chemistry, geology, and sociology just as they shape how and why people get married or wear a particular fashion of clothing. Although scientists *strive* to be objective and use procedures that probably advance them toward that goal, they are still pervasively social creatures. Their scientific work is influenced by the sociocultural (values and interests) as well as the social structural (particularly, the power structure and patterns of dominance and subordination). This raises some very important ethical issues, and sociologists have tried to develop some guidelines on how to resolve them by defining the values upon which ethical research should rest.

Values and the Sociological Enterprise

Chapter 1 discussed the substance of the sociological perspective. Among other things, sociologists study the impact of the social structure on people's lives, and a major concern is the hierarchical nature of the social structure. The sociological perspective focuses on, among other things, the patterns of dominance and subordination in groups, the pervasiveness of inequality in human societies, and the exercise of power that expands some people's opportunities and restricts others'. Furthermore, sociological research has documented that these social structural elements are at least as important in shaping people's life chances and circumstances as are more individual factors such as personality or intelligence.

Chapter 1 also characterized science as the objective and disinterested search for knowledge—or at least it strives toward that model. So, the science of sociology attempts the dispassionate and objective study of the social structure—the dominance and subordination, the patterns of inequality, and the exercise of power that are found among all human groups. This is what I called basic sociology in Chapter 1. In the ideal, basic sociology doesn't try to support, justify, change, improve, or in any other way have an impact on that social structure. It merely says, "Here is how things work."

However, as we have seen, many sociologists, and especially the applied practitioners, lean toward the goal of social betterment or reform. But to reform something implies an image or ideal toward which change should progress. In other words, reform implies a set of values that guides proposals for change. What values do sociologists espouse? There is, of course, considerable variation in personal values among sociologists, and the profession of sociology has not established an official set of values that sociologists should adhere to in their personal lives. However, professional organizations do have codes of ethics relating to their members' professional behavior and these codes are based on certain values. Professional codes of ethics in sociology tend to rest, either implicitly or explicitly, on the following values:

1. The sanctity and worth of the individual as opposed to the group or collective,
2. The right of individuals to self-determination in their lives,
3. The importance of human equality in social relations, and
4. The establishment of fairness and equity in social relations.

The code of ethics of the Sociological Practice Association, for example, explicitly forbids any inhumane treatment of research subjects or discrimination on the basis of race, sex, religion, or a host of other characteristics. This ethical stance derives from the value placed on the worth of the individual and the importance of human equality. These values are also widely held by many Americans and are common themes in both American and Western societies. In other words, the values that underlie the ethics of professional sociologists tend to reflect the cultural environment in which the discipline of sociology emerged.

If you compare the substance of sociology with these values, the contrast between the two should be striking. Sociologists study patterns of dominance and subordination, but they value fairness; they investigate the exercise of power, yet they value self-determination; sociological study points to the pervasiveness of inequality in social relations, but sociologists value equality. This is not to imply that all sociologists would agree on how to achieve equality, fairness, or self-determination in social relations. But there is a sharp contrast between the professional values of sociologists and what they observe in society.

In terms of social betterment, we can begin to see that sociologists' values might affect their vision of what is a social problem and what would constitute the betterment of society. And these sociologists' visions could be quite different from the visions of others. Can or should the sociologists' vision influence their objective and systematic research work? Two of the areas where this can be an issue are advocacy and the exploitative uses of research.

Advocacy Versus Discovery: A Decline in Objectivity?

The mission of basic research is discovery, finding out through observation what exists in the world. This should also be true of applied research. Whether it be program evaluation or social impact assessment, the applied researcher's goal should be to discover whether a program works or on which social institutions a project impacts.

However, the sponsors who fund applied research may advocate for a particular outcome; they want their program to be shown to be effective or to have positive impacts on particular social institutions. Researchers may also advocate for a particular outcome because their personal values may be more compatible with one outcome of their research than another (Doris, 1982).

Advocacy doesn't create a problem, however, as long as the applied researchers are free to design scientifically valid evaluations. The problem arises when advocacy begins to influence the researcher's decisions and judgment. This influence can be very explicit, as when a sponsor tells a researcher to design an evaluation that will produce a particular outcome. More often, however, the influence is subtle, such as when a researcher gets drawn into close relationships with the sponsors and feels some social pressures to help keep their program going. Whether the influence is explicit or subtle the research turns more toward the goal of advocacy rather than discovery. Rather than focusing on an objective assessment of a problem, the research starts to look for *any* evidence that the program works.

This advocacy can influence the research process without, technically speaking, violating any of the canons of scientific research (Kytle and Millman, 1986; Johnson and Hougland, 1990). This happens when research is designed to find evidence that the lay public and program managers find convincing but that most scientists would judge to be very weak. For example, program managers might refuse to allow a control group in the assessment of the effects of an intervention. I discussed the importance of control groups in Chapter 4. The comparison between a treatment group and a control group is a more rigorous test of whether a treatment works. Without the control group, it is impossible to say whether any improvement among people receiving treatment was due to the treatment or to some other factor. So, if a group that goes through a drug education program uses fewer drugs at the end than in the beginning, laypeople may find this to be very convincing evidence that the drug education worked. Without the control group, however, scientists know that this is weak evidence because the reduction in drug usage might have occurred for other reasons, such as an increase in the price of drugs or a drop in their supply. From a technical point of view, the researcher has done nothing unethical by leaving out the control group. But the publication of the research report saying the treatment works provides scientific legitimation that the lay public may find convincing, even though it is actually very weak scientific support. Even if the researcher accurately qualifies the conclusions, some laypeople are likely to miss the subtleties involving weak research design and accept the conclusion—that the treatment works—without reservation.

Another way that an advocate could encourage a poor research design but not violate the technical canons of science would be to have a researcher use many measures of the dependent variable in hopes of finding *any* effect from an independent variable. In many cases, more than one measure of a dependent variable is used. The problem with using many measures, however, is that it increases the possibility that, by chance, one of the measures will show an effect even though there isn't any. An analogous result could happen with multiple choice examinations. If you don't know a body of material and I ask you one multiple choice question, you will probably answer that one question wrong, although with a four-alternative question, you have one chance in four of guessing the correct answer. However, if I ask you 25 questions, you will probably get at least one of them correct, by chance, even though you are unfamiliar with the material. The more questions you are asked, the more likely you are to answer one question correctly just by chance. Likewise, in research, the more dependent variable measures, the more likely it is that one of them will show an effect even if the independent variable has no effect on the dependent variable.

This is known in research as a Type I error: Your research shows that a program works when it actually doesn't (Figure 7.1). You have drawn an incorrect conclusion, but this is an error that some program managers could live with because it doesn't threaten funding for the program—the program appears to work. On the other hand, using only one measure of the dependent variable raises the possibility that even when the program actually works, your single measure cannot detect its effect, which may show up in some other area than the one you have measured. (Analogously, you could know a body of material but still answer one multiple choice question about it incorrectly.) This is called a Type II error: The program works but your research fails to show this. This is an error that no program manager would want to make because it might lead to curtailing a program that actually works.

Type I and Type II errors have to do with statistical analysis and they are complicated, but the basic dilemma is that you can't reduce the likelihood of both errors at the same time. In general, if you design a research project that reduces the likelihood of one type of error, the likelihood of the other type of error increases. Researchers are well aware of this and try to achieve some balance in designing research. A program manager or researcher-turned-advocate might push for designs that increase the likelihood of Type I errors because this gives the greatest likelihood of showing that the program works. However, researchers recognize that this also increases the probability of getting a false positive reading, showing a program works when it actually

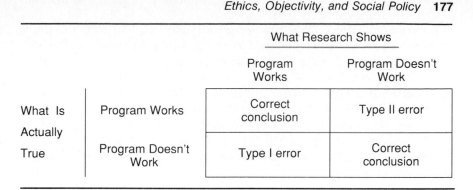

		What Research Shows	
		Program Works	Program Doesn't Work
What Is Actually True	Program Works	Correct conclusion	Type II error
	Program Doesn't Work	Type I error	Correct conclusion

Figure 7.1   Type I and Type II Errors

doesn't. The more Type I error increases, the less confidence scientists have that the conclusions are accurate.

So, the vision—the values and interests—of both applied sociologists and those who sponsor applied research can lead to advocacy and the possibility of bias and misleading outcomes. I hasten to add that there is nothing inherently wrong or unethical about advocating for some outcome. However, people need to be aware that advocacy and discovery are different activities, and the former can interfere with the latter. The line between them is not always clear, but applied researchers need to be on guard for ways in which pressures toward advocacy can threaten the integrity of the research. This is yet another reason for the concern in this book about issues of validity, reliability, and proper research design—all the elements of systematic observation. If a study is properly designed, then researcher advocacy and sponsor advocacy will have less of an effect on the outcome.

Exploitative Uses of Applied Research

Sociologists conducting applied research may find themselves working within hierarchical structures of dominance and subordination. The groups who fund their research have their own visions of what social betterment is, what conditions should be considered problems, and what solutions are best. These research sponsors have a variety of motives for wanting to see particular outcomes in the research. In the public sector, for example, administrators of social programs may want more funds for their programs or a director of a department of corrections may want more effective techniques to control the behavior of prison inmates. In the private sector, a primary motivation of businesspeople is to increase profits and create conditions that are beneficial to their business or corporation. For some sociologists, all of this raises questions about the potentially exploitative uses to which applied sociology could be put. When applied sociologists conduct research for one group in such contexts, are they helping to maintain and extend the patterns of dominance and subordination and working against the interests of other groups? Are they choosing sides? And, because it is virtually always the dominant groups in the power structure that can afford to employ applied researchers, does applied sociology simply become another weapon that the powerful can use to dominate and exploit those subordinate to them? If so, then sociology as an objective quest for knowledge gets turned into a coercive and exploitative tool of government bureaucrats or corporate chiefs.

Now, sociologists recognize that some level of dominance, subordination, and control are common and may even be necessary to maintain the social order. After all, this is at the core of sociological knowledge (see Chapter 1). However, given the values of the profession discussed in this chapter—self-determination, the worth of the individual, equity, fairness—it is not surprising that many sociologists are concerned about *exploitation,* the excessive and unnecessary exercise of power and dominance that benefits one group to the significant disadvantage of another. So, one of the basic ethical dilemmas some applied sociologists address is whether their research will be used to help maintain or extend exploitative patterns of dominance and subordination. After all, as technical expertise, applied sociological research could be used to enhance the control of men over women or to help perpetuate discrimination and prejudice against members of particular racial groups. Sociological knowledge could even have been used by early American slaveholders to control their slaves or by Nazi rulers of concentration camps to induce passivity or conformity among their inmates.

Most people would, justifiably, recoil from such uses of applied sociology. Yet dominance and inequality exist in many less grotesque and more subtle forms. Should applied sociologists assist the school system in gaining greater control over its students or prison officials in exercising social control over inmates? Should applied research be used to enhance corporate profits or strengthen corporate control over employees? Market research (see Chapter 6) is part of a marketing effort to convince people to purchase corporate products, whether people really need them or not. Is it ethical for applied researchers to help market fashionable clothing to people who don't need it or can't afford it? Is it moral for market researchers to help convince people to purchase and consume cigarettes? As I mentioned earlier in this chapter, domination, exploitation, and the exercise of power are inherent features of every social order. However, the question remains of when it is ethical for applied sociologists to jump into this fray and provide services to one group in this struggle—the government agency or the corporation—that may work to the detriment of others—employees, clients, or consumers.

This is an extremely difficult issue to resolve because, although sociologists might value equality or self-determination, they also recognize that some degree of dominance, inequality, and hierarchy are probably inevitable in society and in some situations even legitimate. Where does one draw the line regarding what is ethical in applied research? An example is considered in Research in Action 7.1.

RESEARCH IN ACTION 7.1 ▬▬▬▬▬▬▬▬▬▬▬▬▬▬▬▬▬▬▬▬▬▬▬

Should Sociologists Assist Employee Drug Testing?

These days, corporations routinely use random drug tests as mechanisms of control over their employees, refusing to hire those who test positive and forcing employees who test positive to change their lives or risk losing their jobs. Applied sociologists have been asked to help implement and evaluate such programs, just like the one that determined John was a drug user. Would it be ethical for an applied sociologist to participate in such programs? Is the difference between the concentration camp control over inmates and the corporate control over employees only a matter of degree? If so, where does one draw the line between what it is ethical to support and not to support?

Sociologist David Barrows (1990) has challenged sociologists' participation in such programs. Even though the programs are legal in some cases, Barrows argues, they are still being challenged on constitutional and other grounds. Some people feel that the tests are an invasion of privacy because people are forced to use their own bodies (e.g., to provide blood or urine) in unacceptable ways. Others feel that the tests involve an unreasonable search. The Fourth Amendment to the Constitution states that people have a "right ... to be secure in their persons, houses, papers, and effects, against unreasonable searches and seizures." It is unconstitutional to search a house without permission or without a warrant, yet corporations are allowed to search through and confiscate their employees' bodily fluids. Beyond the constitutional issues, Barrows also argues that the drug tests are of questionable accuracy and have a good probability of wrongly accusing people of illegal drug use.

On the other side of this debate is the argument that corporations have a legitimate right to protect themselves against employee actions that might reduce productivity or represent a danger to other employees or the public. An employee with a substance abuse problem may cost the company money because of absenteeism or may endanger other employees because of carelessness. In addition, the company policy focuses on the use of illegal drugs, which, many people feel, constitutes a serious social problem.

Implicit in this debate over drug testing programs is the issue of whether people are being treated fairly and whether excessive or undue power and dominance are being exerted over employees by the corporation. Is it fair to John to restrict his personal behavior when his job performance has been neither affected nor questioned? Is it fair to restrict John's job opportunities based on a test that is wrong one out of 20 times? What level of corporate control—what level of exercise of power by one group over another—is fair? And, most fundamentally, Barrows questions whether sociologists should offer their knowledge and expertise to the more powerful group in what is a clash of interests between two groups: a corporation with huge resources and relatively powerless employees. Other sociologists would disagree with Barrows that participating in such programs constitutes an exploitative use of applied research. The point here is that the potential exploitative use of applied research is an issue that applied researchers need to address. Each sociologist must then use his or her own professional and personal values to decide how to resolve the debate in particular cases.

The Applied Researcher as "Hired Gun"

Given the issues just described—advocacy and the potential exploitative uses of applied research—some have argued that applied researchers are simply "hired guns": "simple-minded technicians who blindly carry out the mandates of people with funds" (Patton, 1981:4). Since the sponsor of the research decides what research questions are to be investigated and some of the parameters of the research method, some argue that the applied researcher has sold out. The old adage that "He who pays the fiddler picks the tune" seems to apply here. The researcher's role has been reduced to that of providing technical expertise on sampling strategy, research design, and statistical analysis. He or she is like the legendary hired guns of the Old West who merely went after those their employer told them to find. And because it is the powerful and influential in the corporate and government realms who have the funds to support applied research, the applied researcher ends up as the hired gun of the powerful and influential in society.

The real debate here is not over whether this can happen because it can and probably does happen. The real debate is whether applied research is, by its very nature, "hired gun" research. Michael Quinn Patton, who has done considerable applied research himself, argues that even basic researchers are not removed from such pressures: "In basic research the coin of the realm is promotion, tenure, and status within the profession" (1981:4). The basic researcher can be tempted to choose research topics and techniques that are viewed favorably by other sociologists in order to enhance the likelihood of promotion and tenure or finding a better job at a more prestigious university. Or basic researchers might cater to the desires of the major agencies that provide funds for so much basic research, such as the National Science Foundation or the National Institute of Mental Health, and design their research in a way that will be acceptable to these organizations. The basic researcher can become a hired gun who merely does what powerful figures in the profession (senior colleagues or those on promotion and tenure committees or funding review boards) consider to be "good" research. Patton (1981:4) concludes:

> The difference, then, is not that sociological practitioners have less integrity than basic researchers. The distinction is that there are different reference groups available to look to in making decisions about what topic of research to undertake. The basic researchers look to colleagues and disciplinary traditions; the social science practitioner looks to people who have specific questions they need answered in order to take action.

So, the issue of integrity can arise for both basic and applied researchers, but it is a slightly different problem for each. If basic researchers seek guidance from their colleagues, those colleagues share certain professional values regarding how to select research problems and conduct research. In other words, the guidance of these colleagues is likely to be more helpful in shaping a professionally and ethically sound research project. On the other hand, the program managers or corporate chiefs to whom the applied researcher looks do not have the professional training in research methods and ethical practice that sociological colleagues receive. They will be less helpful as guides and may be more likely to push in the direction of inappropriate or unethical topics or techniques. This confronts applied researchers with the task of educating sponsors, a task that basic researchers will probably not have. Ultimately, the applied researcher may have to decline to participate in a project if the sponsors insist on guiding it in a direction that the researcher considers inappropriate. But then basic researchers would presumably face a similar dilemma if their colleagues guided them in a direction they considered inappropriate.

So, hired guns can be found, to some degree, among both basic and applied researchers. Science does, however, provide some checks on this. One is the professional socialization of scientists that trains them to place great value on the integrity of the scientific method described in earlier chapters, which should take precedence over any other influences on their actions. Another check is the peer review process in which other scientists review research to assess its validity and objectivity. A third check is replication: The repetition of studies by different scientists can serve as a check on whether the outcome was biased in some fashion. However, there is probably less peer review and replication in applied than in basic research and therefore fewer checks to detect whether hired gun research has produced invalid or biased results. Although this does not necessarily mean that there is more hired gun research in applied research, it does lead applied researchers to be especially alert to the possibility that their work might, even without their being aware of it, take on some shades of hired gun research.

Resolution of the Ethical Dilemmas

A number of ethical questions have been raised: Can scientists' values result in bias in their research? Should applied sociologists participate in research that is exploitative in nature? Are applied researchers really just hired guns? Although each question must be approached in terms of the specific context in which it arises, there are two distinct approaches to many of the ethical issues discussed here.

The Value-Free Approach. One is a *freedom from values* approach (Kytle and Millman, 1986). Some positivists would claim that they have no values or that their values do not intrude on their scientific work of description and discovery. In this view, science is an objective quest for knowledge and should be, essentially, a value-free quest: supporting no sides in any struggle, but merely accumulating more knowledge about how the world works. This stance is more common among basic than applied researchers. However, as I have tried to emphasize, although science strives toward objectivity as an ideal, it seems to frequently—maybe always and inherently—fall short of the mark. Because science is basically social in nature and values are so pervasive, it seems too simplistic to claim that science can ever be completely value-free. Personal values and group interests will probably always be a threat to the objectivity and validity of research, even when scientists believe they are acting in a value-free fashion.

The Value Clarity Approach. The second approach recognizes that human values can and will influence objectivity and opts for *value clarity*: clearly stating one's values so that others can judge their potential impact on research and interpretation. This does not necessarily solve the ethical dilemma, but it does make it a point of explicit discussion and forces all parties to grapple with it. It reduces the likelihood that research will be pursued with some hidden agenda where some groups benefit and others lose. The value clarity approach avoids the technocratic view of social problems discussed earlier by recognizing that every party to a research situation—researcher and sponsor as well as research subject—can have an interest in a particular outcome. Each has a vision that leads to the designation of a condition as a problem and the choice of particular solutions. Value clarity brings this opposition and conflict of interest into the open. For example, the Sociological Practice Association (1987:5) recommends that when there is a conflict of interest, sociologists should "clarify the nature and direction of their loyalties and responsibilities and keep all parties informed of their commitments." This enables others to make judgments about continuing involvement with the sociologist and about how his or her values might bias the research. The position involves a clear recognition of the political nature of social life, as well as of the role of scientific research. It is sometimes easy to ignore this aspect when applied research focuses on some narrow application, and the client may not be interested in a broader analysis of the problem. However, the fact that the political nature of social problems is not addressed in a research project doesn't mean that it doesn't exist. Policymakers often tend to assume that the technical expertise provided by social scientists means that they are dealing merely with a technical, rather than political, problem. Yet sociologists recognize the profoundly political nature of the process.

Figure 7.2 suggests some of the groups that might be involved in this political process, influencing the research process and potentially being affected by the outcome of applied research. The stake of each of these groups in a particular research project needs to be explicitly addressed. Then it is possible to prioritize whose interests should be given greater weight. Consider the following hierarchy, with those listed first being given higher priority (Kytle and Millman, 1986):

1. The advancement of knowledge (if this is compromised, then scientific research is meaningless),
2. The community (the benefit of society as a whole, if this is relevant, should precede the benefit of any special groups or interests),
3. The professional research community (good research enhances the integrity and legitimacy of research in general),
4. The client (program administrators, corporate executives, or some other special interests who sponsor the research),
5. The individual researcher (researchers who produce valid and useful results might be well paid for their efforts).

So, this hierarchy suggests that the advancement of scientific knowledge should never be compromised in order to advance the interests of a client nor should the interests of a client or an individual researcher be placed before the good of the community as a whole. Obviously, not

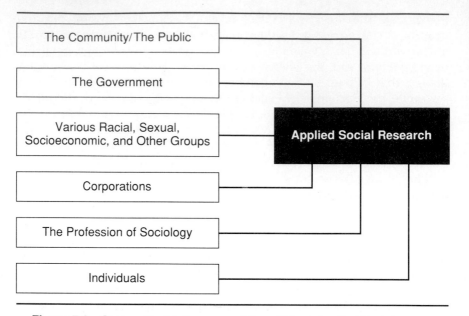

Figure 7.2 Groups That Influence and Benefit from Applied Social Research

all of these interests will be involved in every research project, and some people might arrange this hierarchy in a different order, possibly adding some other interest groups that have not been included. However, the point is not that this prioritizing is the best one or the only one possible. The point is that creating a priority system forces the researcher to think explicitly about which groups might be affected by research and in which way. It clarifies whose values and interests are being given priority and can assist in identifying and resolving ethical dilemmas.

Socially Responsible Research. The hierarchy of interests is a helpful guide in struggling with ethical dilemmas, but it does not point clearly and directly to a solution in every case. Reality is much too complex for that. If we focus just on the exploitative uses of applied research, there are varying degrees of dominance and subordination in organizations, and much of it is quite legitimate. A decision must be made in each case regarding whether research is ethical. After all, applied research in hierarchical settings might be highly beneficial to all or it might be highly exploitative. A hierarchy of benefits can help in making this judgment.

This approach is somewhat analogous to what has come to be called the *socially responsible* investment in the stocks and bonds of corporations. In the 1970s and 1980s, some investors, concerned with issues like environmental pollution and discrimination, decided they wanted to promote what they considered a just world while at the same time earning a profit through corporate investment. The idea was that if they invested in a company that polluted the environment, they were contributing to that pollution. So, these investors made decisions about what corporations to invest in based on the companies' social track records as well as their economic strengths. They bought the stocks and bonds of corporations that didn't pollute the environment, paid men and women equal salaries for equivalent work, and treated their employees with fairness and dignity. In this view, it is perfectly acceptable to share in the profits of a corporation if the corporation exhibits some social responsibility: if it produces healthy products; pays its employees a fair and just wage; doesn't discriminate on the basis of race, ethnicity, age, or gender; and works to protect the environment.

By analogy, it would be ethical to conduct applied research for agencies or corporations that exhibit similar social responsibility and, in addition, would not use the results of the research to unfairly manipulate or exploit their employees, the public, or the consumer. In some sociologists' view, it might be unethical to do market research for a cigarette company because the product is inherently unhealthy. However, it might be perfectly acceptable to help a corporation that sells health care products or a criminal justice system that wants to provide a safer prison environment for inmates and correctional personnel.

A researcher who takes this view must still make judgments about what is meant by social responsibility, how socially responsible a particular agency or company is, and which aspects of social responsibility are more important than others. After all, bureaucracies and corporations have a legitimate right to exercise some authority and control over their employees and those to whom they provide services. Where legitimate authority crosses the boundary into exploitative control is, of course, a matter of considerable judgment and debate. However, this approach does provide a framework for deciding whether participation by an applied researcher in a hierarchical organizational context is ethical. But the guidelines don't tell the researcher what to do; as in other areas of ethical decision making, they only point to some general rules and principles that can be used in applying individual judgment to an ethical dilemma.

Much sociological research has focused on the inequitable distribution of resources in society, and one manifestation of that is the fact that the more powerful groups can fund applied research while the less fortunate in society are more often the subjects of research interest rather than the sponsors of the research. Research in Action 7.2 suggests some ways in which the discipline might deal with this issue.

RESEARCH IN ACTION 7.2 ▬▬▬▬▬▬▬▬▬▬▬▬▬▬▬▬▬▬

Should There Be a Program of "Sociological Aid"?

Chapter 5 described the case of Joan Little, a poor woman accused of murdering her jailer. In one way, she was lucky: Her treatment by the criminal justice system led to an outpouring of sympathy and financial support for her defense. As we saw, this enabled her defense team to include applied social researchers who could use their tools to assist her in getting a fair trial. Normally, only the rich and powerful can afford such a defense. This is typically the case with applied research: The privileged and powerful are more likely to be able to use applied research to their own benefit.

Sociologist Edna Bonacich (1990:7) expressed concerns about this issue in this way:

Many people become sociologists because they want to make society more just. Yet they find themselves either doing research on behalf of existing power structures because that is where funding is obtained; or doing research for their own professional career advancement.

One resolution for this dilemma, she suggests, is for the discipline of sociology to establish a program of *sociological aid,* similar to legal aid. Just as legal aid lawyers provide free or low-cost legal assistance to the poor and others without resources, sociological aid sociologists would provide free or low-cost research expertise to community groups who might benefit from it but cannot afford it. This would provide some counterbalance to the already established tendency for the rich and powerful to put research to work for their own benefit. In fact, in its code of ethics, the Sociological Practice Association (1987:5) calls for applied sociologists to "willingly contribute a portion of their services to work for which they receive little or no financial return." This would make some research expertise available to advocacy groups working for the poor, minorities, and other groups who normally would not have access to the research community.

▬▬▬▬▬▬▬▬▬▬▬▬▬▬▬▬▬▬▬▬▬▬▬▬▬▬▬▬▬▬▬▬

Ethical Obligations in Conducting Applied Research _____

Thus far, the ethical issues discussed in this chapter have been rather broad in nature: namely, *whether* it is ethical to conduct a particular type of research at all. Ethical issues do not end here, however. Once the decision is made that a research project is ethically acceptable, ethics are also important in deciding *how* to conduct research. As two applied social researchers put it:

> The principles of research are important not only as standards of practice but also as an expression of a moral code, a code of ethics. They express what cannot be done and sometimes what should be done ... to the people being studied. (Kytle and Millman, 1986:168)

So, the research principles and techniques discussed throughout this book involve an implied moral code, namely, that ethical research uses the most valid and reliable techniques available, states any weaknesses or limitations in the methods, and treats research subjects and sponsors in an ethically proper fashion. To do otherwise is considered a violation of professional ethical standards. The last point is the focus of this discussion: What is ethical in the treatment of research subjects and sponsors? These ethical research practices build on the personal values discussed earlier in this chapter but also involve some additional values that are widely held in contemporary American society (Sieber, 1982; Tymchuk, 1982; Bruhn, 1991):

1. People have a right to privacy.
2. People are not to be harmed intentionally.
3. Contracts that are moral and have been entered into freely and legally should be honored.

Ethical Treatment of Research Subjects

There are a number of ethical standards that researchers adhere to in their treatment of the people on whom they conduct research.

Informed Consent. Given the value placed on individual self-determination, people should be allowed to decide *whether* their thoughts, feelings, or actions will be used in a research project. This means obtaining their informed consent: telling them about all aspects of the research that might reasonably influence their decision to participate and obtaining their verbal or written agreement to participate. A consent statement might include information on the sponsor of the research, the topic of the research and the use to which the results will be put, any intrusive or uncomfortable procedures or situations that might be involved, and any other information that might influence a person's decision to participate. Coercion or deception should never be used in obtaining consent.

In some cases, informed consent may not be necessary. Most researchers, for example, would balance the desirability of informed consent against both the feasibility of obtaining it and the importance of the research. If informed consent would be very difficult or costly to obtain, if the research goals are clearly very important, and if no harm will come to the subjects, then many researchers would agree that informed consent can be ignored. Informed consent may also not be necessary when organizational records, such as the membership lists of organizations or the case records in the criminal justice system, are used. These records are often the property of the organization rather than the individuals whose lives make up the record, and legally the organization may be able to do with its records as it pleases. Yet some researchers would argue that there is an informed consent issue at stake here: People should be allowed to decide whether records kept on them will be used in research.

Other than these exceptions, however, researchers agree that informed consent is ethically essential. To do otherwise is to deny people the right to determine the uses to which their beliefs and actions will be put. In addition, when considering whether informed consent is necessary in a particular research project, researchers are aware that their judgments about how important the research goals are and whether the research subjects will suffer harm can be influenced by the researcher's personal interests and values—a major point of this chapter. A personal interest in completing a research project might lead one to downplay the significance of potential harm. So, informed consent should be ignored only after careful assessment of these issues, possibly including consultation with other researchers who do not have personal stakes in the particular research.

Privacy. In the United States, personal integrity and self-determination are highly valued. People want control of their lives and the issues that might affect them. Given these values, researchers make great efforts to maintain people's right to privacy. Privacy is the right to control when people will have access to your values, beliefs, or behaviors. After all, in the course of their research, sociologists learn many personal and sensitive facts about people—their sexual preferences, grades in school, or criminal records. People may not want these things to become known to others. Furthermore, sociologists are not always able to say what aspects of life a person will consider sensitive. I might not care whether others know of my grades in school, but another person might perceive school grades as a very personal matter that he or she would prefer that others not know about. For these reasons, researchers use some well-established procedures that, taken together, will effectively protect privacy in the vast majority of cases.

One such procedure is the use of informed consent. This enables a person who does not want personal information revealed to decline to participate in the research. Even when people do participate, however, procedures should be implemented to protect their privacy. Another procedure is the use of anonymous data collection techniques. **Anonymity** means that *it is impossible for anyone, even the researcher, to identify the responses of any particular individual.* For example, a mailed survey would be anonymous if the respondents did not put their names on it and there were no identifying names or numbers on the survey mailed back to the researchers. Then, there is no way for anyone to link the responses on a particular returned survey to any individual.

Anonymity is often difficult to achieve. In some cases, researchers may need to know the names of those who return questionnaires so that those who have not returned them can be contacted (see Chapter 5). In these cases, a third procedure that can be used is **confidentiality,** or *not publicly identifying the responses of any individuals in the research.* The researcher may have the data stored along with the identities of individuals but promises not to report who gave which responses. Once data have been collected, breaches of confidentiality can be reduced if identifying names are separated from the data. Each case can be given an identification number and the names destroyed; after that no one can link names with responses. Or, if it is necessary to keep the names, the project director can keep a master file that links names with identification numbers, but others going through the data file will not be able to do so.

In choosing between anonymity and confidentiality, remember that third parties, including the courts, can seek the names of research participants. The confidence of the researcher-respondent relationship is not considered legally protected, as is the lawyer-client or doctor-patient relationship. Courts have subpoenaed social scientists and insisted that they reveal names and other data in court. Refusal to do so can result in criminal charges. Respondents should always be told if their responses are anonymous or confidential. They should never be misinformed about this in order to increase the likelihood of participation. And procedures need to be carefully reviewed to ensure that they are truly anonymous or confidential. For example, if there are identifying numbers on the questionnaire that are only for purposes of assessing the response rate and will be removed once the questionnaires are received, only confidentiality can be claimed because it is possible for the researcher to link responses to an individual, even though there are no plans to do so.

A final procedure for protecting privacy is to report data only at the group or aggregate level. This is in fact the way most applied research is reported. Usually we want to know what percentage of a particular group were recidivists or what proportion of teens from a particular social background became pregnant. This type of analysis can tell us how effective a program is or how much need there is for a particular service. Rarely would it be helpful to know which particular individuals were recidivists or became pregnant. So, this group level of analysis helps protect the privacy of individuals.

There are some controversial areas where sociologists disagree on the importance of informed consent and protecting privacy. For example, some researchers argue that *public* behavior is not subject to the same demands for informed consent and privacy. A public act, they argue, is available for all to observe, including researchers gathering data. However, there is much disagreement over what is a "public" place. Obviously, one's home is not public. What about one's place of work? What about public rest rooms? One sociologist created a storm of controversy by making disguised observations of men engaging in homosexual actions in a public rest room (Humphreys, 1970). He argued that the rest room was public, the men going there knew that, and so their behavior was observable by any male who went into the rest room, including sociological observers. He did not feel that privacy rights had been violated or that informed consent was needed. His critics argued that the men were clearly trying to hide their behavior by using lookouts who warned of the approach of police or any straight males—sufficient evidence that they did not want their behavior observed. If they had known their behavior was being recorded and would be used for some particular research purpose, they may well have behaved differently. They behaved as they did, in part, because they were uninformed about the uses to which their behavior would be put by someone else. This was a very controversial piece of research, and it shows the difficulty of clearly specifying when certain ethical principles apply.

Deception. The use of deception in research has been a controversial topic because some research cannot be conducted without a degree of deception (Elms, 1982; Baumrind, 1985). For example, people are sometimes misled or misinformed about the research hypotheses because we have learned from volumes of research that people act differently when they know what the hypotheses are. They tend to give researchers the answers they think the researchers want rather than acting naturally. (This is a version of the problem of reactivity discussed in a number of chapters.) However, there is a tension between deception and informed consent: The more a person is deceived, the less informed is their consent. Because of this, some sociologists take the position that all deception is unethical.

Most sociologists, however, would take a less extreme position on this issue, recognizing that eliminating deception entirely would place severe limitations on the kinds and amounts of research that could be done. They argue that deception is acceptable if (1) it is essential to carrying out the research, (2) the goals of the research are important, (3) it will bring no harm to the research subjects, and (4) the information withheld would not likely influence people's decisions about whether to participate in the research. Regarding this last point, research has shown that knowledge of sponsorship and of the overall purposes of the research do influence people's decision to participate (Heberlein and Baumgartner, 1978; Goyder, 1985). There are times when a sponsor might prefer to remain unknown (e.g., a corporation that is trying to influence people to purchase its products), but people should never be deceived about this because it seriously compromises informed consent.

On the other hand, people are often left in the dark as to whether they are in the experimental group or control group because people who are told they are receiving a treatment sometimes show improvement whether or not they actually receive the treatment. If we don't deceive people about this, it is difficult to say if changes are produced by the treatment itself or by people's belief that they are receiving treatment. However, when such deception is used, people are often told, as a part of informed consent, that they might be deceived about this. In addition, when deciding if deception is warranted, researchers should carefully assess whether their personal interests and values are affecting their judgment about whether the deception is necessary or whether the information withheld might influence people's decision to participate. As with informed consent, it may be desirable to consult with other researchers who do not have a personal interest in the decision.

Harm or Distress. Only rarely would social science research expose research subjects to the possibility of physical harm or injury. The possibility of psychological harm or emotional distress, however, can be a real one. For example, people may learn something negative or unsettling about themselves. They may learn that they rank rather low in comparison to others on some test of abilities or that they have low self-esteem or harbor prejudices toward some minority group. The general ethical principle is to avoid exposing research participants to any harm or distress, whether physical, psychological, or emotional. This cannot always be avoided, but if there is harm or distress involved, it must be justified by research goals that are sufficiently important to outweigh the risks involved and there is no alternative way to accomplish the goals. This, of course, is a judgment, and it must be considered very carefully by researchers. In fact, some social scientists would argue that researchers do not have any superior wisdom or insight with which to make this judgment and would reject as unethical any research with a clear risk of harm, especially if the harm could be substantial (Bailey, 1978). If the decision is made to proceed with research involving some risk, then participants must be fully informed so that they can decide whether to expose themselves to it.

When the potential for harm exists, the research design will typically include a debriefing session in which the researcher can assess whether any harm or distress has occurred and alleviate its impact. The harm or distress caused by social science research is typically mild, and it can usually be alleviated through reassurance and an explanation of what the research was about. Even in research where harm is not anticipated, researchers need to monitor for any unanticipated negative reactions that people might have.

Ethics in Sponsored Research

The sponsor of a research project is the person, organization, or agency that provides the funds and other resources that make the research possible. The sponsor of basic research is often a government agency or private foundation (Monette, Sullivan, and DeJong, 1990). For example, the National Science Foundation and the Ford Foundation provide grants for sociological research. These organizations also fund applied social research, but so do private corporations, and large and small human service agencies, such as a department of corrections, a community mental health center, or an agency providing child-care services to a community. Applied research virtually always has a sponsor—an agency or organization that paid to have the research done in order to help solve a problem or answer a question. A major difference between many basic and applied research projects is that with the latter the sponsor almost always wants some very precise recommendations for action from the research. This is only sometimes true in basic research. So, certain ethical considerations arise from this sponsor-researcher relationship.

The Contract. Researchers and sponsors will develop a contract, which is an agreement regarding what research will be done and for what fees. This contract should be as precise as possible to avoid problems. It should detail the precise methodology to be used, such as an experiment or quasi-experiment, and the data-gathering technique, such as a survey or the use of existing data. However, it is not always possible to be this specific because the contract may include provisions for developing the most appropriate design and techniques. The contract should also specify deadlines for accomplishing tasks and precisely what products, such as written or verbal reports, are expected as a consequence of the research. The contract should also include provisions relating to the resolution of any ethical issues in the relationship with the sponsor. Once this contract is agreed to, the researcher is ethically bound to live up to all of its provisions and to complete the research as specified in the contract.

Public Dissemination of Results. In most basic research, even when funded by a sponsor, it is assumed that the full results will be published by the researcher because the goal of the research is to advance our knowledge, no matter what the outcome. However, as we have seen, applied research typically involves more advocacy: Sponsors are desirous of a particular outcome and may not want negative results made public. Control over public dissemination of results should be spelled out in the contract. In some cases, a researcher might not want to agree to a contract if dissemination will be limited. However, it would be unethical for researchers to publish results if they had contractually agreed with the sponsor not to do so.

This issue of public dissemination of the results can create dilemmas for the researcher: What if the research shows some negative consequence of a program but the sponsor prefers not to make that public? What if the research shows that a very expensive program is not achieving its goals or is actually making matters worse? Does the researcher have a moral responsibility to the public or to those served by the program to inform them of the results? Most researchers, in most cases, would say, No. The stronger ethical commitment is to the sponsor with whom the researcher has made an explicit agreement not to release the results. However, if the negative effects of the research are very serious or widespread, and if the sponsor does not respond by making changes in the program to reduce these negative effects, some applied researchers would argue that the researcher must act as a "whistle blower" by going outside of the contract and releasing the results. In addition, if the sponsor makes public a distorted version of the research results, it would be ethically acceptable for the researcher to make public an accurate version. When these sorts of conflicts between sponsor and researcher arise, the Sociological Practice Association (1987:6) provides some guidance by recommending that researchers "attempt to affect change by constructive action within the organization before disclosing confidential information acquired in their professional roles." This offers a strategy that, if effective, would resolve the ethical dilemma. If it doesn't work, then the applied sociologist still has an ethical judgment to make. This is an area of considerable disagreement. Some applied researchers would even refuse to sign a contract that did not allow them to make a full disclosure of results.

Research Outcome. It is considered highly unethical in applied research to promise a sponsor that research will show a particular outcome. As strange as it may seem, I have talked with program managers who said, in effect, "I don't want to pay for research that shows my program doesn't work." Such managers are understandably under pressure to show that the funds expended on their program actually achieve something of value. If they don't, the program may be cut. They might encourage researchers to lie about results, suppress negative findings, report only the positive outcomes, or manipulate the findings (to "lie with statistics") in order to give a favorable impression to the outcome. In addition, many managers are truly convinced that their programs do work. And it is possible for a program to work even if the research fails to show that. This can happen, for example, if the researcher measures variables that the program actually doesn't impact on and fails to measure variables that it does impact on; it can also happen when researchers use measures that are not reliable or valid. So, given managers' belief that their program works and the possible failure of research to show this, it is more understandable why some managers may express reluctance to dole out funds without some assurances about the outcome.

Nevertheless, it is still unethical to promise a certain outcome. To do so would call for the researcher to change the data if they come out negative, and this is never acceptable. It is considered equally unethical to manipulate the data such that there is any inaccuracy or deception in the results reported. Researchers are professionally obliged to give a complete and accurate accounting of the results. The solution to the manager's dilemma is to design the most valid research possible and then be very clear about any of its weaknesses and limitations. Once this is done, researchers are required to report the findings completely and honestly. Inaccurate or deceptive reporting of results threatens the integrity and credibility of all science and research.

Quality Research. Researchers have an obligation to provide the highest quality research for the sponsors with whom they contract. This means developing the most appropriate research design and selecting the most valid data-gathering techniques. It also means that researchers should not agree to conduct research that they do not have the skills and expertise to complete. It can be somewhat difficult for a sponsor to assess the qualifications of a person being considered as an applied social researcher, but there are some criteria that can be used.

One is the candidate's educational attainments: An applied social researcher should have an M.A. or Ph.D. degree in sociology or a related social science discipline. A second criterion is an institutional affiliation, such as working in a research position for a university, a government bureau, a corporation, or a research consulting firm. These institutions have mechanisms for ensuring that only competent researchers are employed. A third criterion is any previous research projects the person has been involved in that document his or her skills. A final criterion includes any professional publications or activities. If the person has published a textbook on social science research methods or conducted seminars to train others in research methods, there can be some assurance about his or her skills.

So, sponsors need to search for researchers with the appropriate skills for their project, and researchers need to be forthright about their qualification to conduct research. An ethical researcher will refuse to contract for research that he or she is not competent to do.

Codes of Ethics

We have covered a lot of ethical territory in this chapter. You should, by this point, be aware of both the complexity and the subtlety of the ethical issues that applied researchers confront. Ethical issues are difficult and controversial because they involve judgment, assessment, and interpretation. To help practitioners with these issues, most professional organizations provide a written code of ethics that can be used in navigating through these very treacherous waters. Although these codes of ethics do not settle all issues, they do provide a foundation and framework that can assist practitioners to carry out ethical practice. Both the American Sociological Association and the Sociological Practice Association have published codes of ethics, and copies can be obtained by contacting them (see the Appendix).

CRITICAL THINKING

The Integrity of the Scientific Method

One point that emerges from this discussion of ethics in applied research is the importance of maintaining the integrity of the scientific method. This, after all, is what sociology contributes to our efforts to understand the world and what this book has been all about: a systematic method of obtaining the most valid, reliable, error-free, and bias-free knowledge of the world around us. We maintain its integrity by insisting on the highest ethical standards and on the strictest adherence to valid and reliable research methods. That is the coin of the realm; that is what we have to offer society: a sound technique for gaining knowledge. Any practice that threatens that integrity—any sociological practitioner, for example, who would promise a sponsor a particular outcome no matter what the data say—is a threat to the very core of applied social research. So, all research decisions and the resolution of all ethical issues focus on maintaining the integrity of that scientific method.

These concerns of researchers relating to ethics, objectivity, and public policy also harbor some lessons for critical thinkers in general. Some of the sociocultural and structural factors that can shape the actions of researchers can also sway the thinking of people in their everyday lives. So, when assessing research or information and arguments that are presented to you, consider the following points:

1. What is your structural position in society? Where to you fit in terms of such characteristics as social class, income, education, gender, race, and so on? How does this status influence your own personal interests and your reaction to research and arguments?
2. In terms of your sociocultural position, what personal values influence your views of information, arguments, or research results?
3. What vision of social betterment seems to underlie your view of the world? What oppositional groups come into play in defining a particular issue as a social problem?
4. In terms of the hierarchy of interests discussed in this chapter, who benefits from particular research outcomes? Society as a whole? Or does the research serve the interests of some groups but work to the detriment of others?
5. As far as you can tell, are there any unethical practices engaged in relating to the treatment of research subjects or research sponsors?

Key Terms for Review _____

anonymity   ethics
confidentiality   public policy

For Further Inquiry _____

William Broad and Nicholas Wade. *Betrayers of the Truth: Fraud and Deceit in the Halls of Science.* New York: Simon & Schuster, 1983.
> This book describes many of the frauds that have been perpetrated by scientists, mostly in the natural sciences. It is interesting to read and suggests the rather disturbing conclusion that fraud may be both easy to carry out and common in science.

L. S. Hearnshaw. *Cyril Burt, Psychologist.* Ithaca, NY: Cornell University Press, 1979.

> Hearnshaw analyzes a classic case in which fraudulent social science research findings were translated into public policy. A psychologist falsified data to show that heredity outweighed environmental factors in producing intelligence, and this was used as a basis for educational policy.

Allan J. Kimmel. *Ethics and Values in Applied Social Research.* Newbury Park, CA: Sage, 1988.

> This book presents a more complete overview of ethical issues in applied research than could be accomplished in this brief chapter.

James B. Rule. *Insight and Social Betterment: A Preface to Applied Social Science.* New York: Oxford University Press, 1978.

> This is an excellent analysis of the nature of social problems and social betterment. Rule goes far beyond this chapter in assessing what role sociology can and should play in this process.

Exercises

7.1. Review some research articles in journals that publish applied social research (see the listing in the Appendix). Can you find any research about which there could be some ethical question about whether the research should have been done at all? State the arguments for and against doing the research.

7.2. For these same research articles, point out the ethical issues that arose in relation to research subjects or sponsors (e.g., privacy) and how they were resolved? Do there appear to be ethical issues that the authors don't discuss in the articles? What are they? How might they have been resolved?

7.3. Obtain the code of ethics from one of the organizations listed in the Appendix. Link up statements in the code with the sociocultural values described in this chapter.

7.4. In regard to such issues as informed consent, right to privacy, and freedom of choice, describe situations where people "volunteer" to participate in research but where there appear to be significant social pressures on them to do so. What about prison inmates, welfare recipients, and others who are in a very subordinate status? What about college students who can get class credit by participating in an experiment their professor is conducting? Can they make a free choice (informed consent)?

7.5. Have a class discussion on what research areas are sensitive to the students. Do they all agree on what is sensitive, or is there variation based on sex, ethnicity, religion, or other factors? Do the same for social research areas that the class believes might do some emotional harm to people.

Journals and Organizations in Applied Sociology

Professionals in most fields, including medicine, law, and applied research, subscribe to professional journals and belong to organizations that keep them in contact with one another and enable practitioners to keep abreast of what is happening in their field. The journals provide a permanent, published record of research that has been done and offer information on how to solve various research design problems. The professional organizations provide a network of assistance and organize periodic conferences where professionals can meet, exchange current information, and cooperate on projects. All of this contact and communication is important because practitioners may spend much of their working lives isolated from others in their field. As an applied researcher works with clients to design and conduct some research project, there may be no need or opportunity to come into contact with other applied researchers. If the researcher happens to be on the faculty at a university, he or she does have an available network of professional contacts. However, the other faculty may not be doing applied work and may thus be of little direct help in solving research design problems or resolving ethical issues. The professional organizations and journals provide the framework for practitioners to stay current in their fields and get the support they need to produce high-quality, ethically sound research.

I have developed a list of the major journals and organizations in the field of applied sociology. For those of you new to the field, these journals and organizations are a vehicle for learning more about the field. For those of you considering a career in the field, the journals and organizations are a way to learn of the exciting opportunities and the varied alternatives you will confront. It may not be a complete list

(I have certainly missed local or regional organizations in parts of the country that I am not familiar with), but it does include many national organizations and journals. Many sociological organizations that are not explicitly concerned with applied sociology and the sociology journals that publish mostly basic research and theoretical articles have not been included. Finally, I have not included journals in fields other than sociology that sometimes publish applied research. These include *Social Work Research and Abstracts, Journal of Alcohol and Drug Education, Journal of School Health,* and many others. Those of you who delve deeper into the field of applied research will gradually discover and make use of these other journals. My list is intended as a beginning, to give you an assist on a journey that will prove to be very rewarding. (By the way, the addresses listed are the most current ones; however, some of these journals and organizations do move from time to time, and they could be outdated by the time you read this.)

Journals and Newsletters ⸻⸻⸻⸻⸻

- *Clinical Sociology Review,* published by the Sociological Practice Association and the Michigan State University Press
- *Evaluation and Program Planning,* published by Pergamon Press, Inc., Elmsford, NY.
- *Evaluation Review,* published by Sage Publications, Inc., Newbury Park, CA.
- *International Clinical Sociology,* published by the International Sociological Association Working Group in Clinical Sociology
- *Journal of Applied Behavioral Science,* published by the NTL Institute for Applied Behavioral Science
- *Journal of Applied Sociology,* published by the Society for Applied Sociology
- *Newsletter,* published by the Chicago Sociological Practice Association
- *The Practicing Sociologist,* a newsletter published by the Sociological Practice Association
- *Public Opinion Quarterly,* published by the American Association for Public Opinion Research
- *SINET: Social Indicators Network News,* published by Abbott L. Ferriss, Editor, P.O. Box 24064, Emory University, Atlanta, GA 30306
- *Social Problems,* published by the Society for the Study of Social Problems

- *Sociological Practice,* published by the Sociological Practice Association
- *Sociological Practice Review,* published by the American Sociological Association

Organizations _____

- American Association for Public Opinion Research (P.O. Box 17, Princeton, NJ 08540)
- American Sociological Association (1722 N Street, NW, Washington, DC 20036)
- Chicago Sociological Practice Association (Andrew Montgomery, Department of Public Health Nursing, University of Illinois, 845 S. Damon, Chicago, IL 60612)
- Clinical Sociology Association, now the Sociological Practice Association
- District of Columbia Sociological Society (William V. D'Antonio, American Sociological Association, 1722 N Street, NW, Washington, DC 20036)
- International Sociological Association Working Group in Clinical Sociology (Jan Fritz, President, 254 Serena Drive, Palm Desert, CA 92260)
- NTL Institute for Applied Behavioral Science (Frederick Nader, President, 1240 N. Pitt Street, Suite 100, Alexandria, VA 22314)
- Society for Applied Sociology (Harold Cox, Department of Sociology, Indiana State University, Terre Haute, IN 47809)
- Society for the Study of Social Problems (Thomas Hood, Executive Officer, University of Tennessee, Knoxville, TN 37996-0641)
- Sociological Practice Association, a professional organization of clinical and applied sociologists (Elizabeth J. Clark, Executive Officer, RD 2, Box 141A, Chester, NY 10918); there are also chapters of the SPA in California, Michigan, Wisconsin, and possibly other states
- Sociologists in Business (Joan Waring, Chair, the Equitable, 42nd floor, 787 Seventh Ave., New York, NY 10019)

More information can be found in the *Directory of Sociological Practitioners* (1991), published by the American Sociological Association.

Graduate Education in Applied Sociology _____

Although there are a few undergraduate sociology programs that emphasize applied sociology, most undergraduate education is nonspecialist education. It is typically not until the graduate level that sociology students begin to specialize in applied sociology or some other area. To help students who are interested in graduate education in applied sociology, sociologists Jeanne Ballantine, Carla Howery, and Brian F. Pendleton have prepared a volume called *Graduate Programs in Applied Sociology and Sociological Practice*. It is available through the American Sociological Association.

Bibliography

Anderson, Curt L., Wayne A. Jesswein, and William Fleischman. 1990. "Needs Assessment Based on Household and Key Informant Surveys." *Evaluation Review,* 14 (April):182–191.

Ards, Sheila. 1989. "Estimating Local Child Abuse." *Evaluation Research,* 13 (October):484–515.

"Arrests of Wife-Beaters Rise in New Policy in Minneapolis." *New York Times,* July 24, 1984:10

Babbie, Earl. 1990. *Survey Research Methods,* 2d ed. Belmont, CA: Wadsworth.

Bailey, Kenneth D. 1978. *Methods of Social Research.* New York: The Free Press.

Barrows, David C. 1990. "The Ethics of an Internship." *ASA Footnotes,* 18 (September):5.

Barth, Steve. 1984. "The Men Who Hit Women." *Coastlines,* 15 (October/November):4–7.

Baumrind, D. 1985. "Research Using Intentional Deception." *American Psychologist,* 40 (February):165–174.

Benton, Ted. 1977. *Philosophical Foundations of the Three Sociologies.* Boston: Routledge & Kegan Paul.

Berk, Richard A. 1981. "On the Compatibility of Applied and Basic Sociological Research: An Effort in Marriage Counseling." *The American Sociologist,* 16 (November):204–211.

Berk, Richard A., Robert F. Boruch, David L. Chambers, Peter H. Rossi, and Ann D. Witte. 1985. "Social Policy Experimentation: A Position Paper." *Evaluation Review,* 9 (August):387–429.

Berk, Richard A., Thomas F. Cooley, C. J. LaCivita, Stanley Parker, Kathy Sredl, and Marilynn Brewer. 1980. "Reducing Consumption in Periods of Acute Scarcity: The Case of Water." *Social Science Research,* 9 (June):99–120.

Betzold, Michael. 1989. "More Arrests Would Curb Domestic Assault, Panel Told." *Detroit Free Press,* January 26:5.

Bonacich, Edna. 1990. "Community Forum Discussion: What Next?" *ASA Footnotes,* 18 (November):7.

Bowles, Roy T. 1981. *Social Impact Assessment in Small Communities.* Toronto: Butterworths.

Bradburn, Norman M., and Seymour Sudman. 1988. *Polls and Surveys: Understanding What They Tell Us.* San Francisco: Jossey-Bass.

Browne, M. Neil, and S. M. Keeley. 1986. *Asking the Right Questions: A Guide to Critical Thinking,* 2d ed. Englewood Cliffs, NJ: Prentice-Hall.

Browne, M. Neil, and James L. Litwin. 1987. "Critical Thinking in the

Sociology Classroom: Facilitating Movement from Vague Objective to Explicit Achievement." *Teaching Sociology,* 15 (October):384–391.

Brownstein, Henry H. 1991. "The Social Construction of Public Policy: A Case for Participation by Researchers." *Sociological Practice Review,* 2 (April):132–140.

Bruhn, John G. 1991. "Ethics in Clinical Sociology." In Howard M. Rebach and John G. Bruhn (eds.), *Handbook of Clinical Sociology.* New York and London: Plenum.

Bullock, Charles S., III, James E. Anderson, and David W. Brady. 1983. *Public Policy in the Eighties.* Monterey, CA: Brooks/Cole.

Bureau of Justice Statistics. 1989. *Recidivism of Prisoners Released in 1983.* Washington, DC: U.S. Department of Justice.

Burgess, R. G. 1984. *In the Field: An Introduction to Field Research.* London: George Allen and Unwin.

Campbell, D. T., and J. C. Stanley. 1963. *Experimental and Quasi-Experimental Designs for Research.* Chicago: Rand McNally.

Carmines, Edward G., and Richard A. Zeller. 1979. *Reliability and Validity Assessment.* Beverly Hills, CA: Sage.

Chaiken, Marcia R., and Jan M. Chaiken. 1984. "Offender Types and Public Policy." *Crime and Delinquency,* 30 (April):195–226.

Collins, Randall. 1989. "Sociology: Proscience or Antiscience." *American Sociological Review,* 54 (February):124–139.

Converse, Jean M., and Stanley Presser. 1986. *Survey Questions: Handcrafting the Standardized Questionnaire.* Newbury Park, CA: Sage.

Corcoran, K., and J. Fischer. 1987. *Measures for Clinical Practice: A Sourcebook.* New York: Free Press.

Darrow, William W., et al. 1987. "Multicenter Study of Human Immunodeficiency Virus Antibody in U.S. Prostitutes." Paper presented at the Third International Conference on AIDS, Washington, DC.

DeMartini, Joseph R. 1979. "Applied Sociology: An Attempt at Clarification and Assessment." *Teaching Sociology,* 6 (July):331–354.

DeMartini, Joseph R. 1982. "Basic and Applied Sociological Work: Divergence, Convergence, or Peaceful Coexistence?" *The Journal of Applied Behavioral Science,* 18 (no. 2):203–215.

de Neufville, Judith Innes. 1981. "Social Indicators." In Marvin E. Olsen and Michael Micklin (eds.), *Handbook of Applied Sociology.* New York: Praeger.

Doris, John. 1982. "Social Science and Advocacy: A Case Study." *American Behavioral Scientist,* 26 (November/December):199–234.

Dunham, H. Warren. 1983. "The Epidemiological Study of Mental Illness: Its Value for Needs Assessment." In R. A. Bell, M. Sundel, J. Apolte, and S. Munell (eds.), *Assessing Health and Human Service Needs.* New York: Human Sciences Press.

Dunning, C. Mark. 1985. "Applying Sociology in Natural Resource Management Agencies: Some Examples from the Corps of Engineers." *Sociological Practice,* 5 (Summer):193–203.

Durkheim, Emile. 1938. *Rules of the Sociological Method.* Translated by Sarah Solovay and John Mueller and edited by George E. G. Catlin. Chicago: University of Chicago Press.

Durkheim, Emile. 1951 (originally published 1897). *Suicide*. Translated by J. A. Spaulding and George Simpson. Glencoe, IL: Free Press.

Edmondson, Brad. 1988. "Hide and Seek." *The Atlantic*, 262 (December): 18–26.

Elms, A. C. 1982. "Keeping Deception Honest: Justifying Conditions for Social Scientific Research Strategies." In T. L. Beauchamp, R. R. Faden, R. J. Wallace, Jr., and L. Walters (eds.), *Ethical Issues in Social Science Research*. Baltimore: The Johns Hopkins University Press.

Ferraro, Kathleen J. 1989. "Policing Woman Battering." *Social Problems*, 36 (February):61–74.

Ferriss, Abbott L. 1988. "The Uses of Social Indicators." *Social Forces*, 66 (March):601–617.

Finsterbusch, Kurt. 1981. "Impact Assessment." In Marvin E. Olsen and Michael Micklin (eds.), *Handbook of Applied Sociology*. New York: Praeger.

Finsterbusch, Kurt, and Annabelle Bender Motz. 1980. *Social Research for Policy Decisions*. Belmont, CA: Wadsworth.

Fritz, Jan M. 1991. "The Contributions of Clinical Sociology in Health Care Settings." *Sociological Practice*, 9:15–29.

Garner, Joel H., and Christy A. Visher. 1988. "Policy Experiments Come of Age." *NIJ Reports*, National Institute of Justice, U.S. Department of Justice, no. 211 (September/October):2–7.

Garrison, Howard H. 1981. "Racial Inequality." In Marvin E. Olsen and Michael Micklin (eds.), *Handbook of Applied Sociology*. New York: Praeger.

Gelber, Seymour E. 1988. *Hard-Core Delinquents: Reaching Out Through the Miami Experiment*. Tuscaloosa and London: University of Alabama Press.

Glaser, Barney, and Anselm Strauss. 1967. *The Discovery of Grounded Theory*. Chicago: Aldine.

Glassner, Barry, and Jonathan A. Freedman. 1979. *Clinical Sociology*. New York: Longman.

Goodwin, Leonard. 1983. *Causes and Cures of Welfare: New Evidence on the Social Psychology of the Poor*. Lexington, MA: Lexington Books.

Gorden, R. L. 1987. *Interviewing: Strategies, Techniques and Tactics*, 4th ed. Chicago: Dorsey Press.

Goyder, J. 1985. "Face-to-Face Interviews and Mailed Questionnaires: The Net Difference in Response Rate." *Public Opinion Quarterly*, 49 (Summer):234–252.

Graham, K., L. LaRocque, R. Yetman, T. J. Ross, and E. Guistra. 1980. "Aggression and Barroom Environments." *Journal of Studies on Alcohol*, 41:277–292.

Greenbaum, Thomas L. 1988. *The Practical Handbook and Guide to Focus Group Research*. Lexington, MA: Lexington Books.

Halfpenny, Peter. 1982. *Positivism and Sociology: Explaining Social Life*. London: George Allen and Unwin.

Heberlein, T. A., and R. Baumgartner. 1978. "Factors Affecting Response Rates to Mailed Questionnaires: A Quantitative Analysis of the Published Literature." *American Sociological Review*, 43:447–462.

Henderschott, Anne B., and Stephen Norland. 1990. "Theory Based Evaluation:

An Assessment of the Implementation and Impact of an Adolescent Parenting Program." *Journal of Applied Sociology,* 7:35–48.

Hirschi, Travis, and Hanan C. Selvin. 1967. *Delinquency Research: An Appraisal of Analytic Methods.* New York: Free Press.

Humphreys, Laud. 1970. *Tearoom Trade.* Chicago: Aldine.

Iutcovitch, Joyce Miller, and Mark Iutcovitch. 1987. *The Sociologist as Consultant.* New York: Praeger.

Jaffe, Harold W., et al. 1983. "National Case-Control Study Of Kaposi's Sarcoma and *Pneumocystis carinii* Pneumonia in Homosexual Men: Part I, Epidemiological Results." *Annals of Internal Medicine,* 99 (August): 145–151.

Johnson, Paul L. 1983. "Human Services Planning." In Howard E. Freeman, Russell R. Dynes, Peter H. Rossi, and William Foote Whyte (eds.), *Applied Sociology: Roles and Activities of Sociologists in Diverse Settings.* San Francisco: Jossey-Bass.

Johnson, Timothy P., and James G. Hougland. 1990. "The Politics of Research in Applied Settings: The Case of Survey Research." *Journal of Applied Sociology,* 7:25–34.

Kairys, D., J. Schulman, and S. Harring (eds.). 1975. *The Jury System: New Methods for Reducing Prejudice.* Philadelphia: Philadelphia Resistance Print Shop.

Kovanis, Georgea. 1989. "Child Abuse Probe Turns to Quiet Boy's Death." *Detroit Free Press,* December 4, Section B:1.

Krueger, Richard A. 1988. *Focus Groups: A Practical Guide for Applied Research.* Newbury Park, CA: Sage.

Kuhn, Thomas S. 1970. *The Structure of Scientific Revolutions,* 2d ed. Chicago: University of Chicago Press.

Kytle, Jackson, and Ernest Joel Millman. 1986. "Confessions of Two Applied Researchers in Search of Principles." *Evaluation and Program Planning,* 9:167–177.

Lake, D. G., M. B. Miles, and R. B. Earle (eds.). 1973. *Measuring Human Behavior: Tools for the Assessment of Social Functioning.* New York: Teachers College Press.

Larson, Calvin J. 1990. "Applied/Practical Sociological Theory: Problems and Issues." *Sociological Practice Review,* 1 (June):8–18.

Lawlor, Edward F. 1986. "The Impact of Age Discrimination Legislation on the Labor Force Participation of Aged Men: A Time-Series Analysis." *Evaluation Review,* 10 (December):794–805.

Lee, Alfred McClung. 1991. "Public Policies and Clinical Sociology." In Howard M. Rebach and John G. Bruhn (eds.), *Handbook of Clinical Sociology.* New York and London: Plenum.

Levine, Saul V. 1984. *Radical Departures: Desperate Detours to Growing Up.* San Diego, CA: Harcourt Brace Jovanovich.

Liroff, R. 1978. *Judicial Review Under NEPA—Lessons for Users of the Water Resources Assessment Methodology.* Vicksburg, MS: Environmental Effects Laboratory, Waterways Experimental Station, U.S. Army Corps of Engineers.

Lofland, J., and L. H. Lofland. 1984. *Analyzing Social Settings,* 2d ed. Belmont, CA: Wadsworth.

Love, Ruth. 1983. "Some Roles of Sociologists in Organizational Decision-Making." *Sociological Practice,* 4 (no. 2):133–149.

McConahay, John B., Courtney J. Mullin, and Jeffrey Frederick. 1977. "The Uses of Social Science in Trials with Political and Racial Overtones: The Trial of Joan Little." *Law and Contemporary Problems,* 41 (Winter): 205–229.

McKillip, Jack. 1987. *Need Analysis: Tools for the Human Services and Education.* Newbury Park, CA: Sage.

McNulty, Faith. 1980. *The Burning Bed.* New York: Bantam.

Maguire, Brendan, and William Faulkner. 1990. "Safety Belt Laws and Traffic Fatalities." *Journal of Applied Sociology,* 7:49–61.

Merton, Robert K. 1973. *The Sociology of Science.* Chicago: The University of Chicago Press.

Meyers, Chet. 1986. *Teaching Students to Think Critically.* San Francisco: Jossey-Bass.

Miller, Delbert C. 1991. *Handbook of Research Design and Social Measurement,* 5th ed. Newbury Park, CA: Sage.

Mills, C. Wright. 1959. *The Sociological Imagination.* New York: Oxford University Press.

Miringoff, Marc L. 1989. *The Index of Social Health, 1989: Measuring the Social Well-Being of the Nation.* Tarrytown, NY: Fordham Institute for Innovation in Social Policy.

Monette, Duane R., Thomas J. Sullivan, and Cornell R. DeJong. 1990. *Applied Social Research: Tool for the Human Services,* 2d ed. Fort Worth, TX: Holt, Rinehart and Winston.

Morgan, David L. 1988. *Focus Groups as Qualitative Research.* Newbury Park, CA: Sage.

Morgan, Skip. 1989. "State-Ordered Research Hinders Workfare." (Riverside, CA) *Press-Enterprise,* February 13, Section B:1.

Nafstad, Hilde E. 1982. "Applied Versus Basic Social Research: A Question of Amplified Complexity." *Acta Sociologica,* 25:259–267.

Palamara, Frances, Francis T. Cullen, and Joanne C. Gersten. 1986. "The Effect of Police and Mental Health Intervention on Juvenile Deviance: Specifying Contingencies in the Impact of Formal Reaction." *Journal of Health and Social Behavior,* 27 (March):90–105.

Palmore, Erdman B. 1982. "Predictors of the Longevity Difference: A 25-Year Follow-Up." *The Gerontologist,* 22 (no. 6):513–518.

Patton, Michael Quinn. 1981. "Reflections on Professional Practice as a Social Scientist." *Mid-American Review of Sociology,* 6 (no. 1):1–15.

Paul, Richard. 1990. *Critical Thinking: What Every Person Needs to Survive in a Rapidly Changing World,* ed. by A. J. A. Binker. Rohnert Park, CA: Center for Critical Thinking and Moral Critique, Sonoma State University.

Peck, Dennis L., and Kimberley A. Folse. 1990. "Teenage Suicide: An Evaluation of Reactive Responses to Change and a Proposed Model for Proactive Accommodation/Adaptation." *Sociological Practice Review,* 1 (June):33–39.

Polich, J. M., P. L. Ellickson, P. H. Reuter, and J. P. Kahan. 1984. *Strategies for Controlling Adolescent Drug Use.* RAND Publication R-3076-CHF.

Popper, Karl. 1965. *Conjectures and Refutations.* New York: Harper & Row.

Rebach, Howard M., and John G. Bruhn. 1991. "Clinical Sociology: Defining the Field." In Howard M. Rebach and John G. Bruhn (eds.), *Handbook of Clinical Sociology.* New York and London: Plenum.

Riccio, James A. 1987. "Participation, Impact, and Benefit-Cost Findings from a Welfare Employment Program in Virginia." Paper presented at the annual meeting of the American Sociological Association, Chicago.

Richardson, Laurel. 1988. "The Collective Story: Postmodernism and the Writing of Sociology." *Sociological Focus,* 21 (August):199–208.

Roberts, Lance W. 1991. "Clinical Sociology with Individuals and Families." In Howard M. Rebach and John G. Bruhn (eds.), *Handbook of Clinical Sociology.* New York and London: Plenum.

Robinson, Michael J. 1976. "Public Affairs Television and the Growth of Political Malaise: The Case of 'The Selling of the Pentagon.'" *American Political Science Review,* 70:409–432.

Roethlisberger, Fritz J., and William J. Dickson. 1939. *Management and the Worker.* Cambridge, MA: Harvard University Press.

Rosenberg, Morris. 1968. *The Logic of Survey Analysis.* New York: Basic Books.

Rossi, Peter H. 1987. "No Good Applied Research Goes Unpunished." *Society,* 25 (November/December):74–79.

Rossi, Peter H., R. A. Berk, and K. J. Lenihan. 1980. *Money, Work, and Crime: Experimental Evidence.* New York: Academic Press.

Rossi, Peter H., and Sonia Rosenbaum. 1981. "Program Evaluation." In Marvin E. Olsen and Michael Micklin (eds.), *Handbook of Applied Sociology.* New York: Praeger.

Rossi, Peter H., James D. Wright, Gene A. Fisher, and Georgianna Willis. 1987. "The Urban Homeless: Estimating Composition and Size." *Science,* 235 (March 13):1336–1341.

Rule, James B. 1978. *Insight and Social Betterment: A Preface to Applied Social Science.* New York: Oxford University Press.

Rutman, L. 1984. *Evaluation Research Methods,* 2d ed. Newbury Park, CA: Sage.

Scheaffer, Richard L., William Mendenhall, and Lyman Ott. 1986. *Elementary Survey Sampling.* Boston: Duxbury Press.

Sherman, Lawrence W., and Richard A. Berk. 1984. "The Specific Deterrent Effects of Arrest for Domestic Violence." *American Sociological Review,* 49:261–271.

Shilts, Randy. 1987. *And the Band Played On: Politics, People, and the AIDS Epidemic.* New York: St. Martin's Press.

Sieber, Joan E. 1982. "Introduction: Critical Value Issues for Applied Social Scientists." *American Behavioral Scientist,* 26 (November/December): 149–158.

Signorile, Vito. 1989. "Buridan's Ass: The Statistical Rhetoric of Science and the Problem of Equiprobability." In Herbert W. Simons (ed.), *Rhetoric in the Human Sciences.* London: Sage.

Simmons, Roberta G., and Dale A. Blyth. 1987. *Moving into Adolescence: The Impact of Pubertal Change and School Context.* New York: Aldine de Gruyter.

Smart, Barry. 1976. *Sociology, Phenomenology, and Marxian Analysis: A Critical Discussion of the Theory and Practice of a Science of Society.* London: Routledge & Kegan Paul.

Smith, Allen G., and Albert E. Robbins. 1982. "Structured Ethnography: The Study of Parental Involvement." *American Behavioral Scientist,* 26 (September/October):45–61.

Smith, T. W. 1987. "That Which We Call Welfare by Any Other Name Would Smell Sweeter: An Analysis of the Impact of Question Wording on Response Patterns." *Public Opinion Quarterly,* 51 (Spring):75–83.

Sociological Practice Association. 1987. *Ethical Standards of Sociological Practitioners.*

Tatalovich, Raymond, and Byron W. Daynes. 1988. *Social Regulatory Policy: Moral Controversies in American Politics.* Boulder, CO: Westview Press.

Turner, Jonathan. 1974. *The Structure of Sociological Theory.* Homewood IL: Dorsey.

Turner, Stephen Park, and Jonathan H. Turner. 1990. *The Impossible Science: An Institutional Analysis of American Sociology.* Newbury Park, CA: Sage.

Tymchuk, Alexander J. 1982. "Strategies for Resolving Value Dilemmas." *American Behavioral Scientist,* 26 (November/December):159–176.

Vissing, Yvonne, and David J. Kallen. 1991. "The Clinical Sociologist in Medical Settings." In Howard M. Rebach and John G. Bruhn (eds.), *Handbook of Clinical Sociology.* New York and London: Plenum.

Weber, Max. 1957 (originally published in 1925). *The Theory of Social and Economic Organization.* Translated by A. M. Henderson and T. Parsons. New York: Free Press.

Weiss, Carol. 1972. *Evaluation Research: Methods for Assessing Program Effectiveness.* Englewood Cliffs, NJ: Prentice-Hall.

Weiss, Carol. 1987. "Evaluating Social Programs: What Have We Learned?" *Society,* 25 (November/December):40–45.

Wheeler, Gerald R., and Rodney V. Hissong. 1988. "A Survival Time Analysis of Criminal Sanctions for Misdemeanor Offenders: A Case for Alternatives to Incarceration." *Evaluation Review,* 12 (October):510–527.

Wilson, Thomas P. 1970. "Normative and Interpretive Paradigms in Sociology." In Jack D. Douglas (ed.), *Understanding Everyday Life: Toward the Reconstruction of Sociological Knowledge.* New York: Aldine.

Woolsey, Theodore D. 1986. "Retiring Chair Shares Thoughts with Council." *News From COPAFS,* 51 (November/December):2–3.

Wright, Susan E. 1986. *Social Science Statistics.* Boston: Allyn & Bacon.

Name Index

Subject Index

Acquired Immune Deficiency Syndrome. *See* AIDS

Action realm. *See* Policy, realm of

Adolescence, 99–101, 159–160

Advocacy, 21–22, 40–41, 174–177, 193

Age, 56–57, 61, 97–99

Age Discrimination in Employment Act, 97–99

Aggression, 123

AIDS (Acquired Immune Deficiency Syndrome), 28, 48–49, 110

Alcohol, 123, 150, 153. *See also* Drug use

Alienation, 157

American Association for Public Opinion Research, 118, 199, 200

American Marketing Association, 118

American Medical Association, 1, 131, 158

American Political Science Association, 118

American Sociological Association, 118, 195, 200, 201

Analysis of data
in available data, 134
ethics and, 189–190
in focus groups, 130–131
in observational research, 124
in surveys, 116–118

Anecdotal evidence, 164

Anonymity, 189

Antecedent variables, 65–66, 69

Anthropology, 10

Applied research
characteristics of, 20–21
compared to basic research, 16–18, 21–22, 145, 180–182, 192–193
education in, 198–199, 201
examples of, 19–21, 82, 90–93, 97–99, 108–110, 125–127
exploitation in, 177–180
interdisciplinary nature of, 10, 21, 150
journals in, 198–200
organizations in, 198–200
and power structure, 172–182
sponsors in, 192–195
techniques, 125–127
theory in, 34–35
types of, 21–22, 29, 129, 140–163
uses of, 2–3, 22, 118, 146–147, 154–155, 168–172
See also Cost-benefit analysis; Needs assessment; Program